ALSO BY JOE SACCO

FOOTNOTES IN GAZA

FOOTNOTES IN GAZA

JOE SACCO

METROPOLITAN BOOKS

Henry Holt and Company ■ New York

Metropolitan Books
Henry Holt and Company, LLC
Publishers since 1866
175 Fifth Avenue
New York, New York 10010
www.henryholt.com

Metropolitan Books® and ⅿ® are registered trademarks of
Henry Holt and Company, LLC.

Some of the material in this book (from the chapters "Rafah's Curse" and
"Worse Then, Worse Now") appeared in another form in "The Underground War in
Gaza," *The New York Times Magazine*, July 6, 2003.

Library of Congress Cataloging-in-Publication data

Sacco, Joe.
    Footnotes in Gaza / Joe Sacco.—1st ed.
        p. cm.
    Includes bibliographical references and index.
    ISBN 978-0-8050-7347-8
    1. Arab-Israeli conflict—1948–1967. 2. Egypt—History—Intervention, 1956. 3. Rafah—
History—20th century. 4. Khan Yunus—History—20th century. 5. Violence—Gaza Strip—
Rafah—History—20th century. 6. Massacres—Gaza Strip—Khan Yunus—History—20th
century. 7. Arab-Israeli conflict—1948–1967—Personal narratives, Palestinian. 8. Egypt—
History—Intervention, 1956—Personal narratives, Palestinian. 9. Interviews—Gaza Strip—
Rafah. 10. Interviews—Gaza Strip—Khan Yunus.   I. Title.
    DS119.7.S29 2009
    956.04—dc22   2009028433

Henry Holt books are available for special promotions and
premiums. For details contact: Director, Special Markets.

First Edition 2009

Printed in the United States of America
3 5 7 9 10 8 6 4 2

To the people of Gaza

FOREWORD

The genesis for this book dates to the spring of 2001 when the journalist Chris Hedges and I prepared to go on assignment to the Gaza Strip for *Harper's* magazine, he as a writer with me as illustrator. We had decided to focus on how Palestinians in one town—Khan Younis—were coping during the early months of the Second Intifada against the Israeli occupation. I recalled a reference I'd read many years before in Noam Chomsky's book *The Fateful Triangle*—basically a short quote from a United Nations document—about a large-scale killing of civilians in Khan Younis in 1956, and Chris agreed that we should add this barely noted historical episode to our story if it turned out to have some validity and current resonance.

Once in Khan Younis, we devoted about a day to gathering eyewitness testimony to what had happened in the town in November 1956 during the Suez Canal Crisis, when Israeli forces briefly occupied the Egyptian-ruled Gaza Strip. Old men and women had stark stories to tell about their fathers and husbands being shot in their houses or being lined up in the streets and killed by Israeli soldiers. One of those we interviewed was Abed El-Aziz El-Rantisi, a senior official of Hamas, the Islamic Resistance Party (who was later assassinated by an Israeli missile). El-Rantisi, who in 1956 was nine years old, told us his uncle had been killed that day. "I still remember the wailing and tears of my father over his brother," he said. "I couldn't sleep for many months after that. . . . It left a wound in my heart that can never heal. I'm telling you a story and I'm almost crying. This sort of action can never be forgotten. . . . [T]hey planted hatred in our hearts."

Chris deemed what had happened in Khan Younis in 1956 a significant part of the town's history, and he included several paragraphs about it in the *Harper's* article. For whatever reason, that section was cut by the magazine's editors.

I found that galling. This episode—seemingly the greatest massacre of Palestinians on Palestinian soil, if the U.N. figures of 275 dead are to be believed—hardly deserved to be thrown back on the pile of obscurity. But there it lay, like innumerable historical tragedies over the ages that barely rate footnote status in the broad sweep of history—even though, as El-Rantisi alluded, they often contain the seeds of the grief and anger that shape present-day events.

To me, the story of the Khan Younis killings was not so easily dispensable. I had done some digging, and almost nothing had been written in English about the episode. I determined to go back to Gaza to research what had taken place in 1956. As I prepared, I began to learn more about another incident that had occurred around the same time, on November 12, in the neighboring town of Rafah, in which scores of Palestinian men were killed. What had happened there? Again, a couple of sentences in a U.N. report were all that saved the incident from outright oblivion. In some ways, the Rafah story began to interest me more. The violence done in Khan Younis was shocking and brutal but, as I ascertained on my initial trip to Gaza with Chris, very straightforward; the killings in Rafah took place over a daylong screening operation for Palestinian guerrillas and soldiers. How had more than 100 people died in what should have been a standard, if complicated, military procedure? Had Israeli soldiers simply "panicked and opened fire on the running crowd," as the U.N. report surmised? Creatively speaking, there were more layers to investigate with the Rafah story, more pieces of a puzzle to put together. In addition, almost all the men of military age were caught up in the sprawling Rafah incident and many survivors would still be alive; at Khan Younis, only a handful of those involved survived being lined up and shot. So this book is broken up into two major though uneven sections—one about Khan Younis and the other, considerably longer, about Rafah.

Most of the on-the-ground field research for this book took place during two trips to the Gaza Strip between November 2002 and March 2003. My main priority was to record the stories of Palestinian eyewitnesses to the events in Khan Younis and Rafah. But 50 years is a long time to wait before asking people what they remember about a particular day. Thus the recollections reproduced here have been scrutinized in light of an inevitable blurring of memory and are compared in their details: Did the survivors recall essentially the same thing? Documentary evidence is usually considered more reliable than oral testimony by historians, but the record is scant and certain unsavory orders and reports are often kept "off the books" or are stored out of reach of even the most diligent researcher. Egyptian military records are closed to most inquiries. Certain U.N. records in Jordan and elsewhere that might shed some light are near unreachable. Still, it was important that available avenues be explored, and to this end I employed two Israeli researchers to go through the Israel Defense Forces archives. One of them also examined the Israel State Archives, the Knesset Archives, a press archive, and the *Kol Ha'am* (Communist Party) newspaper archive for any mention of the two incidents. Translations of key records and a list of Israeli historians and significant personnel consulted are included in the appendices at the end of the book. My hope is that this account will prompt former Israeli soldiers who might have witnessed the events in 1956 to offer their own recollections and points of view. Perhaps an Israeli historian needs to step into the breach.

Besides the problems inherent in relying on memories, addressed more fully in the book, the reader should be aware that there is another filter through which these stories passed before reaching the page, namely my own visual interpretation. In essence, I am the set designer and the director of every scene that takes place in the 1940s and 1950s. In reconstructing what the towns and refugee camps of Gaza looked like, I relied heavily on photographs available at the United Nations Relief and Works Agency (UNRWA) archives in Gaza City. I also drew on physical descriptions related to me by Palestinians. Still, any act of visualization—drawing, in this case—comes with an unavoidable measure of refraction.

My research did not take place in a vacuum. While I was investigating what had happened in 1956, Israeli attacks were killing Palestinians, suicide bombers were killing Israelis, and elsewhere in the Middle East the United States was gearing up for war in Iraq. Among the most critical developments in the daily lives of Gazans at the time was the wide-scale demolition of Palestinian homes in Rafah and Khan Younis, which made its way into the fabric of this book. (Interviews with Israeli military personnel for their take on the matter can be found in Appendix 2.) However, even the present-day stories I tell here quickly fell under the category of history because the situation in Gaza has undergone two major changes since I started this project almost seven years ago.

First, in 2005, Israel unilaterally dismantled all the Jewish settlements in Gaza and left the small sliver of land entirely to its Palestinian inhabitants. However, Israel still tightly controlled Gaza's airspace, coastline, and its entry and exit points save one. (That one was the Rafah terminal, with access to Egypt, which severely limited movement to and from Gaza.) In effect, the Gaza Strip, overcrowded and destitute, had not been freed from the Israeli clamp or the threat of withering attack or retaliation by Israeli forces, as witnessed in the winter of 2008–9.

Second, in 2007, the Islamic group Hamas seized control and has been in charge of Gaza ever since. Hamas, branded a terrorist organization by Israel and the United States, had won the majority of legislative seats in a 2006 election. A national unity government with its rival Fatah was unacceptable to the Israelis, who further tightened the screws on Gaza. When tensions between Fatah and Hamas boiled over, Hamas preemptively seized Gaza ahead of a U.S.-engineered coup by Fatah. What shocked Palestinians, even those disgusted with years of corruption under Fatah rule, was the ruthlessness with which Hamas crushed its Fatah opponents. The tradition of Palestinian militants, regardless of faction, standing shoulder-to-shoulder against Israel and not against each other was at an end. With the Hamas takeover, Israel declared the Gaza Strip an "enemy entity." The blockade of Gaza, which was joined by the United States and the European Union, is, at this writing, almost complete.

As someone in Gaza told me, "events are continuous." Palestinians never seem to have the luxury of digesting one tragedy before the next one is upon them. When I was in Gaza, younger people often viewed my research into the events of 1956 with bemusement. What good would tending to history do them when they were under attack and their homes were being demolished *now*? But the past and present cannot be so easily disentangled; they are part of a remorseless continuum, a historical blur. Perhaps it is worth our while to freeze that churning forward movement and examine one or two events that were not only a disaster for the people who lived them but might also be instructive for those who want to understand why and how—as El-Rantisi said—hatred was "planted" in hearts.

Joe Sacco
July 2009

FOOTNOTES IN GAZA

KHAN YOUNIS

GLIMMER OF HOPE

This is the story of footnotes to a sideshow of a forgotten war.

FOOTNOTES

The war pitted Egypt against the strange alliance of Britain, France, and Israel in 1956;

the sideshow was the ongoing raids and counter-raids across the Gaza border by Palestinian guerrillas and Israeli forces;

and the footnotes—

Well, like most footnotes, they dropped to the bottom of history's pages, where they barely hang on.

J. SACCO 4-05-1-09

8

History can do without its foot-notes.

Footnotes are inessential at best; at worst they trip up the greater narrative.

From time to time, as bolder, more streamlined editions appear, history shakes off some foot-notes al-together.

And you can see why...

History has its hands full.

It can't help producing pages by the hour, by the minute.

History chokes on fresh episodes and swallows what-ever old ones it can.

The war of 1956?

Hunh?

Here we are tonight, for instance, in Gaza, with Israeli pilots circling above us and a Pal-estinian I have just met checking his Browning down below.

J. SACCO 4.05

9

They are a small part of a larger struggle between their two peoples over the same land, linked by a desire or a necessity to kill each other in the here and now.

What does '56 matter to them?

Someone brings in a Kalashnikov.

IT NEEDS TO BE CLEANED.

We go up to the roof.

The unseen Apaches are receding, and their clatter is replaced by the lawn mower buzz of a drone, which circles overhead, relaying images from its see-in-the-dark camera to a command post somewhere.

I've already brushed my teeth and performed my nightly ablutions.

I'd put on pajamas if I had them.

This is the end of my first day in Khan Younis, and I've been operating on less than two or three hours of sleep each of the last few jet-lagged nights.

An Apache's cannon is whirring at something in the distance.

30 MM.

Who is this guy?

Abed, my guide, tells me his name is Khaled.

HE IS 'MUTARAD,' WANTED BY THE ISRAELIS.

They'd snuff him out in a second if they had him in their crosshairs.

Now we hear tanks to the east and their heavy machine guns opening up.

THEY'VE SURROUNDED TWO OF THE EASTERN VILLAGES.

IT LOOKS LIKE THEY'RE GOING TO DEMOLISH THE HOUSE OF TALAL ABU ZARIEFEH.

WHO'S THAT?

AN ACTIVIST. ALSO WANTED.

J SACCO 2-09

ABED

You sort of forget what it's like till you're here again, and then it all comes back to you in a swirl of dust and a tornado of children.

WHAT'S YOUR NAME?

HELLO! WHAT'S YOUR NAME?

Christ almighty, not *this* again!

WHA' YOUR NAME

They don't see many outsiders here in southern Gaza, which makes me exotic, sometimes golden.

I was once one of three in the backseat of a taxi that stopped for a couple more passengers...

one of whom tried to squeeze in next to me—

but the driver would have none of it.

CAN'T YOU SEE HE'S A FOREIGNER?!

Then again, sometimes my presence elicits discomfort, suspicion, perhaps tinged with humiliation.

THEY'RE USING US FOR LAUGHS.

Who am I, after all, snooping around, taking photos, wanting names?

SOMEBODY FROM THE JEWS WILL GET YOUR BOOK AND READ MY NAME AND MY ADDRESS... AND THEY WILL COME HERE IN THE NIGHT AND—

—and demolish your house?

"If they demolish your house," I say, "I promise I will buy you a new one!"

J. SACCO 5-05

13

One day we watch a video from that era.

In it, Israeli vehicles charge defiant Palestinian teenagers who leap out of the way and let loose a torrent of stones.

A nostalgic Abed tells me the First Intifada was truly a popular uprising.

Abed is one of the many Palestinians angered by the agreements the Palestine Liberation Organization (PLO) made with Israel starting in 1993, known as the Oslo Accords, which ended the First Intifada and returned Yasser Arafat and the old-guard Palestinian leadership from exile in Tunisia.

OSLO [CREATED] A KIND OF HYSTERIA.

PEOPLE STOPPED THROWING ROCKS AT THE ISRAELIS AND STARTED THROWING OLIVE BRANCHES.

BUT WE GOT NOTHING FROM OSLO.

Although Israeli soldiers mostly withdrew to their fixed positions, the overall occupation continued and the number of Jewish settlers on occupied land doubled.

DURING THE FIRST INTIFADA, I USED TO THINK WE WERE A GREAT PEOPLE.

NOW I DON'T.

OUR LEADERS, WHEN THEY WERE IN TUNIS, WERE LIKE HEROES TO US.

AFTER OSLO, WHEN THEY CAME HERE, WE SAW THEM FOR WHAT THEY ARE.

THEY PUT THEIR PRIVATE CONCERNS ABOVE THE NATIONAL CAUSE.

THE PEOPLE ARE THE ONES WHO SACRIFICED, AND WHAT THEY CARE ABOUT IS GOING TO TEL AVIV FOR A GLASS OF WINE AND TRAVELING AROUND FREELY.

J. SACCO 5-05

The uneasy "Oslo period," straining under the weight of the interminable occupation and the phenomenon of suicide attacks on Israeli civilians, ended after Israeli opposition leader Ariel Sharon's provocative visit in September 2000 to Jerusalem's Al-Aqsa Mosque compound, which is also the site of the Jewish Temple Mount.

Simmering Palestinian resentments erupted and the Second Intifada was on.

But now the revived stone throwing seems like a quaint echo of the earlier struggle —

the real resistance is in the hands of militant groups armed with infantry weapons and explosive belts.

The Israeli crackdown features tanks, helicopter gunships, and jet bombers.

Evidence of its ferocity is a short taxi ride away in the Toufieh neighborhood, which is near an Israeli settlement and military position. Israel Defence Forces (IDF) periodically destroy refugee homes here, claiming they are Palestinian "gun nests."

Sometimes Abed and I check out the damage wrought by the previous night's bulldozers.

We talk to people sifting through their rubble.

CAN YOU IMAGINE A DIFFERENT LIFE FOR YOURSELF, OR ARE YOU SO USED TO THIS THAT IT'S IMPOSSIBLE?

FOR ME, I CAN.

I WANT TO SPEND ANOTHER YEAR IN GAZA, AND THEN I NEED TO LEAVE, MAYBE FOR THREE OR FOUR YEARS...

NOT JUST TO FINISH MY STUDIES, BUT TO SEE SOMETHING ELSE OF THE WORLD, TO GET DIFFERENT PERSPECTIVES.

On another occasion Abed tells me—

I'D LIKE TO EXPERIENCE SOMETHING OF THE FREEDOM OF THE WEST WITHOUT MAKING MYSELF CONFUSED.

DO YOU FEEL FREE IN GAZA?

IN MY THOUGHTS.

Sometimes he's less philosophical.

I NEED TO DRINK SOMETHING.

TO FORGET ALL THIS.

TO GET DRUNK.

J. SACCO 5.05

17

THE GAZA STRIP

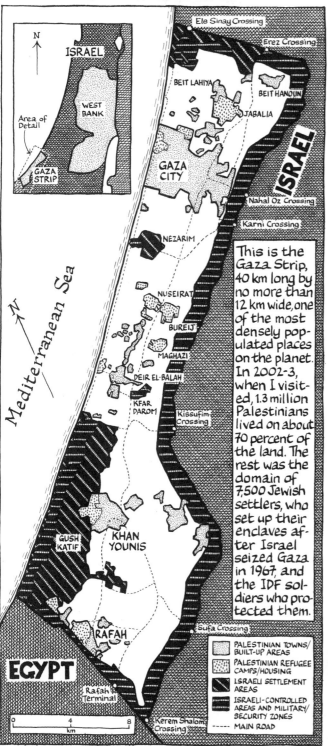

ISRAEL

WEST BANK

Area of Detail

GAZA STRIP

N

Mediterranean Sea

N

Ele Sinay Crossing

Erez Crossing

BEIT LAHIYA

BEIT HANOUN

JABALIA

GAZA CITY

ISRAEL

Nahal Oz Crossing

Karni Crossing

NEZARIM

NUSEIRAT

BUREIJ

MAGHAZI

DEIR EL-BALAH

KFAR DAROM

Kissufim Crossing

GUSH KATIF

KHAN YOUNIS

RAFAH

Sufa Crossing

EGYPT

Rafah Terminal

Kerem Shalom Crossing

0   4   8
km

PALESTINIAN TOWNS/ BUILT-UP AREAS

PALESTINIAN REFUGEE CAMPS/HOUSING

ISRAELI SETTLEMENT AREAS

ISRAELI-CONTROLLED AREAS AND MILITARY/ SECURITY ZONES

MAIN ROAD

This is the Gaza Strip, 40 km long by no more than 12 km wide, one of the most densely populated places on the planet. In 2002-3, when I visited, 1.3 million Palestinians lived on about 70 percent of the land. The rest was the domain of 7,500 Jewish settlers, who set up their enclaves after Israel seized Gaza in 1967, and the IDF soldiers who protected them.

Among the Palestinians here, unemployment was at 50 percent. The number of people below the poverty level — living on less than $2 per day — was at 70 percent.

About two-thirds were registered refugees, the jetsam of the '48 war. Most of these lived in the eight major camps administered by the United Nations Relief and Works Agency — UNRWA (pronounced as one word).

All access to and from Gaza, for Palestinians and foreigners, was controlled and heavily restricted by the Israelis.

J. SACCO 5-05

The placement of settlements, settler roads, and checkpoints allowed the Israelis to easily separate one part of Gaza from another. For example, the south was frequently cut off from the rest of the Strip at the IDF checkpoints at Abu Houli.

DEIR EL-BALAH

KFAR DAROM

GUSH KATIF

ABU HOULI

IDF Chkpt.

IDF Chkpt.

Kisoufim Crossing

ISRAEL

NORTH-SOUTH PALESTINIAN ROAD

SETTLER-ONLY ROAD

Here the settler-only road to the Gush Katif settlement bloc bisected the north-south road used by Palestinians.

When settler cars approached the overpass, or for "security" considerations, or for no discernible reason, Palestinian traffic was stopped here—for ten minutes, half a day, or days at a time.

The two major population centers in the south are Khan Younis and Rafah. We'll get to Rafah later. Right now our headquarters is Khan Younis.

And our command post is Abed's home in the center of town.

Here we plan the day's movements...

THE GUY WILL MEET US AFTER PRAYERS.

SOUNDS GOOD.

and here we eat and sleep.

19

J. SACCO 5-05

MUD, TENTS, BRICKS

Abed has brothers, the names of whom I can hardly keep straight.

One of them, Ossam, is a doctor. Typically he comes in after the night shift and takes the bed Abed has just vacated.

If the three of us are here together, Abed or Ossam sleeps on the floor.

I'm a guest, so I always get a bed.

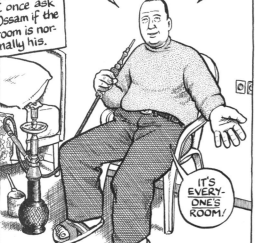

Feeling guilty about the brothers I've displaced, I once ask Ossam if the room is normally his.

MY ROOM?

IT'S IMPOSSIBLE!

WE ARE 12!

IT'S EVERYONE'S ROOM!

It sure is. One night, after a full day's work, and with me looking forward to tucking in before midnight for a change, Abed and I return to find Ossam sitting with their uncle.

The uncle is curious about my '56 project.

No amount of yawning or underarm scratching is going to shake him.

Abed, bless him, launches into his usual explanation.

BUT WHAT ABOUT 1967?

THAT'S ANOTHER STORY.

WHAT ABOUT SABRA AND SHATILA?

THAT WAS IN LEBANON.

IF YOU REALLY WANT TO WRITE A PROPER BOOK ABOUT OUR SITUATION, YOU WOULD START WITH THE ZIONIST CONGRESS IN BASEL.

Basel? The resolution in 1897 calling for a Jewish homeland in Palestine?

It was almost 1:30 a.m. and this guy was beginning to annoy me.

J. SACCO 6-05

WHAT ABOUT 1948?

Okay, okay! His point is finally taken...

and since one must start somewhere, that watershed year, when Israel declared independence and Arab armies attacked the nascent state, seems as logical a place as any.

When the shooting stopped and the U.N. had brokered an armistice demarcation line, the bruised Egyptian army held on to a tiny sliver of Palestine dubbed the Gaza Strip.

Of the hundreds of thousands of Palestinians who fled the fighting or were expelled by Israeli forces, 200,000 ended up in Gaza, tripling its population.

The humanitarian crisis was enormous. Some refugees were housed in public buildings and mosques, but their number was simply too great.

Along the way, over the course of my visits to Gaza, Abed and I collect some stories about that time when the dispossessed came here with nothing and found — what?

WHEN WE CAME FROM OUR ORIGINAL VILLAGES...

MOHAMMED YOUSEF SHAKER MOUSA

"We dug holes and put blankets on the ground, and we lived like that for a short time.

"Some of the people were under tree branches. They covered the branches with blankets and sheltered themselves."

WE WERE SLEEPING UNDER THE TREES...

MAHMOUD MOHAMMED

"We had nothing with which to live. We had no mattresses, no tents. Gaza was like a desert.

"Then the Quakers came, and they put up huge tents."

MOHAMMED YOUSEF SHAKER MOUSA: "Some people were given a whole tent, a big tent. These big tents could be divided for four families. They divided each room from the others with a blanket.

J. SACCO 6.05

"Then they distributed food. Flour, oil..."

RA'ESA SALIM HASSAN KALOOB

WE WOULD GO WITH MY FATHER... TO DIG IN THE GROUND FOR SOME METAL, SOME OTHER MATERIAL, TO SELL.

"And we used to go to the Egyptian positions which were here to buy [the soldiers'] stale bread."

MAHMOUD MOHAMMED: "We cooked our food by burning cactus that we'd dried in the sun."

MOHAMMED YOUSEF SHAKER MOUSA: "They used to cut wood, and God would have to make it burn because the wood wasn't dry."

"No kerosene, no gas. Nothing."

MAHMOUD MOHAMMED: "We dug holes in the ground [for toilets] outside... People could do nothing more than this."

WATER? THERE WASN'T ANY WATER.

OMM AWAD EL-NAJEELI

"We used to walk two kilometers to bring one jug of water... I used to carry my baby and at the same time put the jug on my head."

J. SACCO 6·05

23

MAHMOUD MOHAMMED: "We used to bring the water from a far distance. When we came home, we'd find the water was gone. We'd drunk the water on the way."

RA'ESA SALIM HASSAN KALOOB: "Once when I was a child there was a donkey walking the streets, and I jumped on the donkey. I found the donkey full of fleas.

"And my mother took off all my clothes and burned them. There was a shortage of water, a shortage of soap."

WE USED TO WASH IN THE TENTS.

MARIAM EL-NAJEELI

THE TENT WAS THE KITCHEN AND THE TOILET AND THE BATHROOM AND THE LIVING ROOM AND THE SITTING ROOM.

UNRWA was established in late 1949 to provide for the Palestinian refugees, and it took over from the Quakers in 1950.

IN EACH NEIGHBORHOOD UNRWA BUILT FOUR OR FIVE TAPS IN ONE PLACE.

SO THEY MADE A NETWORK OF WATER PIPES.

MOHAMMED ATWA EL-NAJEELI

MOHAMMED YOUSEF SHAKER MOUSA: "They built groups of toilets. A door for the women, and on the other side a door for the men. Anyone entering these toilets should wear high shoes otherwise he'd sink in the water and sewage."

24

J.SACCO 6.05

YOUSEF ISMAEL FOUDA: "We started to build clay houses ourselves because the tents didn't protect us from the rains... Small rooms, 3.5 x 3.5 meters."

"Fifteen people in this room."

RA'ESA SALIM HASSAN KALOOB: "They used to make bricks and used wooden boxes as a frame. And they lined them up and put them in the sun. When they were dry they used them to build walls."

"No windows, of course. Without a door. A hole in the wall."

MOHAMMED YOUSEF SHAKER MOUSA: "The walls from clay, the roof from palm branches. Over the branches, clay. On top of that they put tar to prevent the clay from getting wet."

YOUSEF ISMAEL FOUDA: "We used to buy mats from Egypt that were full of bugs."

"I'm going to make you laugh. We would use a bit of moist flour to kill the bugs. You'd find bits of flour full of blood."

"UNRWA would spray DDT from time to time."

J. SACCO 6·05

IT WAS A FANTASTIC DREAM FOR ME WHEN I SAW PICTURES IN THE NEWSPAPERS AND MAGAZINES — I WAS JEALOUS WHEN I SAW A CHILD WITH LONG HAIR BECAUSE I COULDN'T LET MY HAIR GROW BECAUSE OF THE INSECTS AND DISEASES.

FUAD FAQAWI

FATIMA EL-KHATEEB: "They opened tent schools for us."

RA'ESA SALIM HASSAN KALOOB: "[I spent] not one day in school. I used to wear my hair back and run like a horse. And run, run!"

MOHAMMED YOUSEF SHAKER MOUSA: "After a long period they demolished those [clay] houses periodically, and they brought brick blocks, and they built houses in groups.

"They gave out rooms according to the number of family members...Each room was 2.5 meters square ...Each [extended] family was surrounded by a wall."

J. SACCO 7.05

26

And so we have taken ourselves from 1948 to the middle of the 1950s—when the camps looked like this.

THE ONLY OPTION

The camp is bordered by the town of the same name. From the late 1960s to 2005, it was hemmed in on its other sides by Gush Katif, the Jewish settlement bloc.

Since the mid-1950s the swollen population of Khan Younis camp has had nowhere to build but into the streets and up.

Palestinian camps all over the Gaza Strip have taken on a look of densely packed permanence, at some places indistinguishable from the towns they abut, with schools, workshops, mosques, and marketplaces...

and at other points the still-common asbestos roofs and the squalor beneath many of them remind a visitor he is among the grandchildren and great grandchildren of refugees who arrived with nothing and for whom nothing fundamental has changed.

The poorest of the poor are designated hardship cases by UNRWA — there are almost 13,000 of them in Khan Younis alone.

A local UNRWA official once invited me to tour a sample home of these unfortunates.

We walked in on a family of 11 living in two rooms.

While the UNRWA guy chased out the neighborhood kids who'd followed us in, the mother of the house agreed to my request to document her shambles.

TAKE PICTURES!

TAKE PICTURES!

They had some blankets and thin mattresses but only one single bed between them.

Their clothes were piled in heaps or hung in plastic bags.

TAKE PICTURES!

J. SACCO 8.05

Work? Would it matter if he **could** work? Is there work in the Gaza Strip?

Perhaps for some small shopkeepers...

and farmers...

Perhaps finding and selling scrap.

Perhaps with UNRWA — teaching the ever-increasing population of refugee children, for example...

or distributing flour to their mothers...

Perhaps as a policeman employed by the Palestinian Authority — known here as the "Sulta" — which in 2003 is still nominally in charge in Gaza, and whose only claim to relevance is the salaries it doles out.

A few, however, manage quite well.

One day we catch up with one of Abed's long-lost friends.

He speaks almost flawless English, he's highly educated, and he works for an American government aid agency.

MY WORK FOCUSES ON DEMOCRATIZATION AND SETTING UP PALESTINIAN CIVIL SOCIETY.

BASICALLY, IT'S BULL-SHIT.

J. SACCO 8-05

He doesn't believe in it, he says, and neither do the other Palestinians who work with him.

He says the Americans spend millions on these projects so Palestinians will focus inward rather than on resisting the Israelis.

Still—

He says there's an opening that pays $1,900 a month, which is a fortune here in Gaza.

IF I DON'T TAKE THE JOB, SOMEONE ELSE WILL.

Is Abed interested?

The answer is no.

Outside, Abed lets loose...

I'M SHOCKED BY HIM.

HERE YOU CAN LOSE YOUR LIFE FROM A BULLET MADE IN THE USA WHILE YOUR SALARY COMES FROM THE USA.

Abed says his friend has traded his national convictions for foreign currency.

Abed himself recently agreed to take a dramatic pay cut — from $900 to $400 a month — when the Palestinian NGO he works for stopped accepting checks from British and American donors.

WE BELIEVE THERE IS A HIDDEN AGENDA BEHIND EACH WESTERN DONOR — ESPECIALLY AMERICAN DONORS...

THEIR IDEA IS TO MAKE US FOCUS ON HOW TO DEMOCRATIZE OURSELVES AND TO FORGET THAT WE ARE STILL SLAVES.

J. SACCO 8-05

Most Gazans don't have the luxury of such assessments. Many covet menial or physically demanding low-wage jobs in Israel, which still pay twice as much as similar jobs in Gaza.

Half of Gaza's workforce once held jobs in Israel, but with the escalating violence Israel weaned itself off Palestinian labor and now imports Thais and Romanians and Chinese and others to do its hot, dusty work.

Mahmoud, Abed's brother-in-law, is one of the few Gazans still holding a permit to work in Israel.

He's just returned home from his job where he finishes wooden furniture.

Besides three Israelis, he works with four Romanians, two Equadorans, and a Russian.

SOME OF THEM SPEAK A LITTLE HEBREW, AND SOMETIMES WE USE HAND GESTURES.

I HAVE NO PROBLEMS WITH THEM.

THEY ARE WORKERS LIKE ME.

THEY HAVE THE SAME TARGET: TO WORK AND MAKE MONEY.

He endures an average of eight hours' traveling to and from his job every day. When he gets home to Khan Younis, he gives himself an hour to shower, pray, and eat before hitting the sack.

He'll be up at 3 a.m. to start all over again.

I tell him that, despite the difficulties, he must feel lucky to have a job in Israel.

I'M NOT LUCKY.

IT'S THE ONLY OPTION.*

J. SACCO 8-05

*AFTER THE HAMAS TAKEOVER IN 2007, IT WAS NO LONGER AN OPTION. ISRAEL SEALED ITS BORDER WITH GAZA.

SIDESHOW

Indeed, what are Mahmoud's other options? He has to provide for a wife and five children.

And what were the options of the Palestinian refugees who had lost their homes and land with Israel's birth and found themselves roaming the sands of Gaza?

Of them, an Israeli Foreign Ministry report in 1949 predicted that "the most adaptable and best survivors would manage by a process of natural selection, and the others will waste away. Some will die but most will turn into human debris and social outcasts and probably join the poorest classes in the Arab countries."

The refugees were landless, destitute, and hungry; they were dependent on meager handouts; the men were unemployed, idle.

Meanwhile, in the fields they had left behind, their crops ripened. In the larders of the homes they had fled there was oil and flour. All of it was a tantalizingly few hours' walk away.

All of it was now in the hands of a new people, the Israelis.

J. SACCO 8-05

In those days the Gaza Strip was not surrounded by an electrically charged fence like it is today. The armistice demarcation line was thinly guarded. The hungriest and the boldest refugees started to slip into what was now called Israel to harvest and scavenge and to bring back all they could carry.

In time, the poorly defended outposts Israel began putting up along the border with Gaza became tempting targets for refugees, who stole livestock and equipment from them.

Refugees also entered Israel to visit family members who had not fled; to transit to the Jordanian-annexed West Bank, where there might be a chance of a better livelihood; or even to move back home.

Israel was absorbing hundreds of thousands of Jewish immigrants.

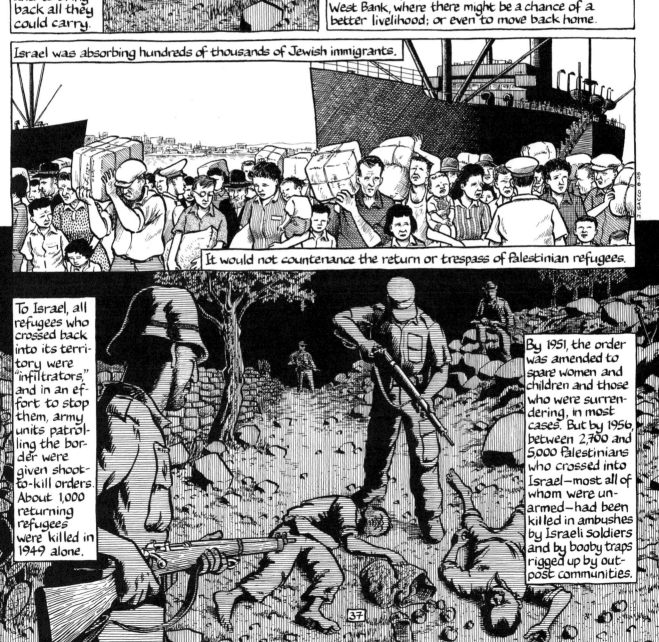

It would not countenance the return or trespass of Palestinian refugees.

To Israel, all refugees who crossed back into its territory were "infiltrators," and in an effort to stop them, army units patrolling the border were given shoot-to-kill orders. About 1,000 returning refugees were killed in 1949 alone.

By 1951, the order was amended to spare women and children and those who were surrendering, in most cases. But by 1956, between 2,700 and 5,000 Palestinians who crossed into Israel—most all of whom were unarmed—had been killed in ambushes by Israeli soldiers and by booby traps rigged up by outpost communities.

J. SACCO B-05

Israel's resolve to deal harshly with infiltrators hardened because they sometimes murdered Jews in chance encounters or killed them out of revenge. Almost 300 Israeli civilians had been killed by 1956.

In Jerusalem, I meet a former military man, Mordechai Bar-On, who was chef-de-bureau to Major General Moshe Dayan, the Israeli army's chief of staff in the mid '50s.

Now a historian, Bar-On explains the policy of retaliation Israel adopted for infiltration and the spilling of Jewish blood.

THE LOGIC OF RETALIATION OPERATIONS IS BASICALLY DETERRENCE.

THE MAIN CONSIDERATION IS YOU'RE HITTING THE OTHER SIDE, EITHER CIVILIANS OR THEIR ARMY.

BUT WHATEVER YOU DO IS TO TRY TO COERCE THE OTHER SIDE'S MILITARY AND POLICE TO CLAMP DOWN ON THE INFILTRATORS.

Israel's initial policy was to strike hard at Palestinian civilians as a way of sending a signal to the Arabs to seal their side of the border.

This approach reached its climax in 1953 in a raid in the West Bank led by Major Ariel Sharon in retaliation for the murder of a Jewish woman and two of her children.

Sharon's orders were to attack the village of Qibya and, specifically, to cause "maximal killing."

38

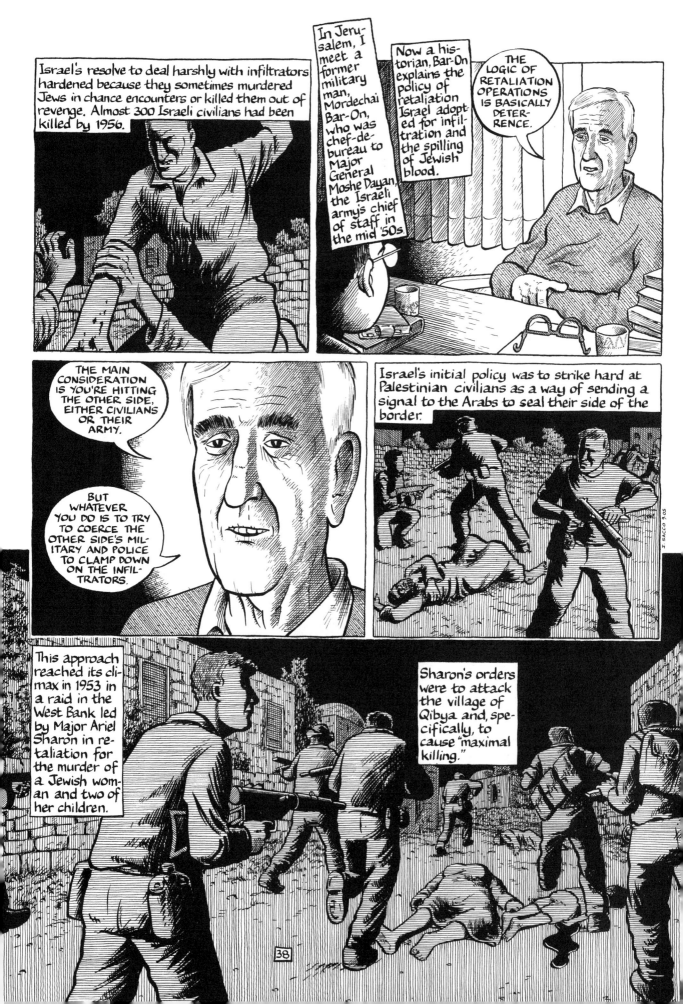

Encountering no resistance in the village itself, Sharon's men shot Palestinians hiding in their homes and then blew up the structures on top of them. Of at least 42 killed in Qibya, 38 were women and children.

But according to Bar-On, the raids on civilians—

—HAD NO EFFECT ON THE EGYPTIANS BECAUSE NASSER COULDN'T CARE LESS WHAT HAPPENED IN THE GAZA STRIP.

The international outcry was such that the Israeli government decided henceforward to focus retaliatory strikes on military and police targets, not civilians.

President Jemal Abdel Nasser!

One of the greatest leaders of modern Arab history!

He had been among the military men who had overthrown Egypt's monarchy in 1952, and he was the chief proponent of pan-Arab nationalism —a single state that would include North Africa, Mesopotamia, and the Arabian Peninsula.

But if Nasser thought events in Gaza weren't really "anything that would endanger his own regime in Cairo," as Bar-On suggests, that was going to change on the night of February 28, 1955.

Which brings us to our first footnote.

J. SACCO 9.05

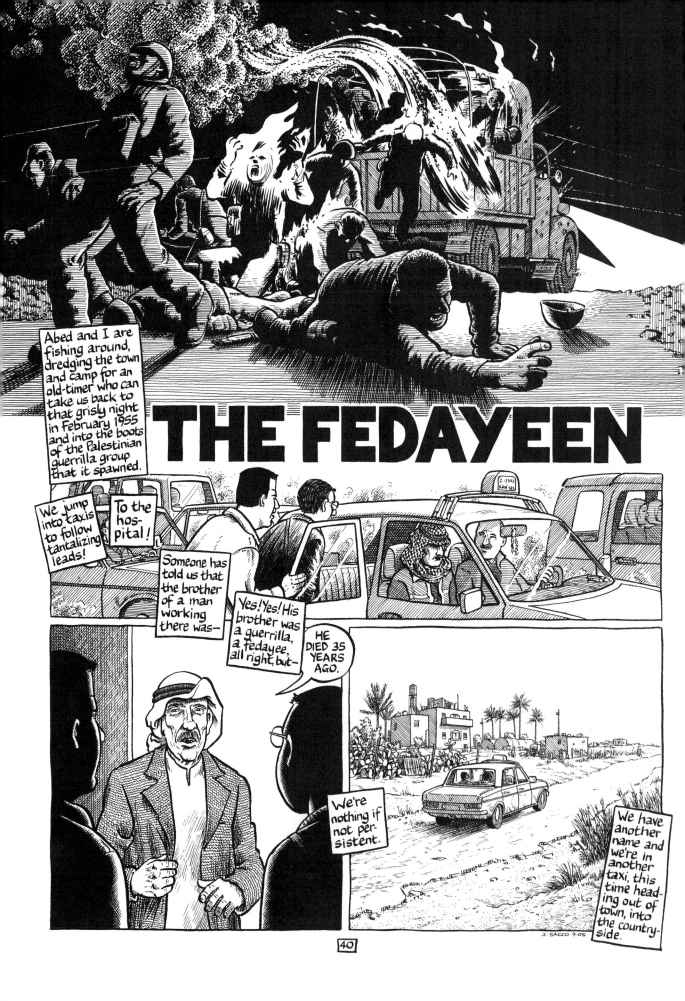

THE FEDAYEEN

Abed and I are fishing around, dredging the town and camp for an old-timer who can take us back to that grisly night in February 1955 and into the boots of the Palestinian guerrilla group that it spawned.

We jump into taxis to follow tantalizing leads!

To the hospital!

Someone has told us that the brother of a man working there was—

Yes! Yes! His brother was a guerrilla, a fedayee, all right, but—

HE DIED 35 YEARS AGO.

We're nothing if not persistent.

We have another name and we're in another taxi, this time heading out of town, into the countryside.

J. SACCO 9-05

And we're in another home, in another room, crossing our fingers, hoping, "inshallah"— God willing— that we're about to meet The Real Thing—

SALAAM ALEIKUM.

ALEIKUM ES-SALAAM.

— and one look tells us we have our man.

We have our man and I have my tape recorder...

and before the last salutation of the obligatory pleasantries has been vollied and returned, I've lobbed my first question into the air.

SO...

WE UNDERSTAND YOU WERE WITH THE FEDAYEEN.

CAN YOU TELL US ABOUT THAT EXPERIENCE?

No, he doesn't want to talk quite yet.

If he talks about the fedayeen period, he'll need to have a cigarette.

Oh, Jesus! It's Ramadan and the sun hasn't set!

HE IS ASKING US TO RETURN IN THE EVENING, AFTER THE FAST.

SO HE CAN SMOKE?

SO HE CAN SMOKE.

And thus begins the aggravating mismatch pitting hapless cartoonist against wily ex-guerrilla.

J. SACCO 9.05

I visit him four times over the months, and each time he runs me ragged between '48 and '67, because he's seen it all and can tell me everything, but I don't want all and everything...

I want the mid-'50s!

The mid-'50s!

The mid-'50s!

But he's not taking orders from me though, let's be clear, he used to take a lot of orders.

He was a soldier's soldier.

He served in the British army during the Second World War and later joined the Transjordan Frontier Force.

He fought against Jewish forces in 1948...

and for a short time after the armistice he found himself in an unlikely role...

I WORKED AS A TEACHER FOR 16 DAYS.

"I went to get my salary; I found it was groceries. Some rice, some corn. I threw down the bag."

MY GOD DIDN'T CREATE ME TO HOLD THIS PEN, BUT TO HOLD A GUN!

J. SACCO 9·05

In 1953, the year after the military coup toppled the Egyptian king, our man joined a newly formed Egyptian-commanded Palestinian militia.

Part of his duties entailed crossing into Israel on intelligence-gathering missions.

BUT WE USED TO GO BEYOND OUR ORDERS.

IN THOSE DAYS THE SETTLEMENTS WEREN'T AS PROTECTED LIKE NOW-ADAYS.

SOME OF US USED TO ENTER THE SETTLEMENTS AND STEAL... COWS AND SHEEP.

At one point scores of Palestinian militiamen were temporarily cashiered for their ties to the Muslim Brotherhood, a militant Islamic group hostile to Cairo and responsible for its own freelance missions of sabotage and revenge in Israel.

AND YOU WERE ONE OF THOSE DISMISSED?

THE FIRST ONE!

YOU, COME HERE!

YOU ARE THE FIRST ONE!

YES, I SWEAR!

But after four months he was called back to service, he says.

His new Palestinian unit began to take over border-guard duties from regular Egyptian soldiers, for whom he had nothing but contempt.

"They were in a room.

"It wasn't a proper military position.

"At night they brought hashish and smoked it through the hubbly-bubbly.

"And they brought alcohol and drank it.

"And slept.

"Anytime the Israelis wanted to kill them, they could have killed them.

J. SACCO 3-05

43

"When I took responsibility, I made a real position, with barbed wire around it and a wall and a trench. A good position. I had 36 soldiers under me."

He and his men watched over a section of the overheated armistice demarcation line, often the site of deadly skirmishes. His orders were to prevent Palestinians from the Gaza Strip crossing into Israel.

The Egyptian authorities implemented stiff jail sentences for those caught doing so. Crackdowns often would intensify after Israeli retaliatory strikes on Egyptian positions in Gaza that usually followed the murder of Jews by Palestinian raiders.

But how far could the Palestinian border guards be trusted to prevent their refugee kin from entering what had until recently been their land?

Not at all, according to Major Mustafa Hafez, head of Egypt's military intelligence in Gaza, who claimed that "Palestinian troops encourage the movement of infiltrators and carry out attacks along the line, and this will lead to an increase in tension."

And our man here is precisely the sort of Palestinian soldier Hafez complained about.

He is drawing a map.

THESE ARE OUR POSITIONS... AND THIS IS THE AREA OF THE ISRAELIS.

HERE, PEOPLE ARE LIVING... FARMERS. THEY WERE PREVENTED FROM COMING CLOSE TO THE LINE.

He relates one incident when he allowed Bedouins to graze their flock across the demarcation line.

J. SACCO 10-05

44

WHEN WE NOTICED A JEEP COMING, WE TOLD THEM TO BRING THE SHEEP BACK INSIDE.

A firefight ensued with the Israeli patrol, and two sheep were killed.

The Egyptian military was not pleased by this unnecessary provocation of the Israelis, and—

—THEIR JUDGMENT WAS THAT I PAY THE PRICE OF THE BULLETS FIRED. (IN FACT, THE OWNERS OF THE SHEEP PAID ME BACK.)

AND I WAS SUPPOSED TO BE PROMOTED TO SERGEANT, BUT THEY STOPPED THE PROMOTION.

But the sheep incident did not end there because—

— I SWORE BY GOD THAT THE PRICE OF THE TWO SHEEP WOULD BE TWO JEEPS.

I am made to understand, elliptically, that he destroyed two Israeli jeeps.

I am hungry for details.

SO THIS OPERATION... IT WAS OBVIOUSLY WITHOUT ORDERS.

YES, THEY WERE MY OWN ORDERS.

DID YOU GO WITH OTHER PEOPLE?

TWO WERE WITH ME.

But he won't tell me about the actions inside Israel that took care of the jeeps except to say he got caught red-handed by UNTSO, the United Nations Truce Supervision Organization, which was charged with the unenviable task of monitoring and if possible preventing cease-fire violations.

"It was our bad luck in the incident over the second jeep... that there was a battle, and the international supervisor came immediately and photographed us. I was carrying a [captured] machine gun."

UNTSO presented the photographic proof that Palestinian troops, supposedly under Egyptian control, were crossing the very border they had been ordered to secure.

"It was impossible to deny this picture.

"This picture was very clear."

J. SACCO 10·05

The Egyptians sentenced him to a prison term in Khan Younis.

And while our protagonist cooled his heels behind bars, the history from which our footnotes dangle was proceeding apace.

In Israel, former Prime Minister David Ben-Gurion came out of retirement and took over the job of defense minister. Together with army Chief of Staff Moshe Dayan, he advocated a hard-line position against the Arabs.

When an Israeli bicyclist was killed by Palestinian infiltrators on February 25, 1955, Ben-Gurion and Dayan were able to convince the less hawkish prime minister, Moshe Sharett, to authorize an attack on Egyptian military positions near Gaza City.

Ironically, in the few months spanning late 1954 and early 1955 the Egyptians had largely succeeded in stopping Palestinian refugees from entering Israel and had halted their own cross-border missions.

Lt. General E.L.M. Burns, the Canadian head of UNTSO, called it "one of the most quiet periods on record."

Dayan promised Sharett that the raid would be nothing out of the ordinary, that it would cause perhaps ten Egyptian casualties.

But let's let Mordechai Bar-On, Dayan's right-hand man, pick up the story...

THAT RETALIATION OPERATION, WHICH WAS ACTIVATED ON FEBRUARY 28, 1955, WAS TO HIT A SMALL MILITARY CAMP AND A BUILDING AT THE RAILWAY STATION.

AND IT WAS TO BE HIT AND RUN.

J. SACCO 10.06

46

The battle was unexpectedly fierce. Israeli paratroopers, commanded by Ariel Sharon, lost eight men, the Egyptian-led defenders about twice as many. Two civilians also died.

Meanwhile, the Israelis had set up an ambush to the south to block enemy reinforcements from reaching the battle.

They caught a truck carrying Palestinian soldiers.

IN THE MIDDLE OF THE ROAD THEY WERE ATTACKED, AND ALL WERE KILLED.

ALL OF THEM WERE PALESTINIAN.*

NATURALLY THE NEWS AFFECTED ME...

I BEGAN YELLING AND SHOUTING.

I STILL HAD 16 DAYS BEFORE I WOULD BE ALLOWED OUT.

*ACCORDING TO UNTSO COMMANDER LT. GENERAL BURNS, 22 SOLDIERS WERE KILLED AND 13 WOUNDED, "MOSTLY" PALESTINIAN.

The incident had immediate repercussions. The next morning riots broke out in Gaza's refugee camps against the Egyptian authorities and the UN. A few Palestinian protestors were shot dead by Egyptian soldiers. Palestinians beat Egyptian troops in the street.

A SEMI-REVOLUTION HAPPENED HERE.

JEMAL ABDEL NASSER HAD TO RESPOND TO THIS ATTACK BECAUSE OF THE PRESSURE OF THE PEOPLE.

And Nasser's dream to unite and lead the Arab world, which depended on his prestige, might have suffered a fatal blow if the Israelis could get away with such an audacious incursion.

OUR SUCCESS MEANT A HUMILIATION FOR NASSER.

J. SACCO 10.06

47

Nasser claimed to have been profoundly jolted by what became known as the Gaza Raid.

He made two fateful decisions.

The first—to buy modern weapons for his army—would have broad implications for the region and the Cold War.

That's the big picture, what gets remembered in history books, and we can skip it for now.

The second decision was to strike back at Israel in a way that would satisfy Arab anger without escalating to an all-out war, which, incidentally, Nasser could not risk until the new arms were available.

One of the instruments of this retaliation was our host here.

NOW THE STORY OF MUSTAFA HAFEZ BEGINS.

(Actually, Hafez's story had already started. He was the same Egyptian intelligence officer who complained about Palestinian troops instigating incidents along the border.

Hafez had been playing a tricky game.

He was entrusted with both stopping Palestinian civilian infiltration and sending authorized military missions into Israel.)

"On March 13, 1955, at 10 o'clock at night, I was alone in my prison cell. I heard footsteps. I pretended to be asleep.

"Then suddenly the light went on. I found Mustafa Hafez standing at the head of my bed.

STAND UP!

PUT ON YOUR CLOTHES!

"Mustafa Hafez remembered me because I was an old soldier—infantry and cavalry.

"I went with him...

J. SACCO 11-06

"I found some people waiting. This group had been assembled by Mustafa Hafez. They said they wouldn't carry out any military operation without me.

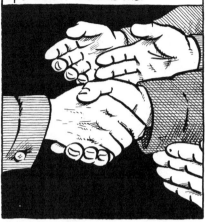

"Mustafa Hafez...gave us the details about the operation we were going to do. Where and when."

THEN WE WENT OUT AND WE SUCCEEDED.

IT WAS A VERY SUCCESSFUL OPERATION.

AND WE LOST NO ONE IN THIS BATTLE.

CAN YOU DESCRIBE THAT OPERATION AT ALL?

I CAN, BUT I DON'T NEED TO.

Over the next few months, the Egyptians recruited a core of militants to establish a Palestinian guerrilla group.

"Most of them came from jail."

"Mustafa Hafez recruited the ones who had been crossing the border...to steal crops and food.

"Some murderers.

"He collected 125 of them and sent them for training."

I ask how he, a professional military man, was able to mix with these recruits, many of whom were criminals.

THEY MADE ME SUFFER.

EACH ONE STARTED TO ACT THE CLEVER FELLOW, TO SHOW OFF AS IF ORDERS DIDN'T APPLY TO HIM.

AT FIRST I CLASHED WITH THEM.

BUT THEN I ABSORBED THEIR MADNESS.

MADNESS.

YES!

J. SACCO 11-06

49

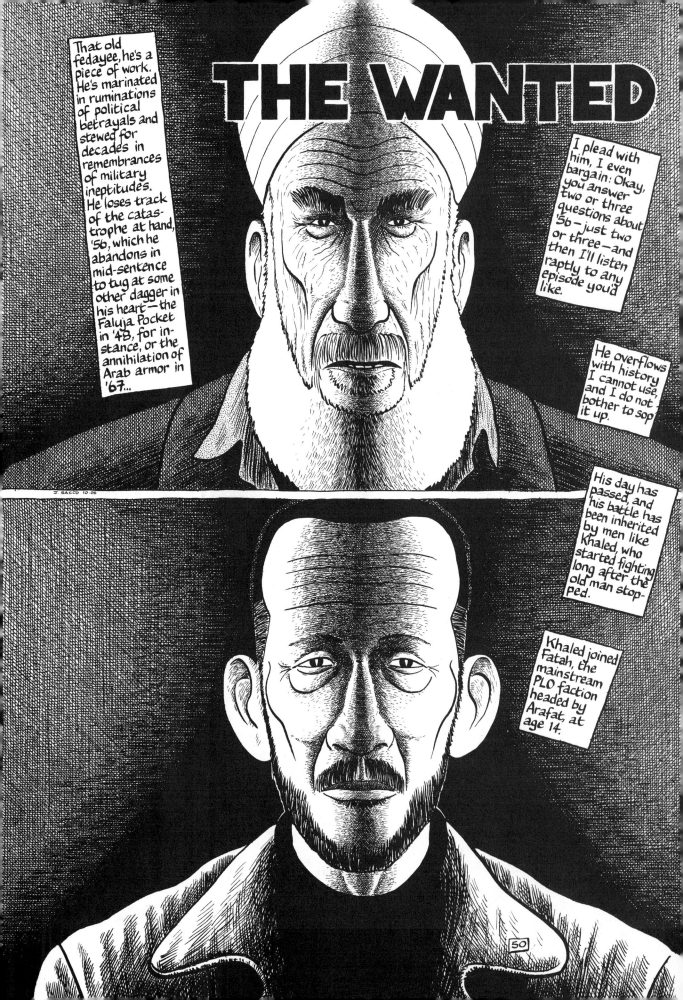

THE WANTED

That old fedayee, he's a piece of work. He's marinated in ruminations of political betrayals and stewed for decades in remembrances of military ineptitudes. He loses track of the catastrophe at hand, '56, which he abandons in mid-sentence to tug at some other dagger in his heart—the Faluja Pocket in '48, for instance, or the annihilation of Arab armor in '67...

I plead with him, I even bargain: Okay, you answer two or three questions about '56—just two or three—and then I'll listen raptly to any episode you'd like.

He overflows with history I cannot use, and I do not bother to sop it up.

His day has passed, and his battle has been inherited by men like Khaled, who started fighting long after the old man stopped.

Khaled joined Fatah, the mainstream PLO faction headed by Arafat, at age 14.

J. SACCO 10·05

50

He proved his mettle in Israeli prisons and in unflinchingly rooting out Palestinian collaborators.

WAS IT HARD KILLING COLLABORATORS?

IT WASN'T HARD AT ALL.

MAYBE YOU COULD SAY IT WAS ONE OF OUR DESIRES.

In the First Intifada, when secret military groups decided to confront the occupation with weapons more lethal than stones, they turned to men like Khaled.

He ended up a high-priority target of the IDF what the Israelis call "wanted."

I asked him when he knew he was wanted. He said Israeli soldiers had once raided his home while he was away...

His father had been used as a shield as the troops searched each room...

And Khaled had been left with a message to give himself up within three days.

He decided to go underground.

"I shook hands with my father and my mother and I stood at the door.

"I took my pistol and shot into the sky.

"My mother started to ululate.

"It was a declaration. Everyone knew then I was wanted. I left. I started a new stage in my life. There was no way to go back on this decision."

He has been on the run ever since.

51

J. SACCO 10·05

Eventually, to reduce the Israeli heat on his family, Khaled decided to escape to Egypt.

Under gunfire, he and three others managed to clamber over an electrified border fence.

He was incarcerated for lack of papers by the Egyptians, who had a peace treaty with Israel and took a sour view of his militant activities. They interrogated him violently. He told them he'd been treated better in Israeli custody.

YOU'RE COMPARING US TO THE JEWS?!

I ACTUALLY CRIED FROM THE INJUSTICE THAT FELLOW ARABS WERE COMMITTING AGAINST ME.

He spent seven months in 13 different Egyptian prisons and jails.

WE HAD TO PAY FOR OUR OWN FOOD, AND OFTEN WE HAD TO PAY OUR GUARDS TO LET US GO TO THE TOILET.

He was deported to Libya, where he joined a PLO training camp.

His wanderings took him as far afield as Sweden and Hungary.

When the Oslo agreements were signed and Israel permitted many Palestinian militants living abroad to return home, Khaled's name was not on the list. He found his own way back to Gaza in a three-month journey that took him from safe house to safe house...

across Egypt's World War II minefields...

and by motorboat to the shores of his homeland.

J. SACCO 11-05

52

He had been gone six years.

"They gave me my Kalashnikov, and I fired into the sky.

"All my neighbors, the old women, came to embrace me.

"My father came out the door, and when he saw me he fainted."

But Khaled knows I'm searching for guerrillas from another time, and he introduces me to his uncle, who might know someone I could talk to.

SALAAM ALEIKUM.

ALEIKUM ES-SALAAM.

Khaled's uncle is a jocular man who was a guerrilla himself as the PLO emerged as the primary Palestinian resistance movement in the 1960's.

J. SACCO 11-05

But his day has passed, too, and his struggle reduced to several well-worn stories and a nod to where his arm used to be.

I ask him what he thinks of his nephew's militancy.

I ADVISED HIM NOT TO BE INVOLVED IN THE RESISTANCE.

IT DOESN'T HELP.

WHEN WE WERE IN JORDAN WE COULD GO IN, SHOOT, AND WITHDRAW.

AND WE HAD MANY MORE WEAPONS.

NOW IT'S CHAOS.

IN THIS FIGHTING IT'S LIKE WE'RE SHOOTING BLANKS.

THEY HAVE MACHINES AND AMERICAN SUPPORT.

HE'S SPEAKING OUT OF FEAR FOR ME.

I AGREE THAT THAT TIME WAS DIFFERENT.

DOES IT MEAN THAT IF YOU HAVEN'T GOT THE MEANS, YOU STOP RESISTING?

Khaled's uncle talks approvingly about the recent ambush in Hebron that killed 12 Israeli soldiers and settler militiamen.

But as to the Jerusalem bus bombing a few days ago—

—IT'S WRONG.

AN OLD MAN? A SMALL CHILD? WOMEN GOING SHOPPING?

WHY KILL THEM?

EVEN A SOLDIER, IF HE GIVES HIMSELF UP, YOU DON'T KILL HIM.

IF YOU GIVE YOURSELF UP TO THE JEWS, THEY TAKE CARE OF YOU.

I'M NEVER HAPPY WHEN I HEAR THAT ISRAELI WOMEN OR CHILDREN ARE KILLED.

LET THEM LIVE.

J. SACCO 1·06

54

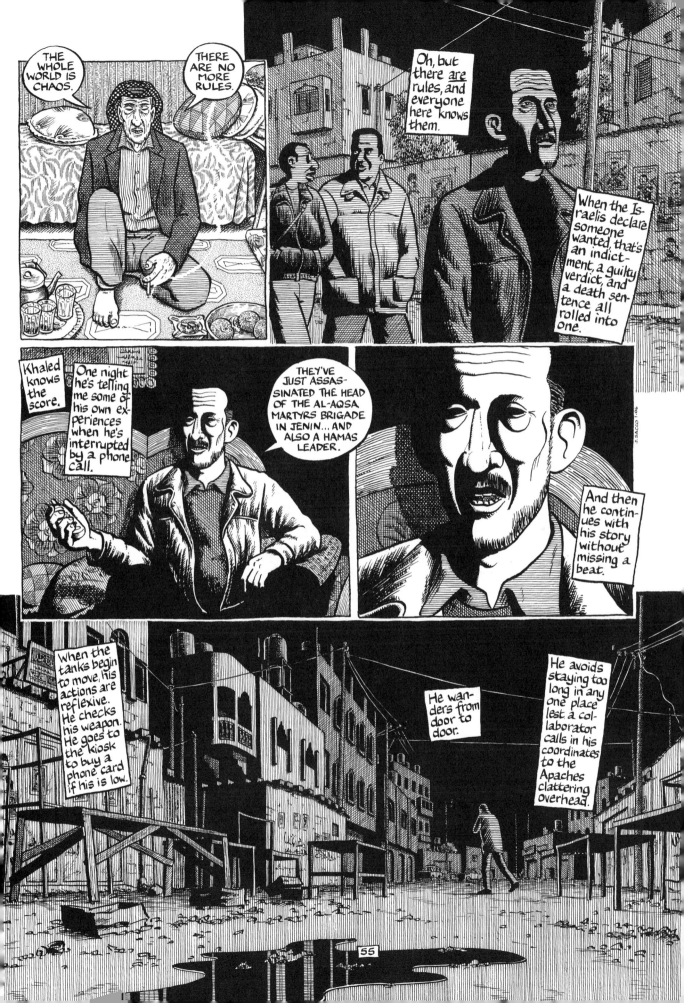

THE WHOLE WORLD IS CHAOS.

THERE ARE NO MORE RULES.

Oh, but there *are* rules, and everyone here knows them.

When the Israelis declare someone wanted, that's an indictment, a guilty verdict, and a death sentence all rolled into one.

Khaled knows the score.

One night he's telling me some of his own experiences when he's interrupted by a phone call.

THEY'VE JUST ASSASSINATED THE HEAD OF THE AL-AQSA MARTYRS BRIGADE IN JENIN... AND ALSO A HAMAS LEADER.

And then he continues with his story without missing a beat.

When the tanks begin to move, his actions are reflexive. He checks his weapon. He goes to the kiosk to buy a phone card if his is low.

He wanders from door to door.

He avoids staying too long in any one place lest a collaborator calls in his coordinates to the Apaches clattering overhead.

J. SACCO 1-06

Sometimes Khaled drops by to steal an hour's rest in the afternoon.

He climbs into one of the beds without removing his pants.

I NEED SLEEP.

I HAVEN'T SLEPT IN TWO YEARS.

He seldom spends the night in his own home.

Two or three times though we visit his house, and once we're up talking till almost two in the morning.

His son is up with us.

SHOULDN'T HE BE IN BED?

Sure, I'm told, but he doesn't get to see much of Khaled. The boy insists on being woken up to play with his dad no matter what time he shows up.

Khaled's wife is expecting again. Khaled says her relatives encourage her to have more children as soon as possible.

They wonder how much longer Khaled has to live.

J. SACCO 1-06

RESISTANCE AND THE SULTA

Last night the Israelis entered northern Khan Younis to destroy the home of a guy who'd blown himself up at the nearby Mawasi checkpoint. Tonight we expect the Israelis to do the same to the home of a second bomber who'd blown himself up in tandem.

We are waiting for news of the incursion at Abed's friend's place when three dudes crash our gathering.

They are moving away from the area the Israelis are expected to attack.

SALAAM ALEIKUM.

They have the same red eyes as Khaled.

J. SACCO 1·06

57

I wonder what Khaled thinks of all that.

I've heard him argue against suicide attacks on civilians.

I've heard him advocate a two-state solution.

I've heard him say he would be willing to cede his "right of return" as a refugee for a chance to raise his family in peace.

But the fighting is not done, and Khaled now belongs to the Popular Resistance Committees, an armed group focused on confronting the occupation aggressively.

I don't know what militant organization these guys belong to.

But here,

in the much-bloodied, achingly poor southern Gaza Strip,

which burns in a tighter circle of hell than almost any other part of Palestine,

—especially here —

whatever differences Khaled has with these men

—political or tactical—

none of them question the basic premise of resisting the common enemy.

In 1996, during the Oslo period, when the Fatah-led Sulta came down hard on Hamas and Islamic Jihad militants for their murderous bombings of Israeli civilians, Khaled refused to participate in the round-ups and interrogations—even though he was an officer in one of the Palestinian security branches.

"Many times they offered me a high rank if I'd get involved," he says because the Sulta knew he had "a lot of information about Hamas and Islamic Jihad."

He couldn't. Those militants were "my friends," Khaled says

Abu Ahmed, who works for a different security service, also refused to participate in the arrests of Islamic militants.

In the First Intifada—

—I ATE WITH THEM AND SLEPT NEAR THEM AND WAS IN PRISON WITH THEM.

AND WE CONSIDERED OURSELVES BROTHERS.

THE GUY WHO USED TO GUIDE MY PRAYERS IN THE MOSQUE WAS FROM HAMAS.

IT'S UNIMAGINABLE THAT I WOULD ARREST HIM.

Abu Ahmed stays away from work for months at a time whenever the assignments don't suit him. However, he proudly threw himself into the Sulta's anti-drug campaign and invited me along on a few swooping raids that busted some dealers and users.

I STOPPED DEALING A LONG TIME AGO.

IF YOU CAN FIND ONE GUY WHO SAYS I GAVE HIM A SINGLE PLANT, I DESERVE TO HANG IN OWDA SQUARE.

Khaled, however, wouldn't even participate in _that_ popular government crackdown because he feared being drawn into more objectionable assignments. To quote an Arabic expression:

THE FIRST STEP TO DANCING IS MOVING.

But, I ask, don't you owe anything to the Sulta for your salary?

I'VE DONE MANY THINGS FOR THIS LAND.

NOT FOR THE SULTA.

BUT I'VE SERVED ALL MY LIFE FOR THE LAND, UNLIKE THE PEOPLE WHO DO NOTHING AND STILL GET SALARIES.

LET ME BE ONE OF THEM.

J. SACCO 1.06

Khaled's com-rade-in-arms, Atlee, also is "wanted" and also draws a Sulta salary.

He, too, is contemptuous of his pay-masters.

They would wish away the resistance to hang on to their ill-gotten gains and the glitzy perks of calm.

ALL THOSE HIGH SULTA OFFICERS HAVE PERSONAL INTERESTS.

THEY TOOK THE COCA-COLA COMPANY. THEY TOOK THE GAS COMPANY.

THEY HAVE BREAKFAST IN TEL AVIV, DINNER IN HAIFA, AND THEY DANCE IN JERUSALEM.

THEY HAVE NO PROBLEMS.

THE RESISTANCE ALWAYS STARTS WITH THE SIMPLE, POOR PEOPLE.

THE RESISTANCE IS IMPOSED ON THE SULTA.

And while the Sulta —which is under great pressure from Israel and America to eliminate homegrown "terrorism"— has muzzled many veteran fighters with jobs and rank in the security services, it hasn't tamed these two.

But, I ask Khaled, couldn't the Sulta just cut off your salary?

It did once, he says, until he threatened to kill someone.

J. SACCO 1·06

IF YOUR SALARY IS STOPPED... YOU SHOOT THEM.

THEY KNOW I'VE KILLED BEFORE.

AND KILLING IS NOT A HUGE THING FOR ME.

Especially in southern Gaza in a place like Rafah, for example, the Sulta's control is tenuous. Says Atlee: "They know we can turn the city upside-down in a few minutes and get the public behind us. Because we are respected among the people."

In fact, Khaled tells me, when the Sulta arrested some comrades in the Popular Resistance Committees, he helped lead demonstrators who freed the men and burned down the building where they'd been held.

So the Sulta teeters, impotent, caught between the occupation and the resistance, neither a proper policeman for the Israelis nor a competent defender of Palestinian lives and land.

Finally, the Israelis have decided to destroy the "terrorists" themselves...

while the Palestinian militants have made it their job to drive out the occupiers.

But no one doubts who has the power and who is winning.

The only question now is how far the Israelis will push their victory or how far the Palestinians can take their defeat.

J. SACCO 2·06

THE FEDAYEEN PT. 2

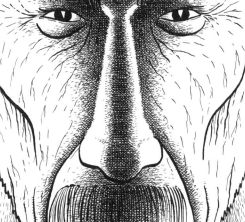

Dear Reader, we have arrived at another losing proposition, the fedayeen campaign of August 1955...

and within inches of my tape recorder, swirling inside the skull of this old man, are perhaps the last extant memories of a participant in that crucial episode along our story's bloody path.

Unfortunately, he is beating around the bush...

THE FEDAYEE'S WORK IS TO ATTACK AND ESCAPE! ESCAPE QUICKLY!

obfuscating...

WHEN WE ATTACKED... IF 100 OF US WERE KILLED AND WE KILLED TWO, WE WERE HAPPY.

holding back...

BUT WE DID VERY GOOD WORK AT THAT TIME, PRAISE BE TO GOD.

CAN I INTERRUPT YOU PLEASE?

I'M LOOKING FOR YOUR EXPERIENCES AS AN INDIVIDUAL.

I DON'T LIKE TO SPEAK ABOUT MYSELF.

NOW WE WILL TALK ABOUT THE REVOLUTION IN '67, THE PALESTINIAN REVOLUTION...

I am a split second from tuning him out for good, but his son, sensing my frustration, steers him back to '55.

IF YOU DON'T WANT TO TALK ABOUT SOMETHING, JUST SAY, 'NO, I DON'T WANT TO TALK ABOUT THAT.'

BUT I WOULD LIKE TO GET AN EXAMPLE OF AN OPERATION.

J. SACCO 2.06

JUST ONE EX- AMPLE.

I FEEL THEY MIGHT READ YOUR BOOK AND DO TO ME WHAT THEY DID TO THAT GERMAN ONE — I STILL REMEMBER HIS NAME — WHO THEY BROUGHT FROM ARGEN- TINA.

EICHMANN?

EICHMANN! EICHMANN!

TO FACE THE FATE OF EICH- MANN!

TAKE CARE! THE JEWS MISS NOTHING!

THEY KNOW EVERY- THING!

THEY KNOW EVERY- THING!

WHEN YOU EN- TERED!

WHERE YOU WENT!

I agree not to use his name, and imme- diately, as if he'd never felt a moment's hesitation, he begins...

BY CHANCE, WHEN WE WERE COMING BACK FROM ONE OPERATION, WE MET A JEEP.

WE DE- STROYED IT COMPLETELY, AND ALL THE SOLDIERS IN THE JEEP WERE KILLED.

"But on their radio, the Israelis said only two soldiers were in- jured. Mustafa Hafez told us—"

YOU ARE LIARS!

WHAT ARE YOU SAYING?

I HAVE BROUGHT SEVEN GUNS FROM THE SOLDIERS.

SHUT YOUR MOUTH!

DON'T SPEAK!

IF SOME- ONE WANTS TO CLAIM SOME- THING, HE SHOULD BRING PROOF.

GO AWAY!

J. SACCO 2-06

ONE OF MY COMRADES, HAMDED ABBAS—HE DIED IN SAUDI ARABIA—

HE DIED?

WE'RE SUPPOSED TO MEET HIM...

—HE WAS OUR GUIDE. HE KNEW THE ROADS.

HE WAS ONE OF THE OLD THIEVES.

"He told me—

LISTEN, I KNOW A WORKERS' CAMP.

THE LEADER ASKED US TO GET PROOF.

DON'T WORRY. LET'S GO.

"We went there. We didn't even come across guards.

"We entered the tents and we killed them all. There was no resistance, nothing.

"The only thing that happened is one of them stood up and stated his nationality.

YOU ARE TURKISH?

WHY DID YOU COME HERE?

GO TO HELL!

"I had a big knife. I cut off their ears.

"It was very easy to cut off their ears with this big knife.

J. SACCO 2-06

65

"We handed Mustafa Hafez the ears."

NOW I BELIEVE YOU.

The old guerrilla doesn't tell me whether this episode took place during this, the first fedayeen campaign. In that week-long assault Israel reported 15 fatalities: five soldiers and ten civilians.

"The goal of most of our operations was to spread panic and fear among those settlements. To prevent more immigrants from coming."

According to Mordechai Bar-On, the fedayeen campaign—

— WAS NEVER CONSIDERED SOMETHING THAT MIGHT DESTROY ISRAEL.

"But it was taken very seriously because of the impact on the general morale, especially on the border. In two or three places settlers evacuated their settlements and new people had to be brought in."

"The fedayeen...were considered something that could not be tolerated."

On the night of August 31, 1955, Israel responded to the fedayeen raids with a devastating attack on the Khan Younis police station.

Hassan Hammad Abu Sitta was there.

He seems like another tired old man in a room full of tired men until I discover he was a policeman on duty that night some 50 years ago.

The memory seems to jolt him awake.

IT WAS 1955, IN THE SUMMER. WE COULD STILL SIT OUTSIDE.

"It was 8 p.m. exactly because we were listening to the news at the time on Nasser's radio station...

THE ISRAELIS ARE ATTACK-ING!

"I entered the building... Everyone who had a gun took his gun.

"...and at that moment the shells started falling.

"Some people who had been outside were going inside for protection, and there were people inside who wanted to get out."

YOU SWITCHED PLACES?

WHY?

HE'S GOING TO DRAW YOU RUNNING AWAY.

THERE WAS A LOT OF CONGES-TION.

J. SACCO 2-06

"I think of how, thank God, I was inside and went out."

"Just outside the station there were Palestinian troops...

"I went into a hole and found four soldiers there.

"There was a lot of shelling. You couldn't see from the smoke and the sand and the dust."

THE RESISTANCE WAS VERY WEAK.

JUST LIKE TODAY. TODAY IT'S THE KALASHNIKOV VERSUS THE MERKAVA TANK.

WE HAD RIFLES. LEE-ENFIELDS WITH FIVE-BULLET MAGAZINES.

"Then there was a big explosion...

"I heard that a tank had come up to the side of the building. They got out, planted explosives, and blew the building up.

"Two floors on the south side collapsed. The whole south side."

I ask what happened to the men inside.

MAY GOD KEEP THAT EVIL FROM YOU.

"They had all been our friends and comrades.

"Most of them were good men, and God bless them.

"You'd find a body crushed by stones and just the legs sticking out.

"There were people who were completely buried."

The Egyptians reported 72 dead, both Egyptians and Palestinians. The U.N. observers confirmed about half that number.

Nasser suspended the fedayeen campaign. His Egyptian and Palestinian forces had shown an inability to repulse Israeli retaliatory raids.

But Nasser remained as determined as ever to tilt the balance of power in Egypt's favor.

In late September 1955 he announced an arms deal with Czechoslovakia, a Soviet satellite, after he'd been stonewalled on a weapons agreement with the Americans.

For the West, this development inaugurated a new and alarming theater—the Arab world—in its Cold War with the Soviets; for Israel, the arms deal was considered a threat to its regional dominance if not a challenge to its very existence.

After general elections, Ben-Gurion replaced Sharett as Israel's prime minister.

The hardliners were now ascendant and determined to start a war with Egypt before it could obtain and incorporate the modern Soviet aircraft and tanks.

According to Bar-On, "many many Israelis, high officials, were clamoring for a preventative strike on Egypt," but Ben-Gurion feared the reaction of the Americans and especially the British, who were treaty-bound with the French to guarantee the borders of the Middle East.

Ben-Gurion, says Bar-On,

WAS TOTALLY OPPOSED TO A PREVENTATIVE WAR, TO INITIATING A WAR OUT OF THE BLUE.

"But he did agree to what Dayan proposed, which was to escalate retaliation operations to the level which would provoke Nasser to begin a war or, at least, would blur... who started it.

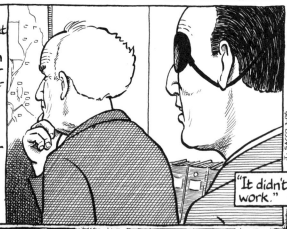

"It didn't work."

Nasser did not take the bait despite continued raids on Gaza and the Sinai that killed scores of Arabs and a deadly strike against Syria, with whom Cairo had recently signed a mutual defense pact.

70

Unable to trigger a war, Israel reverted to a defensive posture, according to Bar-On.

Israel had already started procuring weapons from France to outmatch the quality of the Soviet weapons ordered by Egypt.

A period of relative calm prevailed. Egypt had stopped its infiltrations from Gaza, and despite shooting incidents along the armistice demarcation line, no Israeli had been killed for months.

But over the course of a few clashes in early April 1956, one Egyptian and four Israeli soldiers were killed.

Then, on April 5, a far deadlier incident occurred. According to U.S. Army Lt. Col. R. F. Bayard, chairman of UNTSO's Egyptian-Israeli armistice liaison commission, Israeli mortars fired on an Egyptian position, which led to exchanges of mortar fire along the entire border-line.

Bar-On tells me that the Egyptians fired heavy mortars at "two or three kibbutzim, and it became quite hot," though Bayard reported that UNTSO could not determine which side had fired at civilian targets first.

In any case, five Israeli civilians and two soldiers were wounded that day, and to continue the Israeli perspective...

DAYAN, I THINK, REACTED ALMOST SPONTANEOUSLY.

I WOULDN'T SAY IRRATIONALLY.

J. SACCO 3.06

"He was a rational person, but there was an element of anger, I think: To hell with you! If... you're shelling our kibbutzim, which are civilian targets, I'll show you!"

"And he gave the order to hit Gaza."

"Not much."

"It was one or two barrages."

Israeli heavy mortar shells landed "all along the main street" of Gaza City "at a time when the streets are most crowded," according to Bayard's report, which claimed the Israelis used "the old trick of laying down one or two rounds and waiting several minutes for a crowd to form before returning to [the] original target... Thus many casualties."

About 50 Palestinian civilians were killed and 100 wounded.

According to Bayard, the Israeli claim that they "were firing 120mm mortar at military targets in Gaza is in my opinion an outright lie." The nearest Egyptian military position was one kilometer away.

The attack brought an immediate response from Nasser.

He reactivated the fedayeen.

72

WE WENT TO THE HOSPITAL AND FOUND IT FULL OF PEOPLE INJURED AND KILLED.

WE MOVED QUICKLY TO FORM IN GROUPS...

AND EVERYONE CHOSE HIS TARGET AND ENTERED ISRAEL.

The second fedayeen assault, April 7-12, 1956, cost the lives of ten or 11 Israelis, including children murdered in an attack on a synagogue at Moshav Shafir.

Fedayeen losses were high, and international pressure came to bear on Nasser, who halted the campaign before the Israelis launched an all-out war on Egypt.

J. SACCO 4-06

Nasser!

The mention of the Egyptian leader's name makes the old guerrilla shudder.

WHEN YOU LOOKED AT NASSER YOU GOT SCARED!

HE WAS DARK!

BLACK!

He says Nasser used the fedayeen's limited attacks on Israel to "brighten his face" with the Arab people.

JEMAL ABDEL NASSER EXPLOITED US; HE USED US FOR HIS OWN POPULARITY.

...THE GOALS OF EGYPT'S LEADERS WERE DIFFERENT FROM OURS.

Recall, many of the original fedayeen had been criminals or, like the old guerrilla here, soldiers who had once angered the Egyptian authorities by making freelance attacks on Israelis.

THIS IS A SECRET...AND THIS IS THE FIRST TIME I'VE TOLD IT.

I DISCOVERED THAT THE EGYPTIAN AIM WAS TO GET RID OF ALL OF US BECAUSE THEY CONSIDERED US TROUBLEMAKERS.

And Nasser may have had no interest in creating too potent a Palestinian guerrilla force whose loyalties were not, ultimately, to Egypt.

"Israeli armored vehicles used to chase us...When we...requested anti-tank rifles we were rejected, rejected, rejected. We had the Carl-Gustav rifle. It was useless against those vehicles.

"Mustafa Hafez told us:

I'M WITH YOU, BUT I CAN'T DO ANYTHING ABOUT YOUR REQUEST...I RECEIVE MY ORDERS FROM EGYPT.

"Sometimes Mustafa Hafez got upset. He would locate positions that could be attacked but Egypt told him no."

Whether or not Hafez felt caught between his Egyptian superiors and his mostly Palestinian cadres was of little concern to the Israelis, who assassinated him with a package bomb on July 11, 1956.

"We took him to Cairo and buried him...I cried very much. And his mother was crying with me, trying to stop me from crying...We were crying more than the women. He was very dear to all of us."

MUSTAFA HAFEZ DIED, AND WE DIED.

AFTER HIM, WE DID NO MORE OPERATIONS WORTH TALKING ABOUT.

J. SACCO 4.06

74

Discipline unraveled among a new group of recruits who had joined the fedayeen during Hafez's tenure but who would have been discharged, the old guerrilla contends, had Hafez lived.

"Many rules were broken.

"They made trouble and created many problems.

"They stole gold and attacked women.

"We looked bad before the people."

In his eyes, the Egyptian officer corps was also rotten, starting at the top with the army's chief of staff.

"Abdel Hakim Amer was carousing with women and drinking. We have a proverb: 'If the head of the family is drumming, don't blame the children for dancing.'

"So his officers were just like him.

"Drunkards.

"Drug users."

He says he was convinced the Israelis would retaliate for the second fedayeen campaign.

I BELIEVED THE REACTION OF THE JEWS WOULD BE STRONG.

AND MANY TIMES I SHOUTED AND WARNED THE PEOPLE, 'BE CAREFUL!

'WAKE UP!'

J. SACCO 4.06

75

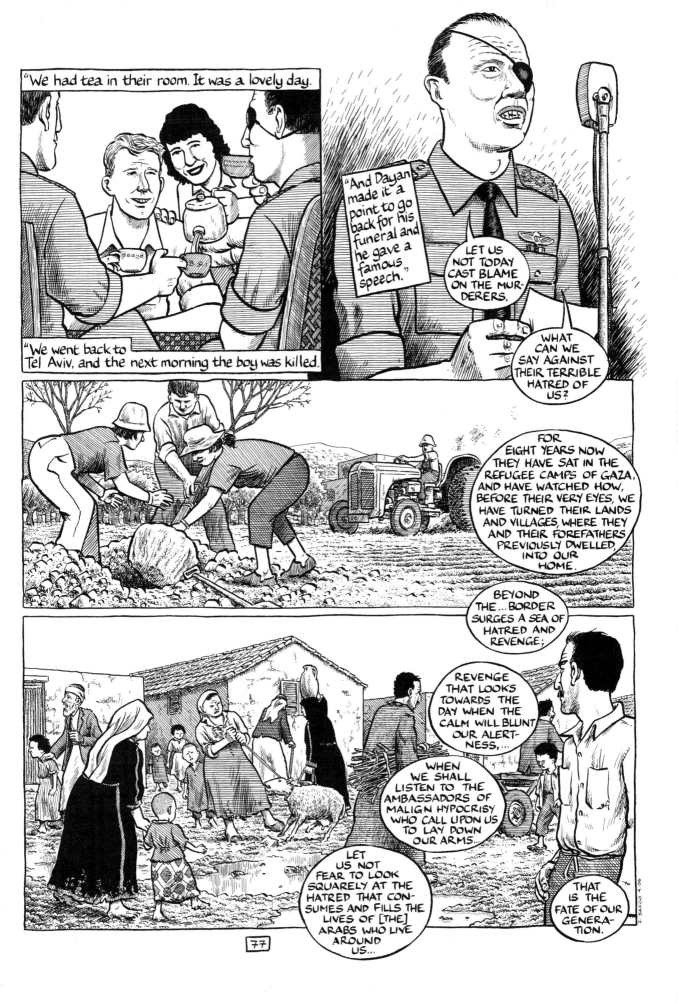

THIS IS OUR CHOICE:

TO BE READY AND ARMED, TOUGH AND HARSH—OR ELSE THE SWORD SHALL FALL FROM OUR HANDS AND OUR LIVES WILL BE CUT SHORT.

YOU COULD SEE IN DAYAN A REALIZATION THAT THE PALESTINIANS HAVE GOOD REASON TO DO WHAT THEY DO ALTHOUGH WE HAVE NO OPTION OTHER THAN TO DEFEND OURSELVES.

According to Bar-On, Dayan had decided that Palestinian infiltrators would have to be stopped once and for all, and that meant one course of action.

HE WANTED TO CREATE A CHANGE IN THE BASIC SITUATION —AND CONQUER THE GAZA STRIP.

Ironically, after trying unsuccessfully to pick a fight, Israel was about to be handed just such an opportunity.

Dear Reader, while we have been focusing on deadly raids and destitute refugees in a sliver of land along the south-easternmost edge of the Mediterranean Sea, overly clever people in London and Paris were hatching a plot that would turn the region upside-down.

The British and French —for their own reasons —had decided to bring down the Egyptian regime.

BRITISH PRIME MINISTER ANTHONY EDEN

FRENCH PRIME MINISTER GUY MOLLET

J. SACCO 4-06

France seethed at Nasser for supporting the costly rebellion against its colonial rule in Algeria.

In fact, by feeding modern weapons to the Israelis, the French hoped to cause problems for Egypt, perhaps even goad Israel into striking Egypt a decisive blow.

78

Britain marked Nasser for removal because his nationalist, anti-colonialist agenda and pan-Arab alliances could have threatened London's client regime in Iraq and British-controlled oil resources there.

Moreover, after vacating its long-standing Egyptian bases by agreement, Britain was angered when Nasser nationalized the foreign-run Suez Canal, the primary waterway for British oil traffic, in July 1956.

Nasser had taken this dramatic step after London, following Washington's lead, broke its promise to fund Egypt's ambitious Aswan Dam project in retaliation for Cairo's arms deals with the Soviet bloc.

Israel, as we have seen, thought war with Egypt was an inevitability.

THE ASSUMPTION AT THAT TIME IN ISRAEL, THROUGHOUT THE '50S, WAS THAT SOONER OR LATER NASSER WOULD ATTACK.

And Israel preferred to strike Egypt first.

Thus, the interests of Britain, France, and Israel overlapped in Cairo.

These nations concocted an elaborate deceit to destroy Nasser, which they outlined in a secret protocol signed in Sèvres, France—the infamous tripartite collusion.

J. SACCO 4.06

The plot called for Israel to attack the Gaza Strip and the Sinai with the chief reason that it wanted to finish off the fedayeen once and for all.

Israel also would make a superfluous parachute drop close to the Suez Canal.

Claiming a duty to protect international shipping traffic, Britain and France would then demand that both Egyptian and Israeli forces withdraw 10 miles from the Canal Zone...

and that Egypt accept the Canal's temporary occupation by an Anglo-French contingent until a settlement could be reached.

The Israelis would comply with the "ultimatum"; Nasser, with Egypt's sovereignty at stake, would certainly refuse it.

The British and French would then attack Egypt.

The scheme started as planned and then quickly unravelled, but let other histories concern themselves with Washington's diplomatic intervention and the subsequent humiliation of Britain and France.

U.S. PRESIDENT DWIGHT D. EISENHOWER

We've got our "human debris and social outcasts" to tend to.

J. SACCO '06

Israel's assault on Egypt began on October 29, 1956.

On November 2, Israeli forces invaded the Gaza Strip.

ATTACK

Fatima Abu Salem was 19 at the time, a mother of two, and living in Khan Younis.

THE ROAD TO EL-ARISH* WAS CUT, AND THE EGYPTIAN SOLDIERS WEREN'T GETTING ANY FOOD.

*EL-ARISH: EGYPTIAN TOWN IN SINAI ABOUT 50 KM WEST OF RAFAH

"They put out chicken coops and asked people to put food in them. A bad situation. No one had food."

"The army was in a complete state of chaos. Soldiers were running into the brush area, taking off their uniforms."

Her husband, a policeman, joined the rout. "He had a uniform," she says. "He was scared...

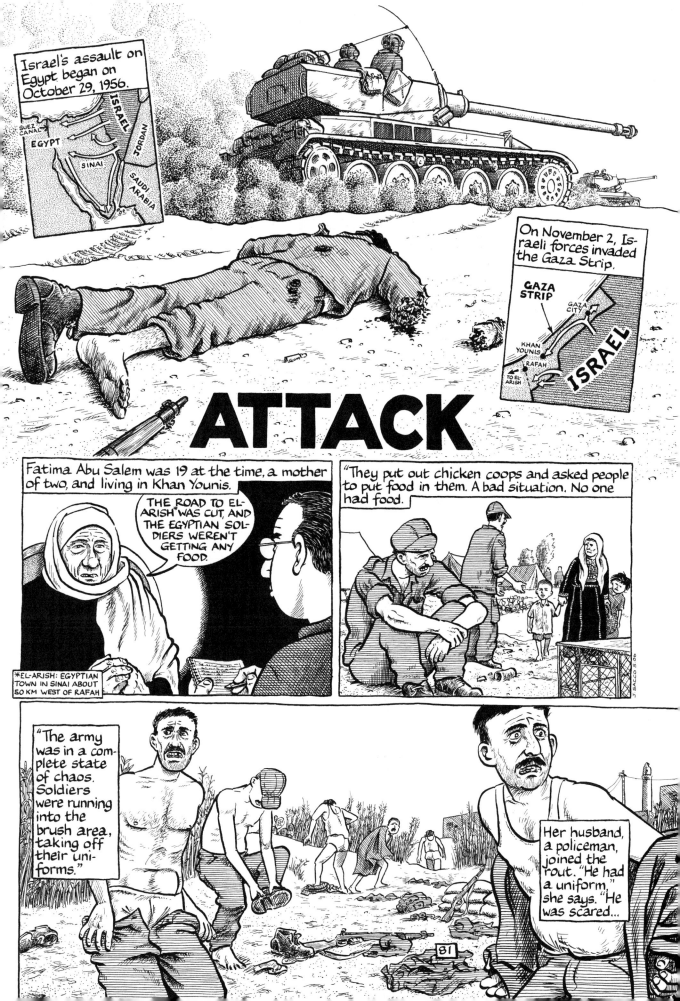

81

"From ships at sea they started shelling the camps. Airplanes were bombing. So we left at night with our neighbors. Everyone was going."

"We walked down to Rafah through the trees and stayed in a sister's house there."

Saleh Shiblaq was a Palestinian in the Egyptian army stationed at an intersection between Khan Younis and Rafah.

THERE WERE ABOUT 55 OF US.

WITH CARL-GUSTAV RIFLES.

WE HAD MACHINE GUNS AND SOME CAN-NONS.

WE DIDN'T HAVE TANKS TO DE-FEND OUR-SELVES.

"We couldn't do anything against planes and tanks."

IT'S JUST LIKE NOW.

WHAT'S A GUY WITH A KALASHNIKOV GOING TO DO AGAINST AN APACHE?

"People started dying. There was an Egyptian officer with three stars who died in front of me named Hanafi ...I was the one who covered him with some sand..."

J. SACCO 5-06

82

"We got orders to withdraw...Everyone went back to his house."

Meanwhile, our old fedayee hurried to Khan Younis with his squad from a mission in Israel to find the defenses already collapsed.

WE RETURNED AND SAW NO PALESTINIAN OR EGYPTIAN FORCES.

WE WERE FEW IN NUMBER. A GROUP OF 11...

"The Israelis outnumbered us...They entered with a huge number of tanks.

"I'd be out of my mind to try to defend with a Carl-Gustav.

"So we escaped to the sea, and we changed our clothes and moved away."

DID THE INVASION OF GAZA BADLY HURT THE FEDAYEEN?

NONE OF THE FEDAYEEN WERE KILLED IN THE '56 INVASION.

ALL OF US ESCAPED.

SOME OF US WENT TO EGYPT AND SOME TO JORDAN.

"The people who suffered were the young men in our cities."

[THE ISRAELIS] TOOK THEM OUT OF THEIR HOUSES AND LINED THEM AGAINST THE WALL AND SHOT THEM.

NOV. 3, 1956

PT. 1: KHAN YOUNIS TOWN CENTER

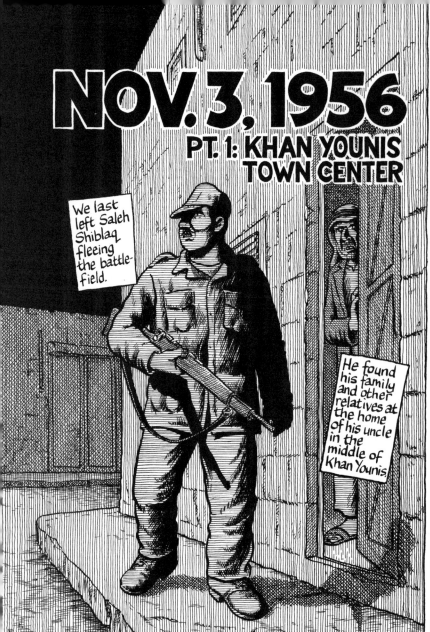

We last left Saleh Shiblaq fleeing the battlefield.

He found his family and other relatives at the home of his uncle in the middle of Khan Younis

I WANTED TO LEAVE THE AREA BECAUSE IT WAS CENTRAL, BUT MY RELATIVES SAID—

STAY HERE!

WE'VE BEEN LOOKING FOR YOU.

The next morning, Saleh could see Israeli soldiers in the street.

Despite this, one of his cousins decided to leave for his own home.

NO, LOOK, THERE ARE JEWS AT THE INTERSECTION THERE.

NO, THEY'RE NOT JEWS.

TAKE IT FROM ME, THEY'RE JEWS.

"He walked toward them, about 100 meters, and they told him to lift his hands...

"and they took him away."

J. SACCO 5.06

84

AFTER A WHILE THE ISRAELIS...STARTED KNOCKING ON DOORS, COLLECTING PEOPLE, SHOOTING THEM IN THEIR HOMES.

NOW, HOW DID YOU KNOW THAT?

DID YOU SEE IT OR DID YOU HEAR IT?

I SAW THE ISRAELIS BANGING ON DOORS AND KICKING DOORS!

AND I COULD HEAR SHOTS...

I WAS WATCHING THEM TAKING THE PEOPLE OUT OF THE HOUSES.

"I had taken off my uniform, but my weapon was with me. I thought I'd take some shots at them, but my father said,

WHAT? YOU WANT TO BE A FEDAYEE NOW?

"They came to where we were...(By this time I had hidden my rifle and some grenades I had under a bed.)

"They came in...and they forced all the women out.

"All the kids...and the old men, too.

"My father was taken out with the women.

J. SACCO 5-06

85

"The other men stayed in the house...

"me,

"my brother,

"and my two cousins ..."

IMMEDIATELY AFTER WE RAISED OUR ARMS, THEY SPRAYED US WITH GUNFIRE.

"I was unconscious maybe half an hour, 45 minutes... I saw that the ones in the room were dead.

"I tried to get up and I fell down."

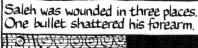

Saleh was wounded in three places. One bullet shattered his forearm.

He still cannot move his arm properly or open his hand fully.

The women of the household carried him to the local clinic the day after the shooting.

From there the Red Cross took him to a hospital in Gaza City.

The cousin who had left the house earlier and been taken by the Israelis was found dead near the Khan Younis castle, one of the town's landmarks.

J. SACCO 5-06

In those days, Misbah Ashour Abu Sa'doni was a handyman living on Jalal Street in the center of Khan Younis, only a couple of dozen meters from where we are talking now.

I WAS WITH MY WIFE, MY MOTHER, MY FATHER, AND MY TWO SONS...

MY SISTER AND HER HUSBAND...

MY BROTHER AND MY BROTHER'S WIFE...

AND ALSO A MAN NAMED SABRI ASHOUR.

SABRI ENDED UP DYING...

THEY CAME TO US BECAUSE OF THE FEAR.

"All of a sudden we heard banging on the door...and by the time we got there they were already breaking it down."

LIFT UP YOUR HANDS!

LIFT UP YOUR HANDS!

The soldiers moved the residents of Jalal Street into the road.

"They divided the men from the women, lining us up on different sides.

"We saw all our neighbors lined up because they were all being brought to the same place..."

Misbah was led away in a group of what he estimates was 30 men.

"We went north a little bit.

"To the bank.

"It was a dentist's office at the time, not a bank."

J. SACCO 5-06

87

In addition, he says, a soldier was standing there with an Egyptian-issue Beretta sub-machine gun.

"I didn't think he had fired at all, but after seven years I discovered a bullet from a Beretta in my leg...

"I sort of went off to the side. I was thinking of escaping.

"Then they started firing.

"I fell down and the bodies began to fall on top of me."

THE SMELL HURT.

THE SMELL OF WHAT? COR-DITE?

YES, FROM SO MUCH FIRING.

IT HURT OUR NOSES.

THEY FIRED A LOT.

"And then there was silence.

"And then we heard them... putting in new maga-zines.

89

"They fired four different times."

THERE WERE MEN WHO HAD BEEN SHOT IN THE FACE AND THEIR SKULLS HAD OPENED UP BECAUSE YOU'RE TALKING ABOUT FOUR TIMES.

THEY WERE HEAVY BULLETS.

"During the fourth burst I felt as though something weighing 50 kilos had been thrown from the top of a minaret onto my back"

"and my spirit went all the way up to the sky.

"I was reciting the Koran...

A bullet had entered Misbah's buttock and exited at his tailbone. He also was wounded in his head and his heel.

J. SACCO 6·06

90

"After it happened, we waited... and then we heard someone say,

NOBODY'S HERE.

"We got up...

"my brother,

"this guy Fayeq,

"and me.

"And there were other people who lived [and] were wounded, but they eventually died.

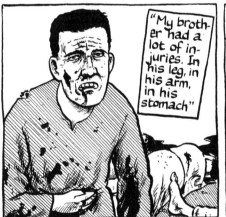

"My brother had a lot of injuries. In his leg, in his arm, in his stomach"

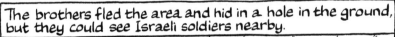

The brothers fled the area and hid in a hole in the ground, but they could see Israeli soldiers nearby.

LET'S GO. LET'S RUN.

"I didn't really want to go. And my brother started to run...

"I tried to start running and would...fall every few meters.

I CAN'T RUN, BUT TAKE CARE OF MY SONS.

THERE'S NO HOPE FOR ME.

J. SACCO 6-06

91

"My brother went...toward the sea. He found someone with a donkey cart who took him to Mawasi.*

*MAWASI: A NARROW STRIP OF LAND ALONG THE SOUTHERN GAZA COAST.

"Three or four months later he died from his injuries."

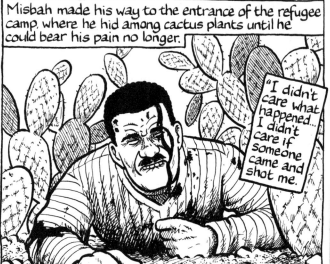

Misbah made his way to the entrance of the refugee camp, where he hid among cactus plants until he could bear his pain no longer.

"I didn't care what happened... I didn't care if someone came and shot me.

"So I started crawling... to get to the road to be face to face with the Israelis."

Instead, Misbah was found by women who had ventured forth to find their male relatives ...

GIVE ME SOME WATER.

and soon he was discovered by his own family...

who tried tending to his injuries the best they could.

PUT COFFEE GROUNDS ON HIS WOUND.

PRESS THE WOUND WITH A HOT IRON...

After three days he was taken to a hospital in Gaza City where he had four operations over four months.

Takreem El-Batta, who resided on the same street as Misbah, was a young boy at the time.

WE WERE LIVING IN THE HOUSE BELOW THIS ONE.

MY MOTHER, MY FATHER, FIVE SISTERS, FOUR BROTHERS, AND THE WIFE OF ONE OF MY BROTHERS.

AND SHE HAD TWO CHILDREN.

"We heard on Israeli radio to stay in our houses and nothing would happen to us."

"Khan Younis was the last place that fell to the Israelis."

"On the 3rd of November, 1956... they came and banged on the door, and my father, who was a sheik, came down and opened it..."

"He asked...if he could wear his [sheik's] clothes...and put his headdress on."

"They said no,

"forget it.

"They said everyone had to come down."

AND RIGHT THERE THEY SHOT MY BROTHER NADEED IN FRONT OF MY MOTHER AND FATHER.

"He was 20 years old.

"He was a student at Al-Azhar University in Egypt, which is a religious school.

"He was on vacation."

93

WAS HE THE ELDEST SON?

NO, HE WASN'T. THERE WAS ONE OLDER THAN HIM, AND HE DIED TOO.

THAT'S COMING.

"They started bringing all the people from the neighborhood to where we were... right in front of our house...

"And then they started taking the men.

"The wife of my brother... [showed] an identity card that said he was just a teacher —Hassan, my brother... And she spoke English well.

HE'S NOT A FIGHTER OR A SOLDIER.

"And they didn't respond.

J. SACCO 7-06

"They took them to the street opposite, where the Bank of Palestine is, and they began to shoot them.

"When we heard the shots, the women began to scream.

"It started around 10 o'clock. We had to stay outside until 2 o'clock.

GO BACK HOME!

"After another hour... soldiers came around the neighborhood banging on the doors saying,

GO GET THEM!

"The women went out to bring the bodies because the [remaining] men were scared.

"My sisters. And the wife of my brother, of course. And the neighbors."

"They lined them up and took them to the castle."

Faris and another boy ran after the young men and their captors.

DIDN'T SOMEONE HOLD YOU BACK? DIDN'T ONE OF THE WOMEN SAY, 'DON'T GO'?

WE WERE CHILDREN AT THE TIME, AND WE JUST RAN.

WERE THE MEN SAYING ANYTHING?

"No."

[THE SOLDIERS] TOLD ME TO GO BACK... I'D MOVE AWAY AND COME BACK AGAIN.

THEY TOOK THE YOUTHS NEAR THE CASTLE...

I DIDN'T REACH THE CASTLE.

I RETURNED HOME.

Half an hour to 45 minutes later, Faris was sent to fetch water despite the curfew.

"I looked to the side as I approached the source of water."

"I saw all the bodies."

J. SACCO 7.06

Almost 50 years later Faris retraces his footsteps to the ruins of the 14th century castle, which now forms one side of the town square.

"I went to the house of one of my relatives, El-Hajj Abdullah. His house was very close to the area.

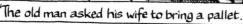
"The old man asked his wife to bring a pallet.

"This is Abdel. "This is Anwar. "This is Abed.

"The old man was checking their faces."

J. SACCO 8-06

Faris leads us through a market, where there was once an open area, to the cemetery where they took the bodies one by one.

I ask him how he feels now, decades later.

I FEEL LIKE I AM THAT CHILD AGAIN.

We arrive at the common family grave—called a fusgeya—into which his cousins were lowered.

"At that time there were hundreds of bodies in one area. You can't bury them individually. You have to hurry and bury the bodies.

J. SACCO 8-06

"The old man, he was experienced, 70 years old.

"He knew that when the [family's] women came and saw their sons and brothers, they would scream.

"So he did his best to bury the bodies before the women came.

"But we only buried a few of them before the women came. They helped us."

The bodies of his relatives were reinterred a few months later.

He tries to recall their names.

He remembers eight names out of twelve.

102

NOV. 3, 1956

PT. 2: KHAN YOUNIS REFUGEE CAMP

We meet Dr. Abdullah El-Horani at his office in Gaza City.

Though he is still a PLO official, he resigned from its Executive Committee after objecting to the Oslo Accords.

He is a harsh critic of those in the Palestinian leadership who would negotiate away the demands of the refugees.

He is a refugee himself.

In 1956 he was a young teacher, an only son who lived with his mother in the Khan Younis refugee camp.

As the Israelis entered the town that day in November, he found shelter with his neighbors.

IN DANGER EVEN ANIMALS SEEK EACH OTHER OUT. HUMAN BEINGS DO THE SAME.

SO PEOPLE WENT TO SIT WITH EACH OTHER ...IN THIS HOUSE OR THAT HOUSE.

AND THAT'S WHY MANY FAMILIES LOST MORE THAN ONE SON.

"Because they were together."

"While we were sitting, we listened to the shooting,

"we listened to the cries.

"We were afraid before they came.

"They entered three rooms. We were in one of these rooms."

'WE'?

APPROX- IMATELY HOW MANY PEOPLE?

I'M TRY- ING...

THE MEM- ORY...

I RE- MEMBER ONLY ONE OF THEM, A TEACHER WITH ME CALLED ATTA EL-OSTAZ.

"I remember he had three or four sisters, and when they took him outside, his mother and sisters cried — but the soldiers did not listen to anybody."

J. SACCO 8.02

104

THEY PUT US AGAINST A WALL IN THE CAMP.

And now Abdullah is up, and in a few steps he is at the wall of his office.

WE WERE AROUND 10,

11,

13,

I DON'T KNOW.

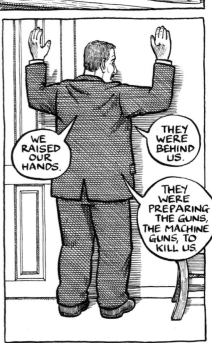

WE RAISED OUR HANDS.

THEY WERE BEHIND US.

THEY WERE PREPARING THE GUNS, THE MACHINE GUNS, TO KILL US.

YOU KNOW, THIS WALL ENDED HERE.

AND HERE THERE WAS A SMALL STREET.

I DID NOT PLAN TO STAND HERE, THE LAST ONE.

BUT I WAS PUSHED...

I CAME HERE.

BY CHANCE!

J. SACCO 8-06

"They started shooting, but I turned into another small street.

"And I ran until I reached the sea.

"Without knowing anything.

"Without looking behind me."

BUT LATER I KNEW THAT ALL [THE OTHERS], UNFORTUNATELY, WERE KILLED.

J. SACCO 7-06

"After the soldiers left, all of the mothers and sisters and children came out looking for their sons and their brothers."

"My mother... searched more than three or four groups looking for me. She was crying all over the camp,

WHERE IS ABDULLAH?

"until I came back two days later."

WHEN I RETURNED ALL THESE THINGS WERE FINISHED. PEOPLE HAD BURIED THEIR MARTYRS.

BUT IN EACH HOUSE I FOUND PEOPLE CRYING.

I STARTED ASKING ABOUT MY FRIENDS.

WE LOST SO MANY FRIENDS.

Omm Nafez was a young woman at the time, married to Abdullah El-Sa'doni. They had three children.

IT IS AS IF IT IS HAPPENING NOW. I'LL NEVER FORGET IT.

On the morning of November 3, she says, a young boy came running from town with a warning.

IF YOU HAVE ANY YOUNG MEN, TELL THEM TO RUN!

THEY'RE KILLING EVERYONE!

J. SACCO 9-06

But Abdullah and three of his brothers were still in the camp, huddled with their families, when the Israelis arrived.

"Two Israeli soldiers stood outside the door, and one came in to get the boys out.

"The first brother who came out was Ibrahim.

"They killed him.

"The next was Subhi. Subhi held a child in his arms.

"They shot Subhi, and as he [fell] they shot the boy, too.*

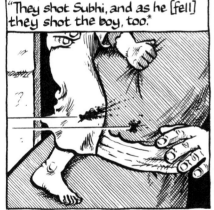

"Then came Abdullah and Khamis. I called:"

MY HUSBAND!

At that point, Khamis made a run for it.

"He jumped over the wall and escaped.

"Abdullah...was trying to escape, but they caught him.

"They took him outside the door ...and they shot him in his side."

* THE INJURED BOY, A NEPHEW OF THE BROTHERS, WOULD LOSE HIS LEG.

J. SACCO 9.06

109

THEY KILLED ABDULLAH AND RAN AFTER KHAMIS.

"Subhi was alive till the next day. He was conscious. He asked about his brothers. I said that they were still alive..."

I KNOW THEY'RE DEAD.

According to Omm Nafez, Subhi asked to be taken to Rafah for treatment, but as the women lifted him—

PUT ME DOWN... PUT ME DOWN...

"Fifteen minutes later he was dead."

"We went to bury them. I went to UNRWA to get something we could carry them with. I held a white handkerchief as a sign—don't shoot me. There was a curfew at the time.

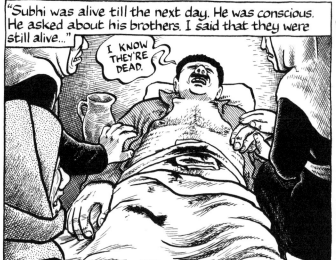

"The soldier at the clinic asked me,

WHAT'S UP?

I NEED SOMETHING TO CARRY THOSE YOU'VE KILLED.

GO HOME, TAKE YOUR DOOR. USE THAT...

THE CURFEW WILL BE OVER IN AN HOUR.

J. SACCO 9-06

"We moved the bodies. Our women, the other wives."

"We dropped Ibrahim once."

WE TOOK OFF THEIR SHOES, AND THEN WE BURIED THEM.

"I covered all the house with ash... from the oven with my hands..."

"I made the house black."

FORGIVE ME, GOD.

YOU'RE NOT SUPPOSED TO MOURN MORE THAN THREE DAYS.

THE ASH REMAINED TILL AFTER THE CHILDREN GREW UP.

WHAT CAN WE DO?

GOD WANTS THIS TO HAPPEN TO US — TO LEAVE OUR LANDS AND COME HERE AND BE KILLED.

MEMORY AND THE ESSENTIAL TRUTH

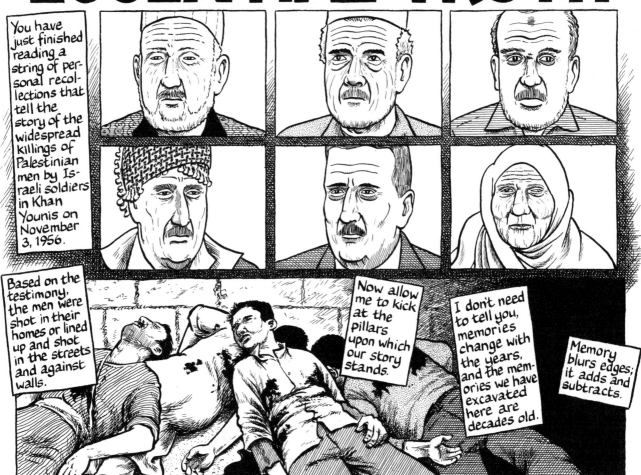

You have just finished reading a string of personal recollections that tell the story of the widespread killings of Palestinian men by Israeli soldiers in Khan Younis on November 3, 1956.

Based on the testimony, the men were shot in their homes or lined up and shot in the streets and against walls.

Now allow me to kick at the pillars upon which our story stands.

I don't need to tell you, memories change with the years, and the memories we have excavated here are decades old.

Memory blurs edges; it adds and subtracts.

Let us take one example, the story of Omm Nafez.

Her story is well known among the camp old-timers because it is particularly tragic.

Four brothers were taken outside to be shot.

Her husband was among them, and he was killed.

One of the brothers, Khamis, escaped.

112

J. SACCO 10-06

Khamis is still alive. His recollections are interesting for the sake of comparison.

For instance, he says he and his brothers were lined up by soldiers before being shot rather than shot one-by-one as they came through the door, as Omm Nafez remembers.

In a separate interview, another witness, Khamis's nephew, Abu Antar El-Sa'doni, who was seven at the time, agrees that the brothers were lined up.*

In fact, Abu Antar's account concurs with Khamis's about the order in which the men stood against the wall — with Khamis nearest the door.

Now let's take up Khamis's story.

He describes how he ran as his brothers were being shot...

RUN, SUBHI!

how he knocked down the soldier pursuing him...

how he jumped over a wall...

and how he fled as soldiers fired at him.

Abu Antar confirms this version so far, down to Khamis's exhortation to Subhi to flee:

AND HE SAID, 'FOLLOW ME, SUBHI!'

* ABU ANTAR'S FATHER, THE FIFTH BROTHER, WAS AWAY IN EGYPT AT THE TIME.

J. SACCO 10.06

Next, Khamis says, Subhi motioned to his family.

TAKE CARE OF THEM.

AND THEN HE DIED.

EVERY TIME IT COMES TO MY HEAD, I SEE IT LIKE A VIDEO.

Khamis's version of Subhi's death generally matches those of Abu Antar and Omm Nafez except on one crucial point.

Both of them say Khamis was not there.

AFTER DAYS, DAYS, WE GOT NEWS... THAT MY UNCLE KHAMIS HAD ARRIVED IN RAFAH, AND THAT HE WAS THERE AND SAFE... AND HE DIDN'T COME BACK TO KHAN YOUNIS FOR TWO MONTHS, AFTER THE WHOLE SITUATION COMPLETELY CALMED DOWN.

HE WAS GONE FOR FOUR MONTHS... I DIDN'T SEE HIM TILL AFTER THE JEWS HAD LEFT KHAN YOUNIS.

What are we to make of this?

J. SACCO 10-06

Is it my place to say that Khamis, who told his story so affectingly before a rapt group of his relatives and neighbors, was not there?

Perhaps Omm Nafez, who was so distraught at her husband's death, has blocked out her memory of Khamis;

perhaps Abu Antar was too young and simply doesn't remember him present.

Or perhaps Khamis has heard the story of his brother's death so often that it has become his own. Maybe Khamis feels he should have been with Subhi.

Khamis survived.

Three of his brothers died, leaving widows and five children.

And that is not all.

In the immediate area 36 people from nine houses, his neighbors and friends, were killed, he says.

OMER EL-HALA

MED ABU AMER

HAMID ABDEL HAFEEZ EL-RANTISI

ABDEL AZIZ NOFAL

AHMED EL-ZAKZA

In moments of calm, he says, he can remember the names of all the dead.

I cannot untangle the twining guilt and grief that envelope a person who survives what so many others did not; nor can I explain what might induce a traumatized individual to recall a brother's death if he was not there — assuming he was not.

J. SACCO 10·06

I only want to acknowledge the problems that go along with relying on eyewitness testimony in telling our story.

But all this should not let us forget the essential truth:

Khamis's three brothers were shot by Israeli soldiers on November 3, 1956.

They were among what a U.N. report alleges were 275 Palestinians killed in Khan Younis town and camp that day.

116

DOCUMENT

You can read that report for yourself at the U.N. archives on East 43rd St. in New York City.

It is the 'Special Report of the Director of the United Nations Relief and Works Agency for Palestine Refugees in the Near East Covering the period 1 November 1956 to mid-December 1956' to the General Assembly.

To the historian, who rubs his hands together as the archivist wheels out a cart loaded with forgotten files, a contemporary document like this can represent a more definitive version of events than decades-old memories.

But the report indicates "there is some conflict in the accounts given as to the causes of the casualties.

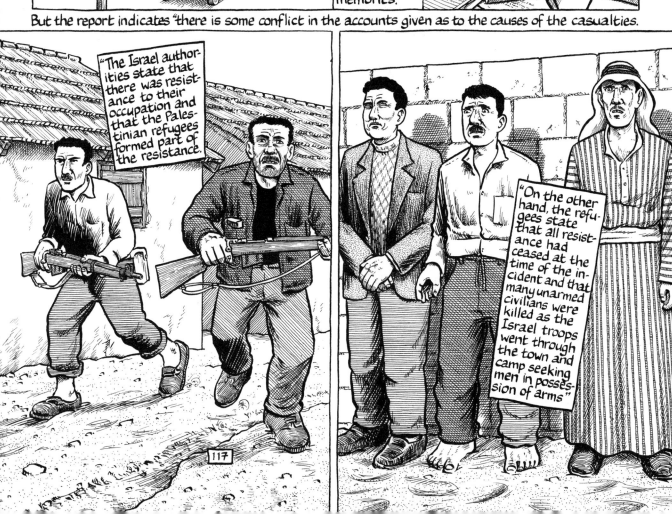

"The Israel authorities state that there was resistance to their occupation and that the Palestinian refugees formed part of the resistance."

"On the other hand, the refugees state that all resistance had ceased at the time of the incident and that many unarmed civilians were killed as the Israel troops went through the town and camp seeking men in possession of arms"

117

The U.N. report presents two incompatible versions of the Khan Younis "incident," and so in this case, as in many others, history-by-document drops us into a muddied soup of "on the other hands" and "possibles" seasoned, perhaps, with a few "probablies."

But clearly the refugees' claim in the U.N. report dovetails with the eyewitness testimony Abed and I gathered many years later. Namely: the fighting had stopped; the men were unarmed; they did not resist.

One former Israeli soldier present in Khan Younis in 1956, journalist Marek Gefen, came forward in 1982 to write about his experiences there.

Gefen reported that when he entered the town he found the streets "completely empty."

"In a few alleyways we found bodies strewn on the ground, covered in blood, their heads shattered. No one had taken care of moving them.

"I felt dreadful. I stopped at a corner and threw up. I couldn't get used to the sight of a human slaughterhouse.

J. SACCO 11-06

"The cleansing of the Strip went on," he wrote, and described a fellow soldier killing an unarmed Arab doctor in an UNRWA clinic during a search for weapons.

WHY?

ONE LESS.

Gefen has passed away, but I manage to locate one of his army comrades in Tel Aviv. Naftali Carni was in the same unit as Gefen.

He remembers some minor abuses of the Palestinian population by soldiers, but says he recalls nothing like the bodies Gefen saw in Khan Younis.

In fact, Carni doubts Gefen's story. He thinks Gefen was prone to sensationalism. "He was a newspaperman," he says by way of explanation.

Well, I'm a newspaperman at heart, and to me it's never been a term of disparagement.

A newspaperman wants the facts, the definitive version, not a bunch of "on the other hands" and "possiblies" or even "probables."

And I swear I'll wrench nothing but the facts from our next batch of eyewitnesses, frail and imperfect as they might be.

We have one more footnote to go.

119

FEAST

CLAUSTROPHOBIA

I hook up with Abed and his pal Hani in Gaza City.

They're good friends.

They met while doing activist work for women's rights, and they studied law together in Egypt.

Abed has news.

He's decided.

IT'S TIME FOR ME TO LEAVE. AT LEAST FOR A WHILE.

He's applying to MBA programs abroad and for scholarships available to Palestinian students.

Abed and I spend the evening at the office where he works to write up his resume and "personal statement."

Why do you want to study abroad? How will it better your prospects?

How will it help you develop your country?

We come up with some sufficiently earnest bullshit.

J. SACCO 12·06

125

Before midnight we hear helicopters and bursts of gunfire.

We turn on the T.V. to see what's up.

Two male nurses have been killed by the Israelis in a Hamas-run rehabilitation center.

The Palestinian cameras don't flinch at the gaping wounds in the nurses' chests.

The next morning, Hani rejoins us.

The office balcony overlooks Shifa Hospital, where the nurses' bodies were brought last night.

Loudspeakers are blaring Islamic songs.

Hani explains that the bodies will be carried to their homes, then taken to the mosque for prayers, and then to the cemetery for burial.

The dead are martyrs, he says, so they will not be washed or redressed.

THE BLOOD OF THE MARTYR HAS THE SMELL OF PERFUME.

THE CLOTHES IN WHICH HE IS KILLED ARE THE BEST CLOTHES IN WHICH HE CAN MEET GOD.

J·SACCO 12-06

126

But we are not sticking around for funerals.

Near the hospital, taxis are lined up for trips to points south — including Khan Younis, where we are going.

The drivers are lucky if they make two roundtrips a day so their place in line is important.

But there's a woman waiting in the front seat of the taxi slated to leave next, and Hani, who is tall for a Palestinian, doesn't want to sit in the cramped rear seats.

Propriety, however, prohibits him from asking the woman to change seats.

Hani's solution is to sit in the front seat of the second taxi in line. We join him in back.

This sets off a shouting match between the first taxi driver, who thinks he's being cheated out of his customers, and Hani.

I've learned that a shouting match in Gaza is not what it seems.

No, actually, it is exactly what it seems:

A bunch of shouting.

Hani gets his way, and soon our taxi fills up and moves.

The ride is smooth until the Abu Houli checkpoint, where we encounter the usual delay.

THE ISRAELIS WON'T LET ANY CAR THROUGH THAT HAS LESS THAN THREE PEOPLE IN IT.

LATELY THEY'VE BEEN SHOUTING, 'YOU HAVE TO HAVE THREE! THREE!' BY LOUD-SPEAKER.

128

Go!

We drive under the bomb-proofed settler bypass bridge to the second tower a few hundred meters away,

where our taxi slows to a non-threatening crawl.

Everyone shuts up again.

Because Abed needs to tend to his applications, we spend the next few days shuttling between Khan Younis and Gaza City, where he has access to the office computers and fax machine.

That means getting through the Abu Houli checkpoint time and time again.

The delay may be ten minutes, or we might find the road cut indefinitely.

"Whenever I'm in Gaza City," Abed tells me, "I prepare myself for being stuck for a day or even a week."

Me, I've learned to bring along a change of underwear.

Once, while we're in Gaza City, we hear of a suicide attack on one of the Abu Houli towers.

Apparently, a Palestinian car, carrying three men so as not to arouse suspicion, suddenly raced at the Israeli position, passengers firing, and detonated.

The Palestinians were killed; a few Israeli soldiers were diagnosed with shock.

J. SACCO 1·07

131

WHO NEEDS TEA, TEA?

WHO NEEDS TEA, TEA?

We expect the Abu Houli checkpoint will be closed for a day or two, but it re-opens in the evening, and the next morning we find ourselves at the familiar jam-up as we try to get back to Khan Younis.

TEA, TEA?

There's a rap on our taxi's window.

The driver behind us is alone, and he needs two passengers to be allowed through.

It's been raining, and the usual shekel boys are nowhere to be seen.

CAN ANYONE COME WITH ME?

Abed and I agree to join him.

His car is stuffed with bags full of biscuits he has to deliver.

The line begins to move, and with each lurch the load threatens to engulf us.

132

J. SACCO 1-07

As we finally reach the checkpoint we look around for signs of yesterday's suicide attack.

MANY MEN HAVE BEEN MARTYRED ATTACKING THESE TWO FUCKING TOWERS.

We're told this is the tower the three men targetted.

Save for a few scraps from the blown-up car, little remains to tell the tale.

The Israeli position is unscathed.

133

The lack of serious Israeli casualties in the Abu Houli suicide attack has disappointed the Palestinians.

ALL OF US WILL GET A BEATING

I pose a question to the table:

IF YOU HEAR THAT A BOMB HAS GONE OFF IN TEL AVIV, WHAT'S YOUR FIRST REACTION?

MY FIRST REACTION IS HAPPINESS.

OF COURSE, ISLAM DOESN'T SANCTION THE KILLING OF WOMEN, CHILDREN, AND OLD PEOPLE.

DO THESE BOMBINGS SERVE ANY STRATEGIC PURPOSE AT ALL?

EVERY ISRAELI IS A SOLDIER.

THEY GO INTO THE ARMY AT AGE 16*, AND AFTER THEIR MILITARY SERVICE, THEY STILL DO 40 DAYS OF SERVICE A YEAR.

YOU HAVEN'T ANSWERED MY QUESTION.

* IN FACT, THE AGE OF CONSCRIPTION IS 18.

I'M NOT TALKING ABOUT THE MORALITY OF THESE ACTIONS.

I'M ASKING IF THEY SERVE THE PALESTINIAN NATIONAL INTEREST.

THEY MAKE THEM FEARFUL.

I'm still not satisfied, and Hani is getting flustered.

I DON'T WANT TO TALK ABOUT IT ANYMORE.

LET'S EAT!

134

Khaled, the wanted man, hears I am back in Khan Younis and has shown up for lunch.

He sinks into a seat and is still.

It seems he's shifted into some sort of lower gear, like an animal dropping its heart rate to conserve energy.

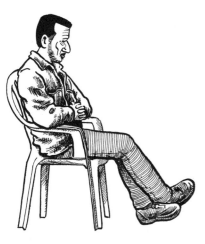

I ask him how things have been in the months since I've seen him.

IT'S WORSE THAN BE-FORE.

THERE'S NO POLITICAL HORIZON AT ALL.

We catch the news whenever we can.

On CNN the anchors seem giddy about the prospect of a war between Iraq and a coalition led by the United States.

War!

The word twirls around their tongues like a chocolate mint.

Bush appears on the set brimming with determination.

Everyone laughs when he refers to Iraq as "a prison."

Do they laugh because they don't think Iraq is a prison? Or because they believe they are the ones living in a prison?

"The game is over," Bush tells the world.

A night or two later, gunfire and explosions keep me awake.

The Israelis are demolishing eight homes in Khan Younis; a woman reportedly dies of a heart attack.

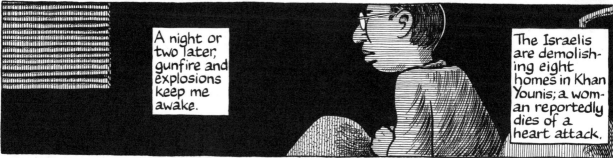

In a taxi the next morning, one passenger mutters to himself for a few seconds, and then...

THE SULTA VIOLATES OUR DIGNITY, AND THE ARAB REGIMES ARE USELESS.

THE AMERICANS TAKE TURNS STEPPING ON OUR HEADS AND THE HEADS OF THE IRAQIS!

AFTER IRAQ THEY'LL ATTACK SYRIA UNTIL ALL OF US WILL GET A BEATING!!

J. SACCO 1-07

136

We've suspended our research for a few days.

No one wants to sit down for an interview about '56 during Eid El-Adha, the feast which commemorates Abraham's readiness to sacrifice his son Ishmael to Allah.

FEAST

Over the last week goats and rams have been coaxed and pulled down the streets of Khan Younis in a lonely, sad trickle.

But this is the eve of the feast, and now the bulls are arriving.

A BULL IS COMING!!

A BULL IS COMING!!

TOY

The animals are made to jump out of vehicles and are driven into empty stores, where they'll spend their final night in solitude...

or taken to back lots where they'll have the company of delighted children.

J. SACCO 1.07

The street, as they say, is running with blood, and the kids use the goo to make handprints on the walls.

Meanwhile, we're still waiting for the butcher.

Bored, Abu Hamed asks what I'm doing in Gaza.

Abed explains my '56 project.

'56?

He was six years old then, he says, but he remembers.

"Before the Israelis entered Khan Younis," he tells us,

I WAS IN A MARKET WHEN WE CAME UNDER AIR ATTACK.

I RAN FROM SHOP TO SHOP BETWEEN PLANES.

A half century has passed, and things seem just as bleak.

WE MAKE A SACRIFICE OF THE BULLS, AND SHARON* MAKES A SACRIFICE OF US.

*ARIEL SHARON, THEN PRIME MINISTER OF ISRAEL

Finally, the long-overdue butcher pulls up.

WAS HE IN FRANCE OR WHAT?

The butcher is with his son. They have other appointments this morning so the store is opened right away to reveal the bull.

This is nothing personal, but the bull knows something is up.

The butcher sharpens his knives while his son expertly lassoes a front leg and then the opposite hind leg.

Now everyone gets in on the act. The ropes are crossed and pulled...

and the bull goes down.

J. SACCO 2-07

When the butcher is satisfied that the animal cannot right itself, he steps forward.

IN THE NAME OF GOD...

He strikes three times before he breaks through the hide.

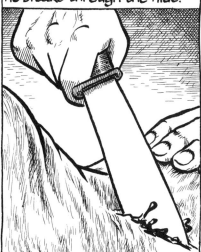

The son takes the father's place.

He has a small knife, but he drives it in so deep that his fists disappear into the bull's throat.

As he hacks, the butcher works to extend the cuts to the sides.

The bull has stopped kicking.

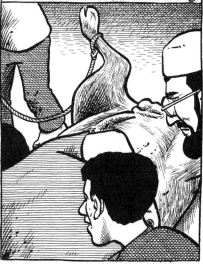

The other men join in, cutting through the neck and twisting off the head.

Cinder blocks are brought in to support the carcass which is flayed...

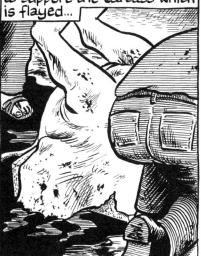

while the legs are cut off at the knee joints.

J. SACCO 2-07

The bull is split open and the organs are removed.

The stomach and intestines are dumped on the sidewalk.

The toxic spleen is handed gingerly to a boy who throws it like a grenade into the street.

J. SACCO 2-07

The hide is given to a poor spastic man who has asked for it. He might fetch 50 shekels ($10) from a dealer.

The bull has been quartered, and the butcher prepares to go.

I'VE DONE MY JOB.

No, no!

You've been paid to divide the bull further!

Grumpily, he cuts away a while longer before leaving for his next $50 appointment.

The pieces of the animal are taken a couple of doors down to be hung up and washed.

The men begin slicing off chunks and dropping them into buckets.

It's time for a smoking break at a nearby shop where Mahmoud is earning a little money making kebabs for neighbors who bring meat from the animals they've just slaughtered.

To entice more customers, Mahmoud throws fat on the coals and fills the street with the smell of his grilling.

J. SACCO 2·07

143

Abed is staring absently at a poster depicting a couple of martyrs.

MY FRIEND WAS KILLED AND I DIDN'T EVEN KNOW.

WHO?

THE ONE ON THE LEFT.

AMMAR.

I ONLY LEARNED ABOUT IT AN HOUR AGO.

HOW COME YOU DIDN'T KNOW?

I'VE BEEN WORKING IN GAZA CITY. I'M THERE MOST OF THE TIME.

His pal had been resisting a recent Israeli incursion.

HE WAS WOUNDED AND DIED LATER.

AMMAR.

We finish our Cleopatra cigarettes and join the final stage of the butchering.

The meat has been separated into piles representing the different parts of the animal and is cut up into even smaller bits.

The pieces are divided into seven equal portions, one for each household.

With all the family heads assembled, the portions are distributed by lot.

J. SACCO 2-07

The entire process, from butchering the bull to allotting the meat, has taken four hours.

But there's more. Each household must now further divide its portion: a third is for the family; a third is passed out to close relatives and friends; and a third goes to the poor.

Abed's step-dad meticulously weighs each share.

Abed's mother hands plastic bags full of meat to one of her sons and mentions the name of an old woman.

MAKE SURE YOU PUT IT IN _HER_ HANDS.

An hour later, Abed and I are eating our first meal from the bull.

The next day Abed jokes that I ought to interview bulls about _their_ massacre.

YOU COULD GO AROUND AND THEY'LL TELL YOU, 'THIS IS WHERE THEY KEPT ME.'

AND SINCE YOU DON'T SPEAK BULL, YOU'LL HAVE A BULL TO ACCOMPANY YOU AS A TRANSLATOR.

A hard rain has begun just as everyone hoped.

While Israeli bombers roar low and unseen overhead, it washes the blood from the streets.

J. SACCO 2-07

HANI

A day or so later, Hani pays us a visit from Rafah, where he lives in the refugee camp.

He says the butcher was late to his place, too, and in the end he decided to take care of the killing himself.

BUT I COULDN'T DO IT.

THE COW WAS TREMBLING AND DIDN'T RESIST.

I DIDN'T HAVE THE HEART TO GO THROUGH WITH IT EVEN THOUGH THE COW WAS DOWN AND I HAD ALREADY SAID, 'IN THE NAME OF GOD, GOD IS GREAT.'

EVERYONE LAUGHED AND MY FAMILY TEASED ME.

Eventually the butcher came and did the deed.

But Hani took no part in skinning or cutting up the carcass.

He couldn't bring himself to eat from the cow, either.

Hani has put himself in charge of logistics for the next phase of my investigations, which will be centered in Rafah.

On my introductory visit to the camp there, the kids follow me around as usual—

HOW ARE YOU?

HOW ARE YOU?

—until Hani politely tells them to shove off.

J. SACCO 1-07

But when we are sitting in his front room and they climb the wall to peer inside, he blows his top.

DON'T EMBARRASS ME!

I'LL TELL YOUR FATHER TO BREAK OPEN YOUR HEAD!

When Hani returns, he has already calmed down.

IT'S NOT JUST A MATTER OF YOU BEING HERE.

THEY WERE CLIMBING UP TO THE WINDOW, AND THIS IS MY PRIVATE SPACE.

During the First Intifada, when Hani was in his mid-teens, he was jumped by an Israeli under-cover unit while he was spray-painting slogans and shot seven times at close range.

He's shown me the scars.

THEY TOOK ME BY HELICOPTER TO AN ISRAELI HOSPITAL.

NOT BECAUSE THEY WANTED TO SAVE ME, BUT BECAUSE THEY WANTED INFORMATION.

After he recovered, he was put in prison.

I WAS KEPT IN A TINY ROOM FOR DAYS.

THEY THREW URINE ON ME.

AND THE INTERROGATOR WOULD BANG MY HEAD ON THE WALL.

147

His story goes on and on...

In the end, Hani tells me he confessed to nothing.

He's proud of that. He's a Bedouin, and proud of that as well; he enjoys explaining Bedouin traditions.

He's proud of being an Arab.

Once, he takes me to see a friend of his, a teacher of Arabic named Abu Mohammed, who is interested in my '56 project and contends that Arabs don't know their own history.

ARABS DON'T READ.

Hani takes exception to this, but Abu Mohammed is insistent.

THE CULTURAL PRODUCTION OF ONLY ONE COUNTRY—SPAIN—IS MORE THAN THAT OF THE ENTIRE ARAB WORLD.

DICTATORSHIPS AND UNEMPLOYMENT MAKE ARABS THINK MORE ABOUT THEIR STOMACHS THAN THEIR MINDS.

Everyone erupts, especially Hani.

COLONIZATION AND OCCUPATION ARE AT FAULT! WHERE DOES OUR ECONOMY COME FROM?

He answers his own question:

FROM THEM!

The colonizers and occupiers!

J. SACCO 3.07

148

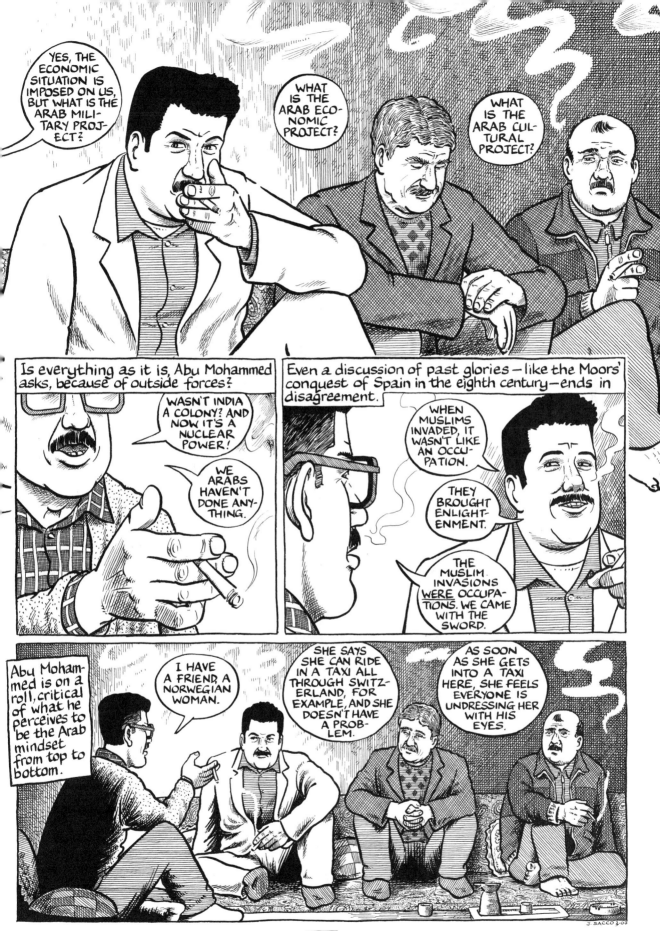

RAFAH

HOUSE HUNTING

It's time to find a place in Rafah, and Hani is insistent.

He doesn't want me living in the refugee camp.

He steers me toward the town proper where we look at a couple of apartments.

IT'S GOOD. YOU'RE CLOSE TO EVERYTHING HERE.

I STILL WANT TO LIVE IN THE CAMP.

Khaled, the wanted man, also tries to dissuade me.

YOU MIGHT COME UNDER SUSPICION.

THE CAMP HAS AREAS OF RESISTANCE.

IT'S BETTER THAT YOU STAY IN A PLACE HANI SUGGESTS.

YOU COULD EVEN FIND A PLACE THAT HAS A DOORMAN.

A DOORMAN?

Abed and I explain the journalistic imperative of being in the thick of things, and in the end Khaled relents.

Two or three calls later, he's found a place for me in the camp center.

The next day, on our way to look at the apartment, we pay Hani a visit.

He's not pleased I've gone behind his back to secure a dwelling in the camp.

WHAT ABOUT HIS SAFETY?

HE IS IN RAFAH NOW!

I AM RESPONSIBLE FOR HIM!

153

J. SACCO 3-07

J. SACCO 3·07

We're staying in a relatively safe area, but the sounds of conflict are ever present, especially after dark.

The eerie squeaking of treads lets us know Israeli vehicles are on the move.

Shooting punctuates the night.

Blasts rattle the walls and set roosters to crowing.

I wear earplugs, but sometimes I'm jolted upright.

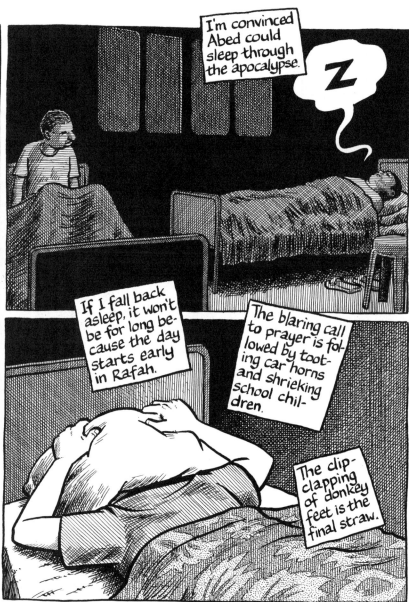

I'm convinced Abed could sleep through the apocalypse.

If I fall back asleep, it won't be for long because the day starts early in Rafah.

The blaring call to prayer is followed by tooting car horns and shrieking school children.

The clip-clapping of donkey feet is the final straw.

I'm wide awake now.

J. SACCO 3-07

156

I head up to the roof from where I can see all the vehicles and people and animals that make up Rafah's full orchestra.

We are in the Yibna neighborhood, so named because most of its first refugees came from the Palestinian village of that name.

Across the street are the winding alleyways of Shaboura.

Other neighborhoods are commonly referred to by their official UNRWA designations: Block J, Block O, etc.

J. SACCO 3.03

We look down into the face of the dead boy.

He is a martyr, felled by an enemy bullet.

Someone fires a single round into the air.

In four minutes the entire column has gone by.

"Halas," as they say here.

Finished.

Sea Street slowly begins to fill up with its shoppers, cars, and carts again.

The noise of the day resumes.

J. SACCO 2·07

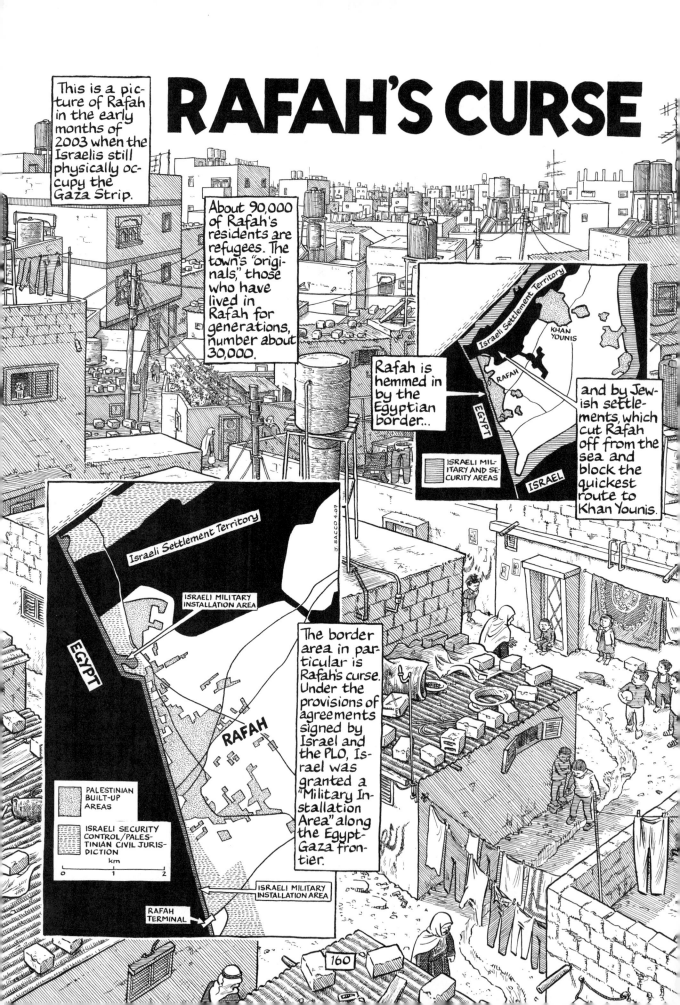

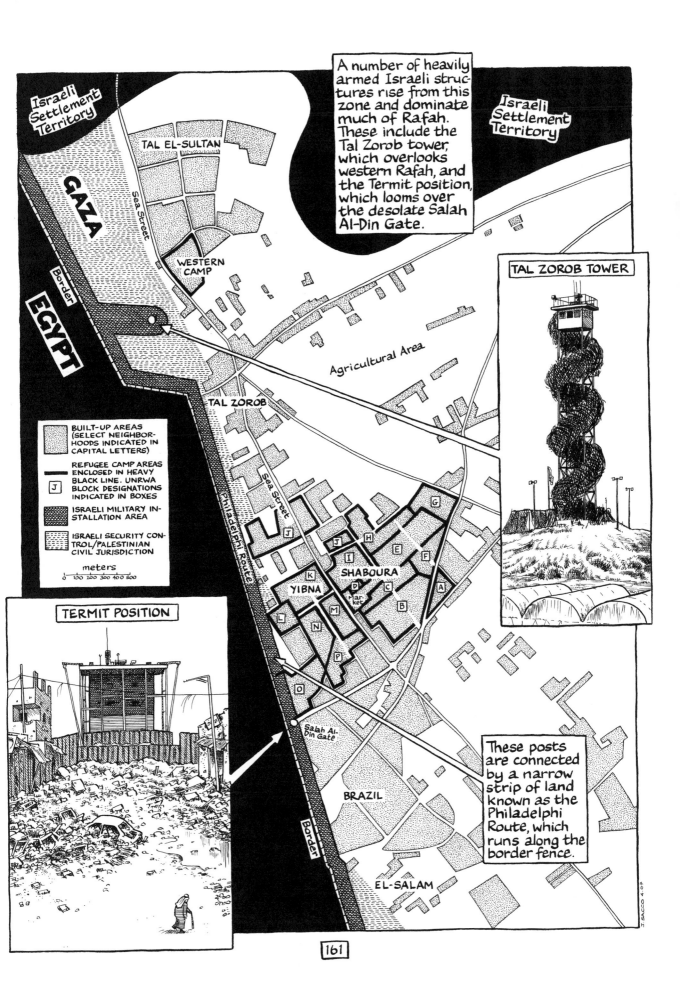

Israeli Settlement Territory

TAL EL-SULTAN

GAZA

Sea Street

WESTERN CAMP

Border

EGYPT

A number of heavily armed Israeli structures rise from this zone and dominate much of Rafah. These include the Tal Zorob tower, which overlooks western Rafah, and the Termit position, which looms over the desolate Salah Al-Din Gate.

Israeli Settlement Territory

Agricultural Area

TAL ZOROB

Philadelphi Route

Sea Street

BUILT-UP AREAS (SELECT NEIGHBORHOODS INDICATED IN CAPITAL LETTERS)

REFUGEE CAMP AREAS ENCLOSED IN HEAVY BLACK LINE. UNRWA BLOCK DESIGNATIONS INDICATED IN BOXES

ISRAELI MILITARY INSTALLATION AREA

ISRAELI SECURITY CONTROL/PALESTINIAN CIVIL JURISDICTION

meters
0 100 200 300 400 500

TAL ZOROB TOWER

J

J H G

I E F

k D C A

YIBNA D Market B

SHABOURA

L M

N

P

TERMIT POSITION

O

Salah Al-Din Gate

BRAZIL

Border

These posts are connected by a narrow strip of land known as the Philadelphi Route, which runs along the border fence.

EL-SALAM

J.SACCO 4.03

161

Since the Second Intifada the IDF has erected an eight-meter high metal barrier on a long stretch of the dusty path to protect its vehicles from Palestinian attack.

EGYPT/GAZA BORDER

IDF POSITION

RAFAH

PHILADELPHI ROUTE

BARRIER

Israel controls the Rafah Terminal, the entry point to Egypt, but the border is not completely sealed. The Palestinians have dug tunnels under the Philadelphi Route to Egypt.

The tunnels have been big business for certain Rafah families who smuggle in Egyptian cigarettes and other goods that are in short supply.

But increasingly, Palestinians have brought in weapons and ammunition to fuel their resistance.

The IDF routinely raids Rafah to uncover tunnel "piers."

Any home hiding a tunnel or used to resist the Israeli incursions is destroyed.

Israel claims these are the only reasons it has demolished hundreds of Rafah's dwellings.

The demolition of houses is an almost daily occurrence.

162

J. SACCO 4-07

And on one of our first tours of the camp, to the sound of gunfire and shelling, we find it happening again.

An armor-plated Caterpillar is crashing into houses in Block O.

A couple of armed Palestinians show up to add to the fray.

Meanwhile, a woman nearby motions us into her home.

She's wrapped up in layers of clothing, ready to run.

THERE'S ONE HOUSE MORE ON THE OTHER SIDE OF OURS.

THERE'S NO ONE LEFT IN THIS ROW OF HOUSES BUT US.

J. SACCO 4·07

163

J. SACCO 5.07

THE FALL OF RAFAH

The demolition of Rafah's houses is the present-day white noise over which we are listening for the sounds of another time, 1956.

The distant voices of the conquerors, at least, still come through loud and clear.

And so while the nighttime gunfire stammers and the armored vehicles rumble over the Philadelphi Route wasteland, Abed loses himself in my English-language translation of Moshe Dayan's wartime memoir, 'Diary of the Sinai Campaign.'

It's jammed with orders of battle, inventories of artillery pieces, and combat maps with attack arrows stabbing in various directions.

One of these maps, with no less than six thrusting arrows, represents the Israeli capture of the Rafah area.

"If El Arish and Rafah fall to us," Dayan wrote, "the Gaza Strip will be isolated and unable, alone, to hold out."

In fact, Dayan considered the attack on Rafah important enough to personally accompany the 1st Infantry Brigade's assault, which began in the early hours of November 1, 1956.

Abed and I track down Mohammed Ismael El-Sbakhi, one of the Palestinian soldiers on the receiving end of the Israeli attack.

I WAS IN THE BACK POSITIONS, IN HEADQUARTERS.

I COULD READ AND WRITE, WHICH WAS WHY I WAS IN HEADQUARTERS.

[IT] WAS CLOSE TO THE ROAD THAT LEADS TO THE EASTERN VILLAGES.

Rafah's defenses collapsed within hours.

"When we felt it going wrong, we entered the fields of cactus. We escaped before the road was cut.

"All the high-ranking Egyptian soldiers took off their uniforms."

By mid-morning, Dayan was already on the way to his next objective.

He later wrote, "As soon as we left Rafah, the excitement and tension suddenly vanished, giving way to the same serenity I used to feel after a jump during my parachute days."

But those left in his dust felt anything but serene.

J SACCO 5.07

169

In the small warehouse in the back of his carpet shop on Sea Street, Mohammed Yousef Shaker Mousa remembers joining the thousands from Rafah who fled from the Israelis to the coast, where some continued on into Sinai.

MY FATHER AND MY MOTHER REFUSED TO LEAVE, AND THEY REMAINED IN THE HOUSE.

"[The Israelis] ran after the people up to the sea.

"They were searching for the soldiers, for the ones wearing uniforms...

"With my eyes I saw six or seven people that they killed in the sandy area of Sinai.

"They were cowardly soldiers, but the Arabs were more cowardly.

J. SACCO 5·07

"The Israelis called to the people to go back to their houses through loudspeakers.

ANYONE REMAINING OUTSIDE IS IN DANGER!

"Their aim was to get the people to come back so it would be easier to gather them."

I CAME BACK BECAUSE THERE WAS NO HOPE [OF ESCAPE].

AND I ALSO STARTED TO THINK ABOUT MY FATHER AND MOTHER.

As an uneasy occupation settled in, Israeli troops took control of the only school in Rafah for local children, which in those days was referred to as the "official" or "government" school to distinguish it from the UNRWA schools for refugee kids. Constructed in the 1930s, the original building still stands and now serves as a preparatory and primary school for boys. Today it is commonly called the El-Ameeriah School.

The school is the crucible of our final footnote.

But before we take you into its fire, we sit shivering in a playground in Shaboura with a man who won't give his name and clearly does not want us to see where he lives.

He tells us something about the atmosphere in Rafah at the time.

WE HEARD ABOUT THE KHAN YOUNIS MASSACRE FROM SOME PEOPLE, FROM PEOPLE WHO HAD ESCAPED.

THEY TOLD US THAT THE JEWS ENTERED THE CITY AND TOLD THE YOUNG MEN TO GET OUT OF THEIR HOUSES AND LINED THEM AGAINST THE WALLS AND SHOT THEM.

WE FELT HORRIBLE FEAR AND TERROR.

"The walls of our houses were very low, and some of the soldiers would look over the walls.

"When you went outside into the yard and saw them, you got scared and went back to your rooms.

"We turned off our lamps and lay down... In the night, no one would light his lamp.

"They gave only two hours daily, from eight to ten, for the people to leave their houses. The people went out quickly to get their food.

"About five minutes to ten...they would start shooting everywhere... shooting in the sky to frighten the people..."

Those who had not reached their homes in time were sometimes shot, he tells us.

ONE PERSON WAS KILLED IN FRONT OF OUR HOUSE.

"He was shot in the back, and he began screaming and shouting, but no one could help him. I saw this with my eyes.

"And there weren't any ambulances at the time. The injured always bled until they died."

172

J. SACCO 5·07

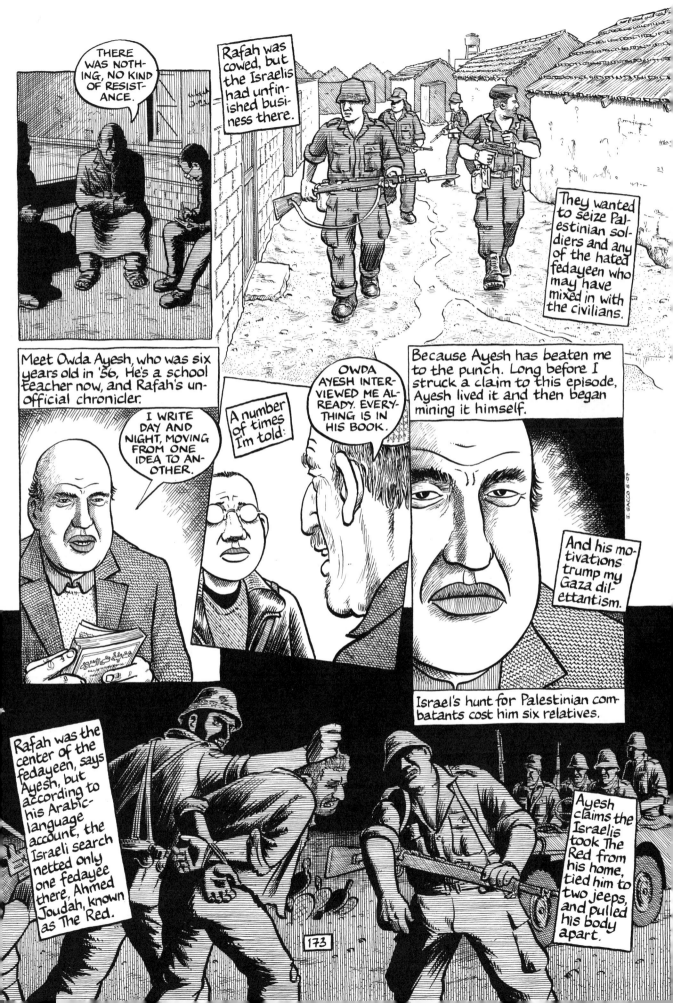

THERE WAS NOTH-ING, NO KIND OF RESIST-ANCE.

Rafah was cowed, but the Israelis had unfinished business there.

They wanted to seize Palestinian soldiers and any of the hated fedayeen who may have mixed in with the civilians.

Meet Owda Ayesh, who was six years old in '56. He's a school teacher now, and Rafah's unofficial chronicler.

I WRITE DAY AND NIGHT, MOVING FROM ONE IDEA TO ANOTHER.

A number of times I'm told:

OWDA AYESH INTERVIEWED ME ALREADY. EVERYTHING IS IN HIS BOOK.

Because Ayesh has beaten me to the punch. Long before I struck a claim to this episode, Ayesh lived it and then began mining it himself.

And his motivations trump my Gaza dilettantism.

Israel's hunt for Palestinian combatants cost him six relatives.

Rafah was the center of the fedayeen, says Ayesh, but according to his Arabic-language account, the Israeli search netted only one fedayee there, Ahmed Joudah, known as The Red.

Ayesh claims the Israelis took The Red from his home, tied him to two jeeps, and pulled his body apart.

173

Abed and I manage to track down The Red's nephew, Zaki Mohammed Abdullah Joudah.

Zaki remembers how his uncle slipped into the camp just after the Israelis occupied Rafah.

HE RETURNED TO TAKE CARE OF HIS FAMILY, TO TAKE CARE OF HIS BROTHERS. MANY PEOPLE TOLD HIM TO HIDE.

...HE USED TO SAY, 'I THINK I'LL BE THE FIRST TO BE KILLED IN RAFAH.'

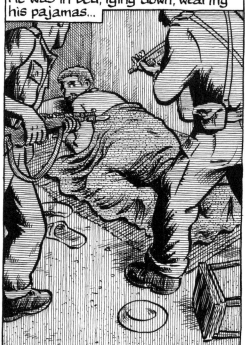

"Around the Isha prayer, the last prayer [of the day], the Jews came... He was in bed, lying down, wearing his pajamas..."

"We stayed inside. We were panicked, full of fright, because we'd heard what had happened in Khan Younis.

"After five minutes we heard shooting.

"We realized it was him."

UNTIL NOW WE DON'T KNOW THE REAL STORY.

NO ONE SAW WHAT HAPPENED.

WE NEVER FOUND THE BODY.

Yes, he knows the rumor that his uncle was pulled apart, but Zaki thinks The Red was probably shot trying to escape.

HE WAS A HERO TO ALL THE PEOPLE, NOT JUST TO ME.

HE HAD DISTINGUISHED HIMSELF IN OPERATIONS INSIDE ISRAEL.

But remember the old fedayee in Khan Younis? He told me that all the fedayeen had escaped the Israeli dragnet in Gaza. So what about The Red?

He chuckles.

AHMED JOUDAH?

HE WASN'T A FEDAYEE. HE WAS MY FRIEND.

HE WAS KILLED BY MISTAKE.

HE WANTED TO SHOW OFF, AND HE LOST HIS LIFE.

TAKING TOO LONG

So who was Ahmed Joudah, The Red? A hero of the resistance? A terrorist? A man playing at something way over his head?

For whatever reason, the Israelis wanted to get their hands on him.

Decades later, Khaled, too, is a marked man, but his credentials as a fighter are not in dispute.

Beyond that, he is considered "clean"—meaning incorruptible—and his word in local disputes carries great weight.

One day Khaled leads us around, showing us places in Rafah where he fought the Israelis,

where he ducked a hail of bullets that killed his friend, another resistance fighter...

J. SACCO 6·07

It didn't, but Khaled still believes in a two-state solution, still supports the framework of the Oslo accords.

The question though is whether they can live with him.

I HATE THE JEWS, BUT I COULD LIVE WITH THEM.

THE JEWS NEVER CLEAR ANYONE'S RECORD.

"Personally," Abed once told me, "I think Khaled is tired."

Tired of fighting, tired of running, tired of how small his life has become.

One day we return from our interviews and find Khaled in our room, red-eyed.

He needs to talk.

He has no prospects here, he says, nothing but his salary from the Sulta.

I FIGURE IT WILL TAKE ME 20 YEARS TO BUY A HOUSE AND A SMALL CAR— AND THAT'S WITHOUT SPENDING ANYTHING.

MAYBE MY WIFE CAN GET EGYPTIAN PAPERS BECAUSE HER PARENTS HAVE EGYPTIAN PASSPORTS.

MAYBE SHE CAN GET OUT WITH THE KIDS, AND MAYBE I COULD FOLLOW.

I'D HAVE TO SLIP INTO EGYPT ILLEGALLY AGAIN, AND PROBABLY THAT WILL MEAN ANOTHER YEAR IN AN EGYPTIAN JAIL, BUT THAT WILL PASS.

ON THE OUTSKIRTS OF CAIRO WE COULD BUY A PLACE FOR $3,000.

J. SACCO 6.07

We could spend time there until the kids are educated and their personalities are built, and they could always return here.

Or we could move to Syria. Or Switzerland. Or Sweden.

If I make it to Sweden, they would put me in jail for being illegal, but in the end they might grant me political asylum. I know other guys who've managed that.

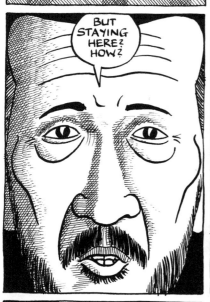But staying here? How?

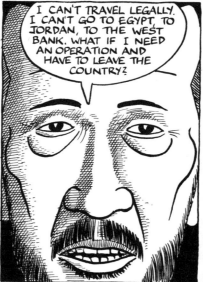I can't travel legally. I can't go to Egypt, to Jordan, to the West Bank. What if I need an operation and have to leave the country?

The other day my daughter asked me, 'Are you coming home tomorrow?' And that hurt me. I can't say when I'm coming home.

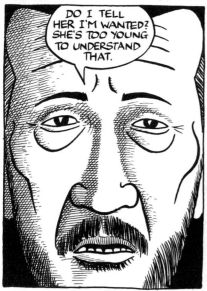Do I tell her I'm wanted? She's too young to understand that.

I expect to be killed, I expect to be assassinated, but now it's taking too long.

J. SACCO 5-09

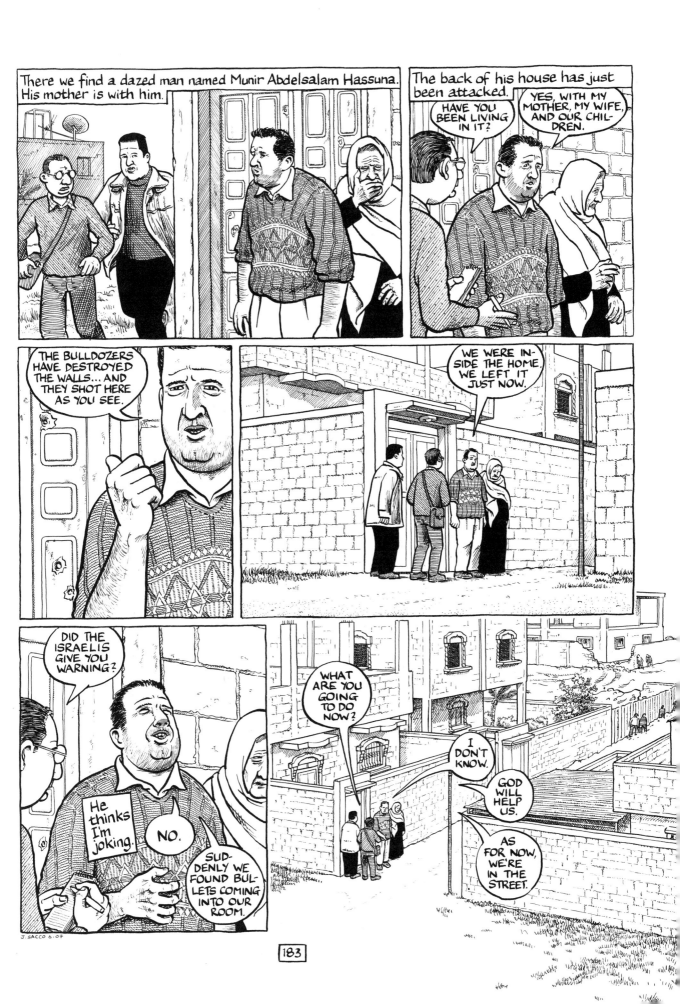

There we find a dazed man named Munir Abdelsalam Hassuna. His mother is with him.

The back of his house has just been attacked.

HAVE YOU BEEN LIVING IN IT?

YES, WITH MY MOTHER, MY WIFE, AND OUR CHILDREN.

THE BULLDOZERS HAVE DESTROYED THE WALLS... AND THEY SHOT HERE AS YOU SEE.

WE WERE INSIDE THE HOME. WE LEFT IT JUST NOW.

DID THE ISRAELIS GIVE YOU WARNING?

He thinks I'm joking.

NO.

SUDDENLY WE FOUND BULLETS COMING INTO OUR ROOM.

WHAT ARE YOU GOING TO DO NOW?

I DON'T KNOW.

GOD WILL HELP US.

AS FOR NOW, WE'RE IN THE STREET.

J. SACCO 6·07

He wants to show me the damage to his house.

He peeks through a bullet hole in the door—

THE TANK IS IN-SIDE.

We wish him luck and hurry to catch up with the others.

We make our way around some buildings to get a view of the bulldozer, which is churning up the ground behind a large house.

Another Israeli vehicle is sending a twirling shaft into the ground.

A powerful blast momentarily scatters the watching crowd.
The driller is detonating underground explosives to collapse any tunnels that might be nearby.
TV
Meanwhile, the bulldozer is still churning...
churning...
and finally!
Some of the teenaged boys start lounging out in the open on a heap of earth pushed up during an earlier bulldozing.
TV
They're showboating for their friends.
J. SACCO 7-07

She grabs at a couple of kids who are passing by.

WHERE WILL THESE CHILDREN GO?

They squirm out of her grasp, and now a photographer steps forward and his camera whirls in her face for ten seconds...

before he turns away without a word to take pictures of something else.

But now another local resident shows up.

WHY ARE YOU TAKING PICTURES?

WHAT ARE YOU GOING TO PHOTOGRAPH?

THE HOUSES?

I'LL HOLD YOU RESPONSIBLE IF I SEE MY HOUSE ON T.V.!

Then he notices a couple of militants near his home.

The man doesn't give a damn about the AFV, which is sending out rounds every minute or two.

He strides across an open area toward the fighters.

J. SACCO 7-07

He yells at them!

He doesn't want them shooting at the Israelis from anywhere close to his house.

(The Israeli policy, remember, is to flatten any home from where they say they've taken fire.)

And now the party is joined by a new group, foreign activists with the International Solidarity Movement.

There are a handful in Rafah—Europeans and Americans—and they stay in those homes that seem most at risk of getting demolished.

While everyone else is taking cover, they stand in the open, unfurl a banner, and start shouting at the bulldozer.

When the coast seems clear Abed and I cross the field to get closer to the action.

J. SACCO 7.07

190

On the way, we find a man tearing at the vegetation.

IT'S FOR MY SHEEP.

We come across the homeowner who screamed at the photographers and militants.

He's wound up, pacing back and forth.

For the photographers his house is an image.

For the militants it's cover.

For the internationals it's a cause.

For the bulldozer operator it's a day's work.

But for him?

I want to have a word, human to human. I put away my notepad and walk up.

He shakes my hand reluctantly. But he won't look me in the eye. Or talk.

He knows it's rubble that's brought me, too.

J. SACCO 7.07

191

It's time for a smoke.

For now we're more or less pinned down.

The AFV is stitching holes in houses on one side of us...

...and sometimes races around to fire a burst on the other side, too.

The activists keep trying to impose their peaceful demonstration on the situation.

STOP DEMOLITIONS!

WE ARE INTER-NATION-ALS!

The militants keep angling for a shot.

They snap at the kids:

Stop following!

Y'know what'll happen if your path crosses a bullet's?

YOU'LL BE ROLLING ON THE GROUND LIKE A FOOTBALL!

192

Oh, shit!

Don't look now!

Teenaged boys headed our way!

Before they can start hassling me I ask them what they think of the internationals.

I DON'T LIKE THEM. THEY'RE NOT MUSLIMS. AND GOD KNOWS IF THEY ARE WITH US OR AGAINST US.

WE ARE INTERN

He asks if I happen to be a Muslim.

NO, I'M NOT A MUSLIM.

THEN YOU'RE GOING TO HELL.

DOES IT MAKE YOU ANGRY THAT I'M NOT A MUSLIM?

He has to think about it.

NO... YOU'RE NOT MY ENEMY.

BUT I'M NOT YOUR FRIEND, RIGHT?

THAT'S RIGHT.

We shake on our accord.

I ask the other boy what he thinks of the internationals.

I'D LIKE TO BE AN INTERNATIONAL.

Good one!

REALLY, THOUGH, I THINK IT'S GOOD THEY'RE AROUND.

J. SACCO 7.07

A couple more boys join our conversation.

They want to know what I'm doing in Rafah so I describe my 1956 research.

WHAT GOOD DOES IT DO?

HE CAME FROM ABROAD. WHAT DOES HE KNOW ABOUT PALESTINE?

One of them motions to the sound of the Israeli vehicles.

WHY DO THEY COME HERE AND DO THIS?

THEY DEMOLISHED MY HOME A MONTH AND A HALF AGO.

WHERE ARE YOU LIVING NOW?

WE RENTED A FLAT. IT'S NOT FAR FROM HERE.

WHY IS OUR COUNTRY LIKE THIS?

BE-CAUSE WE'RE NOT CLOSE TO GOD.

I ask what they think is the best way to resist.

GET CLOSE TO GOD.

WITH BOMBS.

DO YOU LIKE US?

194

ASHRAF

Early the next day we're heading back to the site of the Israeli attack when we're stopped by a shout of recognition.

We've run into one of Abed's long-lost pals.

A loud greeting!

Kisses on this and that cheek!

And bear hugs!

Then Abed endures an ear-bashing.

Why haven't you stayed in touch?

Your behavior is shameful!

You don't know I'm married?

That I have a daughter?

I've seen this scenario repeated half a dozen times in Rafah, where Abed, apparently, has lost touch with some old friends.

This one's name is Ashraf.

He teaches English in Khan Younis.

Abed explains that we're on our way to check on Munir, the man whose home was damaged yesterday

MY HOME WAS DAMAGED, TOO.

In fact, it turns out Ashraf's house was the very one we saw being crashed into by the bulldozer.

I'M GOING THERE NOW MYSELF.

195

Abed and Ashraf do some catching up on our way to Munir's.

Munir invites us in.

We greet his mother.

THE SONS OF DOGS.

THEY'VE DESTROYED IT.

Well, not quite. The master bedroom has taken some large caliber rounds, and the bathroom wall has been cracked open by the bulldozer.

Most of the damage is around back where rubble from previously destroyed houses has been pushed against and broken the wall.

Munir says he's been hanging on to his house despite the constant Israeli operations.

His family has been sleeping in the rooms which don't face the Philadelphi Route to put some walls between them and Israeli gunfire.

A neighbor encourages him to continue holding out.

But for Munir this is the end of the line.

I'LL LOOK FOR A NEW HOME AND RENT.

I'VE BEEN UNEMPLOYED A LONG TIME.

I'LL GET LOANS TILL UNRWA PROVIDES ME WITH FUNDS.

WE'LL MOVE THE FURNITURE OUT AND LEAVE IT WITH OUR NEIGHBORS.

196

THERE USED TO BE 20 HOUSES IN THIS AREA.

I tell Munir I want to follow his "story."

I SUGGEST YOU GET A TENT AND LIVE NEXT TO ME.

But I won't follow Munir's story. Soon I'm swamped by stories like his and Ashraf's.

We walk over to Ashraf's place a little further down.

Whatever dwellings stood between his house and the Philadelphi Route have been returned to the sand.

Israeli bullets started striking the house soon after the intifada began, Ashraf says. He and his wife left and rented in Block J. The rest of the family eventually followed.

BUT MY FATHER COMES HERE EVERY DAY.

We meet his father, Talal, at the side entrance. His sons are coming and going, removing light fixtures and flourescent lamps.

J. SACCO 8-07

We inspect yesterday's damage to a back room and a pillar.

Talal is a building contractor and he built this house himself. One floor is completely finished. His family paid bit by bit for each new addition, each new door, each new window.

But six windows were shot out, they tell me.

"It was either leave the house or someone dying," says Talal.

I ask about the smuggling tunnels. Their destruction is the main reason the IDF says it operates in this area.

THEY PRETEND THAT THERE ARE TUNNELS IN THIS AREA BUT THEY ARE LIARS.

IS ALL THIS AREA FULL OF TUN-NELS?

J. SACCO 8·07

198

I ask about the militants I saw yesterday. Do they think their actions are effective resistance against the bulldozers.

THOSE GUN-MEN HAVE DESTROYED EVERY-THING.

THEY'RE USE-LESS.

THE JEWS USE THEM AS A PRETEXT TO DEMOLISH THE HOUSES.

Yesterday, Talal says, he had a long argument with some militants before they moved away from his home.

I ask if they intend to repair the pillar.

THIS HOUSE IS GOING TO BE DEMOL-ISHED.

THE WHOLE AREA!

Ashraf gives us a short tour of the unfinished rooms that make up the second floor.

THIS WAS GOING TO BE MY FLAT WITH MY WIFE AND CHILD.

MAYBE IN PARA-DISE I'LL GET A GOOD FLAT.

As we leave, two young men nego-tiate a bed frame out the door.

Yesterday was the first time Ashraf's house and Munir's were hit by a bulldozer.

Both houses received minor dam-age, essen-tially a grazing.

But perhaps this was a message from the IDF.

A warn-ing.

A way of saying, it's time to take out everything you can.

199

TIME MANAGE-MENT

Every week or so, Abed and I stop by the neighborhood confectionary to stock up on pastries, especially the honey-drenched variety that so well compliment our morning-noon-and-night coffee fixes.

The kid behind the counter has seen me in here a bunch of times. Finally, he asks what's up?

Abed, good fellow, explains my '56 project once again.

The kid is not impressed.

FORGET THE PAST. WHAT ABOUT NOW?

"One day," I tell him, "50 years from now, they'll forget about you, too."

But that's the way it goes: The young ones don't want to hear about '56; and the old ones —

— as witnesses, the old ones are not always very professional.

THE JEWS ENTERED BUREIJ...

This woman, for example, can't keep anything straight.

She tells us about Egyptian soldiers killed in the schoolyard, but her daughter-in-law interjects.

SHE'S TALKING ABOUT 1967.

THE EGYPTIAN ARMY CAME TO DEFEND PALESTINE.

Her grandson tries to keep her focused.

WE'RE TALKING ABOUT '56.

AFTER THEY KILLED THEM THEY LEFT THEM.

Her tower of memories has collapsed. She gropes around to offer us a piece of her rubble.

HE WAS SHOT IN THE HEAD.

Hunh?

But she's referring to one of her sons, killed during an Israeli raid in 1954.

I SAID, 'FOR GOD'S SAKE LET ME SEE HIM.'

THEY REFUSED TO LET ME SEE MY SON.

HE USED TO ASK ME, 'WHAT DO YOU NEED MOTHER?'

'SHALL I BRING YOU FISH?'

If other old-timers are sharper, they might have just as little to offer. We're often referred to this one or that one,

but this one wasn't even in Rafah during the period in question...

and that one was hiding in the dunes and didn't see a thing.

Eventually, worn out by fruitless chases to Rafah's far corners, Abed and I screen potential subjects whenever possible.

YES, COME IN, COME IN...

Nothing doing!

Before someone puts the kettle on and we're trapped for another half hour, we require a quickie synopsis of your story here at the threshold.

201

At home Abed and I drink coffee and eat those honey-drenched pastries while we go over the interviews.

How did this last story compare with Number 19's?

Number 20's?

Speaking of Number 20 — and, by the way, I've numbered all the interviewees because I can hardly keep anyone's name straight — what did you think of his story?

ABOUT HIS FRIENDS BEING KILLED?

The more we hear, the more we fill in our picture of that day in '56, the more critical we become of each tale we hear.

I THINK HE'S EXAGGERATING.

Abed is getting as sucked into this as I am.

We light up another Cleopatra, and perhaps I mark more details on the chart.

I enter name...

residence...

and then I jot down brief notes into columns labelled "announcement"...

"moving to the school"...

"entrance"...

"waiting"...

"screening"...

etc.

Abed and I are running a very organized investigation over here, and we've broken down the main event into its component parts.

The chart allows us to make quick comparisons between the testimony of each witness.

And so,

once again,

refreshed and recharged,

we don our shoes,

walk downstairs,

J. SACCO 9-07

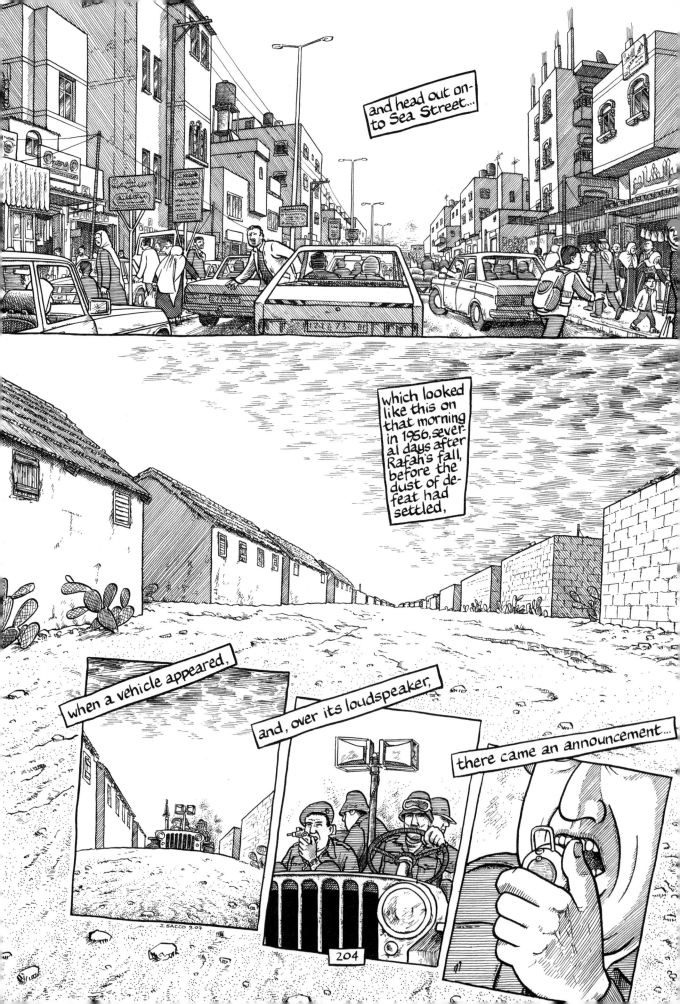

and head out on- to Sea Street...

which looked like this on that morning in 1956, several days after Rafah's fall, before the dust of defeat had settled,

when a vehicle appeared,

and, over its loudspeaker,

there came an announcement...

"It was an unforgettable day.

"November 12, 1956.

"It is written in my brain.

"It was a Monday...

"The Jews called through the loudspeaker for men between 15 and 60 to go to the school."

AWADALLAH AHMED AWADALLAH

ANNOUNCEMENT

IN THE MORNING, 6 OR 6:30, A LOUDSPEAKER CALLED ALL THE PEOPLE TO GO TO THE OFFICIAL SCHOOL IN RAFAH. FROM THE AGES OF 16 TO 60.

KHALIL AHMED MOHAMMED IBRAHIM

...THEY CALLED AT NIGHT, 'FROM THE AGES OF 15 TO 60, GO TO THE OFFICIAL SCHOOL OF RAFAH.'

MOHAMMED YOUSEF SHAKER MOUSA

...WE HEARD THE LOUDSPEAKERS CALL THE YOUTH FROM 15 TO 50, 'GO TO THE SCHOOL.'

MOHAMMED JUMA' EL-GHOUL

THE LOUDSPEAKER SAID, 'ALL THE PEOPLE FROM 16 TO 60 GO TO THE SCHOOL.'

AHMED KHALIL EL-BAWAB

THEY STARTED CALLING ALL THE PEOPLE BETWEEN 15 AND 50 TO GO TO THE SCHOOLS. EACH AREA HAD ITS OWN SCHOOL.

MOHAMMED ABU AMMRAH

THE LOUDSPEAKER CALLED UPON US, THE MEN FROM 15 YEARS OLD — I FORGET IF IT'S 14 YEARS OR NOT — ALL SHOULD GATHER IN EL-AMEERIAH SCHOOL.

MOHI ELDIN IBRAHIM LAFI

J. SACCO 9-07

I WAS IN MY HOME. I HEARD SOMEONE RUNNING.

ZAKI HASSAN EDWAN

WHAT HAS HAPPENED?

THERE'S A LOUDSPEAKER CALLING.

YOU HAVE TO GO TO THE SCHOOL.

IN TEN MINUTES YOU MUST BE THERE.

GHANIM MAHMOUD SHA'AT: "[My cousin] Elabed told me to wait until my brothers came.

...AND WE'LL GO TOGETHER.

"We saw my brothers coming with wood on their backs. People were already walking in the streets.

"Elabed shaved.

"He dressed...

LET'S GO.

"We didn't panic. We didn't know what was going to happen."

J. SACCO 9-07

207

SEA STREET

Ayesh Abdel-Khalik Younis has been hard to pin down.

First he was away on a hajj, and then he needed several days to receive guests and distribute small gifts as is customary after the pilgrimage to Mecca.

After that he required a few days' rest.

Now, finally, we are sitting in his cold front room, and he is telling us about that November morning.

THE SUN SHINED THAT DAY WITH YELLOW RAYS WHICH DECLARED THE RAYS OF DEATH WERE COMING.

But we're not interested in rhetorical flourishes honed by his years as a mukhtar counseling his clan and resolving disputes.

We want to see those hours through the eyes of the 21-year-old UNRWA teacher he once was.

I WAS WOKEN BY THE VOICE OF MY COUSIN TELLING ME, 'WAKE UP OR THEY'LL KILL YOU!'

"I felt it was shameful for me as a teacher to go through the door and into the street in my pajamas.

LEAVE!

THERE ISN'T ANY TIME!

"But I changed my clothes and then went out.

"My house was exactly on Sea Street.

"I found some soldiers in the street. They were shooting, firing from all sides.

"And I started running with all my strength."

WE WALKED TO THE SCHOOL IN A GROUP.

ANONYMOUS 1

"I reached Sea Street, where the fire station is today.

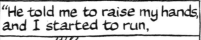

"I was walking normally.

HURRY UP! HURRY UP!

"And he fired at me...

"He told me to raise my hands, and I started to run,

"and the people behind me started to run."

J. SACCO 9-07

209

AND THEY WERE SAYING, 'RUN! RUN!'

VERY QUICK! VERY QUICK!

ABDUL-MALIK MOHAMMED KULLAB

"It was just like ants... People... Everyone from the camp."

Some younger boys were too frightened to remain in their homes.

THERE WAS SHOOTING FROM EVERY-WHERE SO I WENT WITH MY FATHER.

HAMDI HEJAZI

"We walked to the main street, and every few meters you'd meet a group of soldiers with their sticks tell-ing you,

HURRY UP! HURRY UP!

"I wasn't hit myself. I saw many people beaten with sticks."

"The soldiers were on both sides of the street to prevent people from turning into other streets, and the soldiers were [elsewhere] in the camp. There was shooting in the camp."

J. SACCO 9-07

Khalil Ahmed Mohammed Ibrahim, a policeman at the time, left for the school dressed in his uniform.

WHEN THEY SAW ME IN MY UNIFORM, THE PEOPLE CAME TO ME AND SURROUNDED ME BECAUSE THEY WERE AFRAID.

"We met the army. They were firing arbitrarily...

WHAT SHOULD WE DO? WHAT SHOULD WE DO?

GOD WILL HELP US.

JUST WALK AND WE WILL SEE.

"One of the Israelis spoke to me in Arabic.

GO BACK AND BRING THOSE PEOPLE WITH YOU!

"I thought when I turned my back he'd shoot me. My left side froze.

COME!

COME!

"The people who had been with me at first kept on walking.

"And now a different group of people walked with me."

J. SACCO 9-07

MOHAMMED ZIDAN:
"I was with my two uncles and their boys. With some of our neighbors, about 30 people ...We went to the main road... There was heavy firing throughout the town. We felt moving in a group would be safer for us.

"We saw the vehicle with the microphone coming from the eastern side...toward us.

"[A soldier] told us to raise our hands and start running to the school.

"We found a body... on the side of the road...

"His name was Abed Atiyah Sha'at.

"He was about 35 years old.

"And three women came and pulled the body inside a house.

"We stood for awhile thinking to [go] back... And we re-entered the narrow streets of the camp.

"The military vehicle... came back.

"A group of us... went to the jeep and told them that they were shooting people in the street."

WE SAW A BODY IN THE STREET.

SHOOTING, SHOOTING, NEVER MIND.

YOU HAVE TO GO TO THE SCHOOL.

WE ARE GOING TO LOOK FOR MEN INSIDE THE HOUSES, AND IF WE FIND ANY-ONE, WE WILL KILL HIM.

MY UNCLE AND I LEFT THE HOUSE TOGETHER.

ABDEL HADI MOHAMMED LAFI

"I heard the shooting and came back...but my uncle went.

"They shot and killed him. I didn't see it.

"The children and women...convinced me to go to the school...

"I found some of my neighbors and I accompanied them."

MANY SOLDIERS WERE IN THE STREETS AND AT THE CROSSROADS.

ANONYMOUS 2

"I thought it was up to [them] whether they shot or didn't shoot the people...

"I didn't know whether the soldiers had been ordered to do that or whether it was just their mood..."

AHMED KHALIL EL-BAWAB

AND THE SOLDIERS WERE SAYING,

THIS ONE IS FEDAYEE!

THIS ONE IS FEDAYEE!

J. SACCO 10-07

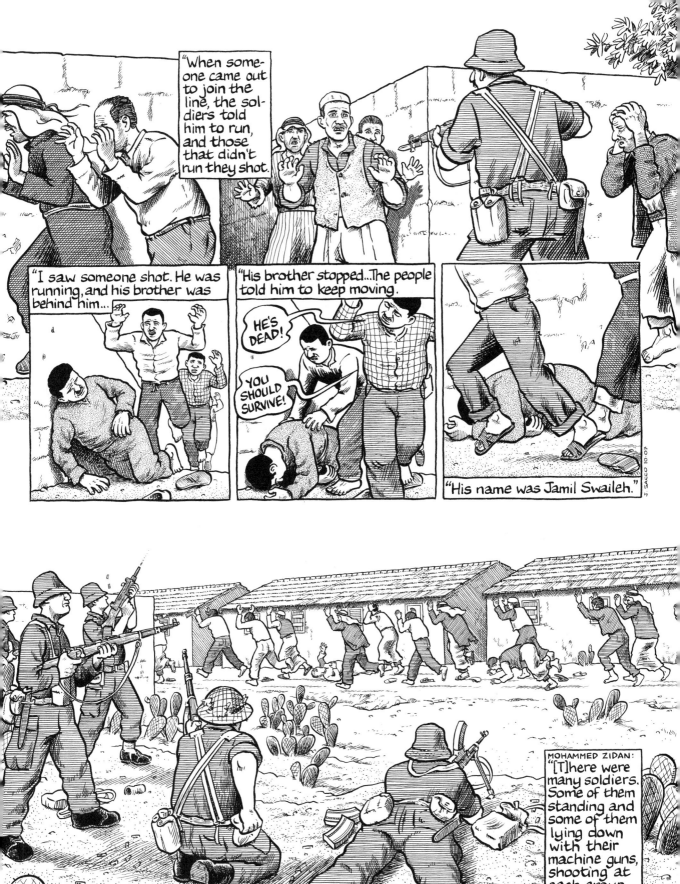

"When someone came out to join the line, the soldiers told him to run, and those that didn't run they shot.

"I saw someone shot. He was running, and his brother was behind him...

"His brother stopped...The people told him to keep moving.

HE'S DEAD!

YOU SHOULD SURVIVE!

"His name was Jamil Swaileh."

MOHAMMED ZIDAN: "[T]here were many soldiers. Some of them standing and some of them lying down with their machine guns, shooting at each group that passed in front of them."

215

"Anyone who was injured or shot, the people left him and kept running. I might have seen three or four bodies on this road. And in each group one or two men were killed.

"When I reached the [UNRWA food] distribution center, I saw a funny sight.

"The shoes of the people filled the street..."

We are back with Ayesh Abdel Khalik Younis. His memory is strong and, with the aid of a map, we want his recollection of how Israeli soldiers directed the human traffic coming eastward along Sea Street toward the school.

THE FIRING WAS FROM ALL SIDES. I RAN UNTIL I REACHED THIS POINT—

NEXT TO OUR FLAT. IN THE MIDDLE BEFORE THE CAR PARK.

FIELD
CAMP
SCHOOL
SEA STREET
U.N. DIST. CNTR.
CAMP
CAMP
CAMP

MAPS NOT TO SCALE

J. SACCO 10-07

"And there I saw some soldiers with heavy machine guns, Bren guns, lying on the ground, and from time to time they shot at the people."

DID THEY SEEM TO BE SHOOTING RANDOMLY INTO THE CROWD?

"To be honest, from my point of view, they were shooting just to terrify the people, but afterwards people told me that the killing had sometimes been on purpose.

216

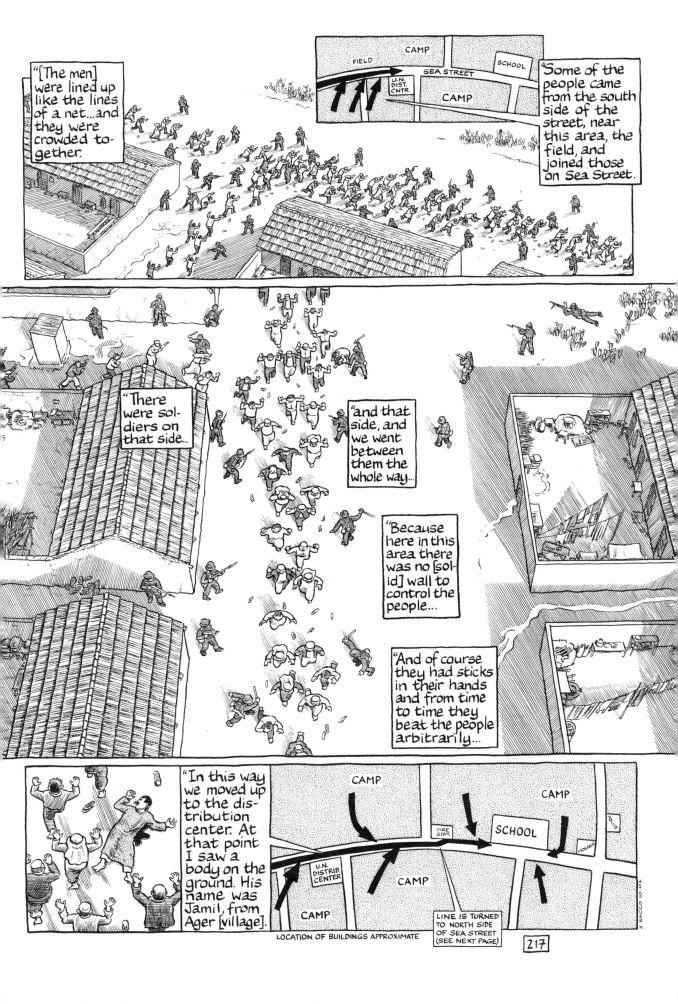

"[The men] were lined up like the lines of a net...and they were crowded together.

CAMP
FIELD
SCHOOL
SEA STREET
U.N. DIST. CNTR.
CAMP

"Some of the people came from the south side of the street, near this area, the field, and joined those on Sea Street.

"There were soldiers on that side...

"and that side, and we went between them the whole way...

"Because here in this area there was no [solid] wall to control the people...

"And of course they had sticks in their hands and from time to time they beat the people arbitrarily...

"In this way we moved up to the distribution center. At that point I saw a body on the ground. His name was Jamil, from Ager [village].

CAMP
CAMP
CAMP
U.N. DISTRIB. CENTER
FIRE STAT.
SCHOOL
POLICE
MOSQUE
CAMP

LINE IS TURNED TO NORTH SIDE OF SEA STREET (SEE NEXT PAGE)

LOCATION OF BUILDINGS APPROXIMATE

J SACCO 10-01

"We moved this way, on the south side of the street, until we reached the [present] fire station... There exactly... we [were] moved from the south side to the north... by pushing and heavy sticks and shooting."

When we last saw Ghanim Mahmoud Sha'at, he was leaving the house with his two brothers and his cousin Elabed.

GHANIM MAHMOUD SHA'AT:
"We went through the narrow roads. Elabed was in front, I was in the back.

"When we reached the corner of the school, I took out a cigarette.

"Suddenly we saw two jeeps coming...

RAISE YOUR HANDS DONKEY!!

SPEAK!

SAY SOMETHING!

218

J. SACCO 10·07

"While I was sitting with him, the jeeps were coming back.

"A woman came out of a house and pulled me from behind and shut the door.

"When the jeeps had gone, she brought a blanket and, with another woman, we carried the body... and returned to the camp.

"We brought the martyr back to his house. Elabed's father asked,

WHAT'S THIS?

WHAT ARE YOU CARRYING?

"He started screaming and shouting.

"The old men told me to go to the school."

SAVE YOUR LIFE. WE DON'T WANT TO LOSE TWO PEOPLE.

NO. I WILL NOT GO.

THE SOLDIERS HAVE ENTERED THE CAMP!

The old men escorted Ghanim to his own house, which he found full of female relatives and neighbors.

"I washed my hands and my face and lay down.

"And I left the outside door open."

J. SACCO 10-07

219

Mohammed Atwa El-Najeeli is a jocular man, well known in Rafah for his incredible story.

I FOUND A GROUP OF SEVEN OR EIGHT PEOPLE FROM THE MASAMHA FAMILY...

I JOINED THEM.

"We walked up to Sea Street, with our hands raised, toward the school...

"I saw one of my neighbors. Swaireh the barber.

"He'd just been shot by the Israelis.

"And we were walking in front of the distribution center... There were soldiers standing in the streets...

"When [one of them] noticed that there were young men in our group,

"he started shooting.

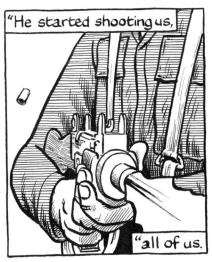

"He started shooting us,

"all of us.

"Now we are on the ground and people are coming from behind, walking on our bodies.

"Now I feel that I am going to die.

J. SACO 11-07

221

"I tried to pinch a person also lying on the ground, but got no response."

"The one behind me, the same. Nothing."

"All of them dead. I am alive. Only one bullet."

"But all the people walking on my neck!"

I WAS WEARING GOOD CLOTHES AND LOOKED GOOD.

AT THAT TIME I DIDN'T DESERVE TO BE SHOT.

BUT NOW I DESERVE IT.

"I took off my... hatta and told the soldier:

COME HERE AND SHOOT ME.

"He didn't come.

"For the second time I asked him...

COME HERE.

COME HERE.

COME AND SHOOT ME.

I AM STILL ALIVE.

"He prepared his gun, put in a full clip,

"and came towards me...

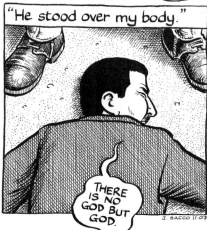

"He stood over my body."

THERE IS NO GOD BUT GOD.

J. SACCO 11·07

222

AND HE SHOT 36 BULLETS IN MY HEAD...

THIRTY-SIX.

IN YOUR HEAD?

A FULL CLIP.

THIRTY-SIX BULLETS IN MY HEAD.

HE WAS A BAD SOLDIER.

HE WASN'T PROFESSIONAL.

IF I WAS HIS INSTRUCTOR, I'D DISMISS HIM.

"I turned on my back.

"My eyes, my mouth, my head were full of blood.

"The Jews asked the people to take us aside to clear the street.

"They dragged me from my legs, and my head was bumping on the ground.

223

"I could feel them...searching through my clothes to find my identification—"

—AND IF THERE WAS SOMETHING ELSE, MAYBE TO TAKE IT.

"The blood poured from every part of my body.

"I sank in the blood."

FROM 1956 UP TO NOW, I'M SUFFERING.

THE OLDER I GET, THE MORE PAINFUL IT GETS.

Back at our place, I can't get my head around the improbability of surviving 36 bullets shot at pointblank range.

Still...

HANI GOT SHOT SEVEN TIMES BY A GUN RIGHT UP AGAINST HIS BODY. I'VE SEEN THE SCARS.

THERE'S A GUY IN KHAN YOUNIS WHO WAS SHOT 42 TIMES IN HIS STOMACH. HE CARRIED HIS INTESTINES TO THE HOSPITAL.

IT'S A WELL-KNOWN STORY.

But I'm very skeptical that Mohammed could have survived so many bullets to the head. And how would he know how many had been fired? Automatic fire is too rapid to count, especially, I bet, while being shot.

Exaggeration or not, I don't doubt he was hit by bullets.

Just before we left him, he insisted I finger one or two of the indentations made in his skull.

J. SACCO 11-07

224

While Mohammed Atwa El-Najeeli lay badly injured, the main current of Rafah's men reached the school where they were funneled into another segment of the gantlet.

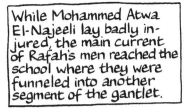

...I WAS SURPRISED TO SEE PEOPLE HOLDING THEIR HANDS UP AND LINED AGAINST THE WALL OF THE SCHOOL

KHALIL AHMED MO-HAMMED IBRAHIM

Today the wall is jammed with small shops selling everything from cassette tapes to handbags

J. SACCO 11-07

In those days it was a bare, crumbling structure that reached just above head height.

225

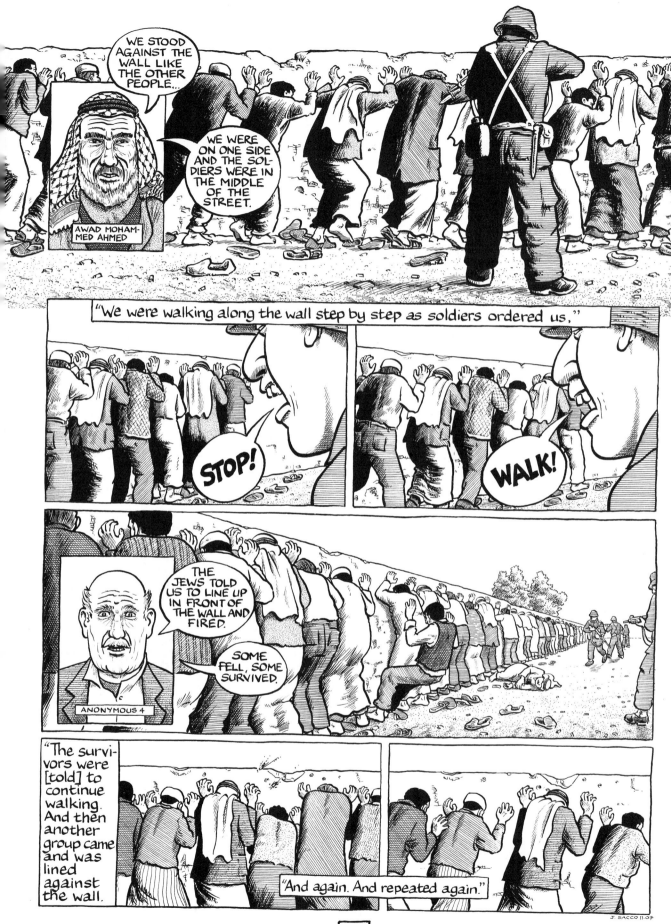

J. SACCO 11.07

I STOOD MANY TIMES AGAINST THE WALL.

WALK AND STOP!

SHOUTING AT ME TO STOP!

STOP!

WALK!

STOP!

WALK!

THE WHOLE TIME MY HANDS WERE IN THE AIR.

MY FACE TO THE WALL.

MOVING AGAINST THE WALL.

SHOOTING WAS CONTINUOUS WHILE WE WERE MOVING...

"There were many bodies on the ground, and we were walking over the bodies..."

DO YOU HAVE ANY IDEA HOW MANY BODIES YOU SAW, APPROXIMATELY?

AT THAT MOMENT I COULDN'T SEE ANYTHING.

OOOH, VERY FEARFUL.

CAN YOU IMAGINE THAT ONE WHO IS VERY FEARFUL CAN SEE ANYTHING?

J. SACCO 11.07

MOHAMMED ZIDAN: "And they started shooting, sometimes over our heads and sometimes at our feet.

"A colleague of mine, his name was Ahmed El-Abed, the bottom of his ear was shot while he was standing at the wall...

"I saw the blood running from his ear...

"They were stopping us... shooting arbitrarily at the people, and then telling us to enter the school—and then they received another group.

"When the soldiers finished shooting at the people, they told us,"

RUN NOW! RUN!

228

ZAKI HASSAN EDWAN

WHEN WE CAME NEAR THE SCHOOL IT BEGAN TO GET CROWDED BECAUSE THE PEOPLE WERE ENTERING THE SCHOOL ONE BY ONE.

"Where could we go? Fly away? Jump over the wall?"

"We didn't know where to go..."

"I wish the wall had collapsed so I could have gone in."

IT WAS VERY DIFFICULT TO WALK BECAUSE THERE WERE SO MANY SHOES. ALL THE PEOPLE LEFT THEIR SHOES ON THE GROUND.

KHALIL AHMED MO- HAMMED IBRAHIM

BEFORE I REACHED THE SCHOOL GATE, TEN METERS MAYBE, A MIL- ITARY JEEP CAME.

LET THEM ENTER THE SCHOOL.

J. SACCO 11-07

[MY BROTHER-IN-LAW] SALEH HASSAN AWAJA— THE SOLDIERS TOLD HIM TO STOP AND TO STAND AGAINST THE WALL, AND TWO OR THREE SOLDIERS BEAT HIM WITH THEIR GUNS.

AHMED KHALIL EL-BAWAB

I WAS STANDING NEAR HIM, AS CLOSE AS THIS CHILD.

THEY WERE STOPPING HUGE GROUPS OF PEOPLE AT THE GATE OF THE SCHOOL, AND THEN THEY'D OPEN UP THE BARBED WIRE AND LET THEM IN.

WE HEARD SHOUTING TO STOP US, BUT WE WENT INTO THE SCHOOL.

ABDELWAHAB MAHMOUD ABDELWAHAB EL-ASMAR

THE SCHOOL GATE

Why this?

Why this forcing the men of Rafah to stand against the wall, to run, to stand, to run?

To terrorize them?

To control the number of men entering the school at any one time?

To allow for the removal of bodies?

The ones who arrived at the school first were not confronted at the wall by soldiers in this way.

Some who lived in the area across from the entrance avoided the shootings on Sea Street and the line-up against the wall entirely.

One of them was Mohammed Yousef Shaker Mousa.

He retraces his steps that day, showing us how he, his father, and others took a narrow trail through a cactus field to enter Sea Street almost directly facing the school gate.

"When the Israelis noticed people using this corridor, they came and stood at the two sides...

"And they beat everyone who came through."

I RECEIVED A BEATING AT THE END OF THE CORRIDOR.

THAT WAS THE FIRST ONE.

J. SACCO 12·07

"The street was full of people running toward the school. So they were beating people randomly.

"Some were jumping into the school, entering over the eastern wall, because it was a low wall at the time.

"Because the people outnumbered them. A lot of people came to the school from all sides."

He motions to Fatima El-Khateeb Street, which runs into Sea Street.

WHERE THAT RED CAR IS.

"I saw 10 or 11 bodies on the ground.

"All of them were killed. I didn't see the killing, but I saw the bodies.

"They were thrown on the ground without any order.

232

"None of the people cared about the others...The only goal was to enter the school.

"I saw many people falling on the ground...

"They were falling on each other.

"The entrance was very small and many people were crowded in this entrance."

He tells us the gate was corrugated zinc back then, not the sturdy iron door we see today.

He says when the men of Rafah reached the school gate, they found a ditch and barbed wire obstructing their path.

233

J. SACCO 12·07

And here we come to a part of the story that remains burned into even the most age-dulled minds.

Though some of the men don't remember the barbed wire and others don't remember the ditch, almost to a man they remember something else at the school entrance—

the soldiers with the heavy sticks.

I WAS BEATEN AT THE GATE.

AND STILL I HAVE THE MARK ON MY HEAD.

"The blood was flowing from my head. Blood was flowing from other people also.

"I jumped over the barbed wire...

"and went to the people and sat with them."

J. SACCO 12·07

THEY BEAT ME ON MY HEAD.

MY HEAD OPENED.

SOMETIMES IT GIVES ME PAIN UP TO NOW.

UP TO NOW.

ISMAEL ABDULLAH FARAHAT

"In front of me there was barbed wire.

"It helped that I was young, active, and strong,

"and could jump over the barbed wire."

THERE WAS A SOLDIER INSIDE...WITH A HEAVY STICK.

WHEN YOU WENT IN YOU COULDN'T SEE THIS SOLDIER.

MOSA ABDULLAH EL-HAJJ MOHAMMED

"Now the three of us are entering the school.

"The soldier hit the first one on his head.

"The second one escaped."

NOW IT'S MY TURN.

I MADE LIKE THIS.

"And I jumped over the ditch."

J. SACCO 12-07

AT THE SCHOOL THERE WAS BARBED WIRE AND A HOLE IN THE GROUND.

AYESH ABDEL-KHALIK YOUNIS

"One had to enter the school quickly, and if he fell in that hole, he'd be killed..."

"I kept my body close to the wall. So I was free to move, not like the other people.

"When I got to the gate, I just broke away and went through."

J. SACCO 12-07

The policeman Khalil Ahmed Mohammed Ibrahim was nearing the school entrance when he was joined by a colleague.

HE WAS A POLICEMAN [TOO], BUT HE WASN'T WEARING HIS UNIFORM.

THE DISTANCE BETWEEN ME AND THE SCHOOL GATE — ABOUT FOUR OR FIVE METERS...

WHEN I GOT TO THE GATE I LOOKED TO THE RIGHT...AND SAW TWO BODIES, TWO MEN WHO HAD BEEN KILLED.

"Up Fatima El-Khateeb Street, about 15 meters away. I thought they might be friends because...I had friends in that area."

WHEN I SAW THOSE BODIES, I DIDN'T KNOW HOW I KEPT ON WALKING.

I FORGOT MYSELF.

NOW I AM WALKING WITH MY POLICEMAN FRIEND.

I HAVE TO GO INTO THE SCHOOL.

J. SACCO 1·08

"When we reached the [police] station they took us to...a room nearby... They put us inside and locked the door and put a guard on us."

"And every few minutes...he fired just to panic us.

"Just to let us know he was there."

Their intimidation notwithstanding, the Israeli army considered local policemen as assets. Their cooperation would soon be enlisted to help consolidate the occupation of Gaza.

AT THE [SCHOOL] GATE THERE WAS A HUGE [NUMBER] OF SHOES.

MOSA AHMED EL-QEESI

"Whoever arrived thought everyone was supposed to take off his shoes...

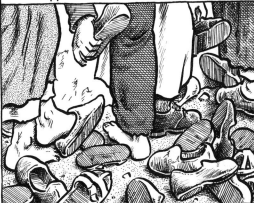

"While they were taking off their shoes, they were getting beaten."

I TOOK OFF MY SHOES.

ABDULLAH [MOHAMMED AHMED EL-ARGAN] WAS IN FRONT OF ME, AND WE WERE WALKING CLOSE TO EACH OTHER.

SALEH MEHI ELDIN EL-ARGAN

"A Jewish soldier came and beat him on his head with the stick.

"He fell down on his face."

J. SACCO 1-08

241

"They pulled his body to the other side of the street..."

"There were people carrying the bodies from the street and putting them in cars like bags of flour."

WE'RE WALKING WITH YOU, OKAY?

ABDUL-LAH IS IN FRONT OF YOU.

ABDULLAH WAS HIT AND YOU KEPT GOING?

I KEPT GOING.

I EN-TERED THE SCHOOL.

I LEFT ABDULLAH AT THE GATE BLEEDING.

Awad Mo-hammed Ahmed sketches the scene in front of the school gate into my notebook.

THERE IS A CORNER HERE.

TWO JEEPS STOOD AT THIS CORNER.

SCHOOL

SCHOOL WALL

SEA STREET

FATIMA EL-KHATEEB ST.

J. SACCO '08

242

"If someone fell, the soldiers took him to the jeeps. Whether he was alive or dead.

"They put four people in each jeep.

"And they took them to the western side."

DID YOU SEE THE JEEPS YOURSELF? DID YOU SEE THEM CARRYING THE BODIES?

I SAW THEM TAKING A GROUP OF BODIES. I SAW THEM ONCE.

"One [man] was dressed in a mukhtar's clothes, and one, his name was Abdullah Argan."

Awad motions with a hand down his skull.

A head split open.

AHMED HASSAN EDWAN

ANYONE WHO WAS BEATEN AND FELL DOWN, HE WAS DEAD.

"Even if he was still alive, they shot and killed him."

DID YOU SEE ANY OF THAT WITH YOUR EYES?

YES, I SAW MANY BODIES ON THE GROUND BEFORE JUMPING OVER THE TRENCH...

"and because I was tall and strong, I jumped quickly..."

243

IT WILL NEVER LEAVE MY MIND.

MOHI ELDIN IBRAHIM LAFI

"A young man was entering the school in front of me,

"and they beat him on his head."

...HE FELL DOWN AND MOVED ON THE GROUND AND MADE SOUNDS LIKE A SLAUGHTERED CHICKEN.

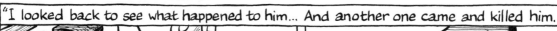
"I looked back to see what happened to him... And another one came and killed him.

"With a stick to his head."

WHAT WAS HIS NAME?

I DON'T KNOW HIS NAME.

AT THE TIME IT WAS DIFFICULT.

IT WAS LIKE JUDGMENT DAY.

J. SACCO 1-08

244

SHLOMO

Nineteen fifty-six or not, life goes on, the present needs tending, and Abed must beat the deadline for his university and grant applications—so we're back in Gaza City where I'm trying to help him finish up his essays.

But it hasn't been easy.

Not with that racket coming from out back!

A mourning tent!

Loudspeakers are blasting patriotic songs!

Messages of condolence!

Exhortations to jihad!

Six Hamas militants were blown to bits yesterday under mysterious circumstances.

Assassinated?

Killed in a "work accident"?

Depends which side you listen to.

With helicopters and a drone buzzing in our ears, we fall asleep.

At 5 a.m. heavy shooting erupts.

Eleven Palestinians are being killed.

Seven here in Gaza City.

Four in nearby Jabalia refugee camp.

J. SACCO 1·08

245

The next day we're heading back to southern Gaza, and our driver is worked up about the "security talks" Palestinian representatives are having with Israelis in London.

THEY SIT AND TALK WITH US, AND THEN THEY COME AND KILL US!

WHY'D THEY COME INTO EL-SHEJAYA* ANYWAY?

WHAT'S THERE?

*EL-SHEJAYA: THE GAZA CITY NEIGHBORHOOD ATTACKED THAT MORNING

THEY DEMOLISHED THE HOME OF A GUY FROM ISLAMIC JIHAD.

21527 TAXI

HE BLEW HIMSELF UP AT THE KFAR DAROM SETTLEMENT ABOUT A YEAR AGO.

When we get to Abu Houli, we find the checkpoint closed.

THEY KILL 11 OF US, AND THEY'VE BLOCKED THE ROAD, TOO!

IT WILL TAKE US FOUR HOURS TO GET TO RAFAH!

IN FOUR HOURS WE COULD REACH AMERICA!

J. SACCO 1-08

Oh well.

We're not going anywhere for a while.

Might as well stretch our legs.

A number of taxi drivers give up.

They disgorge their passengers and return to Gaza City.

The passengers have to fend for themselves, hitch other rides.

Half an hour later the line starts moving...

and stops after we've gone another two dozen meters.

IT'S CLOSED AGAIN!

WHO CLOSED IT?

SHLOMO.

J. SACCO 1-08

Ashraf invites us to the apartment he's renting now in Block J. He says he can add a piece to our '56 story. He says his grandfather was killed in Rafah.

But Ashraf has it wrong.

Like many younger Palestinians who live today's events, his grasp of yesterday's is mixed up.

His grandfather was killed in Khan Younis, not Rafah.

His mother, Wasfeya, tells us the story.

I WAS SITTING WITH MY FATHER LIKE YOU ARE SITTING WITH ASHRAF NOW.

SUDDENLY A SOLDIER ENTERED THE ROOM AND STARTED SHOOTING WITHOUT ANY WARNING.

NOWADAYS IT'S WORSE THAN IN '56.

THOSE DAYS WERE MORE DIFFICULT BECAUSE THE MEN WERE KILLED IN FRONT OF THEIR FAMILIES.

HE REMINDS YOU OF MANY BAD THINGS.

But Wasfeya is lost in thoughts of her father.

I HARDLY KNEW HIM.

J. SACCO 2.08

'56 WASN'T THE END OF THE STORY.

THEY'RE STILL RUNNING AFTER US.

WE WISHED TO LIVE WITH THE JEWS AS NEIGHBORS.

EVEN THOUGH ABU AMMAR* OFFERED THEM A LOT, WE ACCEPTED THAT.

BECAUSE OF THE PEACE WE BOUGHT LAND AND BUILT A HOUSE FOR OUR SONS' FUTURE.

*ABU AMMAR: YASSER ARAFAT

IF THAT HOUSE IS DEMOLISHED IN FRONT OF MY EYES, WHAT PEACE ARE WE TALKING ABOUT?

ALL THE WORLD JUDGES US AS TERRORISTS.

THOSE WHO ARE INSIDE THEIR HOUSES WHICH ARE DEMOLISHED ON TOP OF THEM, THEY'RE CONSIDERED TERRORISTS!

Ashraf's dad brings out some documents, including copies of permits from the municipality of Rafah to start building and to hook up to the electrical and water grids.

The cost of the paperwork, the land, and the house was 40,000 Jordanian dinars, almost $57,000.

ALL MY LIFE HAS BEEN LOST.

MY SON IS SUPPOSED TO GET MARRIED.

WHERE AM I GOING TO FIND A FLAT FOR HIM?

FIND HIM A TENT.

I'VE RENTED TWO STOREROOMS TO HOLD MY FURNITURE.

I CAME TO LIVE WITH ASHRAF BECAUSE THERE'S NO HOUSING.

IT'S EITHER LIVE WITH MY SON OR ON THE STREET.

MAYBE I'LL EXPEL HIM.

J. SACCO 2-08

HOW LONG CAN WE STAY LIKE THIS?

A MAN WITHOUT A HOME IS A MAN WITHOUT DIGNITY.

YESTERDAY WE WENT LOOKING TO RENT A FLAT, BUT IT ISN'T POSSIBLE.

I SAW TWO ROOMS AND THE OWNER ASKED US 1,000 JD AS A DOWNPAYMENT!

But why do you still visit the home you have fled?

I JUST WANT TO CONTEMPLATE THE THING I SPENT ALL MY LIFE DREAMING ABOUT.

WHAT DID I DO TO HAVE MY HOME DEMOLISHED?

AM I A TERRORIST?

PREPARE YOURSELF FOR A SUICIDE BOMBING.

WE WEREN'T SAFE BEFORE THESE SUICIDE OPERATIONS.

IMAGINE WITH THEM.

Just then someone calls from outside.

Ashraf disappears for a few minutes to talk to the visitor, a man who sold them building supplies and wonders when he'll be paid.

PEOPLE AREN'T KIND.

JUST A FEW DAYS AGO THEY ATTACKED OUR HOUSE, AND NOW HE'S COMING FOR MONEY.

LET HIM TAKE THE HOUSE.

I TOLD HIM NOT TO COME ASK FOR A WHILE.

251

J. SACCO 208

THE WILL OF GOD

One night we're trying to get through an interview with one of Rafah's "originals" in the Tal Zorob area.

IT'S DIFFICULT TO REMEMBER '56 BECAUSE OF THE DAILY EVENTS.

WHY?

BECAUSE EVENTS ARE CONTINUOUS, ONE AFTER ANOTHER.

His son listens to our interview with growing agitation. Finally —

WHY ARE YOU WRITING ABOUT '56?

IT'S MUCH WORSE NOW. EVEN MY FATHER SAYS SO.

OF COURSE IT'S BAD NOW, BUT THAT DOESN'T DIMINISH WHAT HAPPENED THEN.

'56?

OKAY, WRITE YOUR BOOK.

On our way out, however, he grabs my wrist. He wants to show me his home across the alleyway.

But before we reach the door, he stops me at a poster.

SEE HIM?

THAT'S MY COUSIN.

HE WAS KILLED JUST DOWN THE ROAD...

J. SACCO 2-08

A few floors up, he shows us bullet scars in his home.

In one room...

...and another...

...and another.

WHEN DID THIS HAPPEN?

EVERY DAY!

He says the rounds came from the Zorob tower, which we see as two lights in the dark about half a kilometer away.

'56?

'56?

The bathroom window faces the tower.

THE KIDS ARE AFRAID TO GO TO THE TOILET.

THIS IS WHERE THE KIDS USED TO STUDY.

BUT A TANK WAS RIGHT THERE THREE DAYS AGO!

RIGHT THERE!

EVERY DAY HERE IS '56!

'56 IS DEAD.

'56 IS FOR MY GRANDFATHER AND GRANDMOTHER.

BUT THIS ONE—

HE IS ALIVE!

AND I AM ALIVE!

J. SACCO 2-08

IS THIS THE SAME PLACE WE VISITED LAST TIME?

YES. HERE'S THAT FRIDGE.

We come across a woman named Sabha sitting nearby.

We met her last month when her home was partially destroyed.

Now it has disappeared.

WE'VE RENTED A PLACE IN THE CAMP.

UNRWA KNOWS OUR HOME IS DEMOLISHED, BUT UP TO NOW WE HAVEN'T RECEIVED COMPENSATION.

THE GOVERNORATE KNOWS ABOUT US, TOO.

WHAT CAN I DO?

WHY DO YOU COME BACK HERE?

THE RENTED FLAT IS SMALL. I CAN'T STAY IN THAT SMALL PLACE.

I SPEND THE TIME IN THIS AREA IN ORDER TO BREATHE.

TWELVE OF US LOST OUR HOME HERE.

THERE IS NO GOD BUT GOD.

257

We go back to the main street where we find Khaled with one of the self-styled defenders of Khan Younis.

I remember meeting this guy before—an odd fellow who had showed off his hand grenade.

Abed recognizes a woman shuffling by.

When we visited her some weeks ago she told us how she managed to stop a bull-dozer operator from demolishing her home by yelling that people were living inside.

But two days ago the bull-dozers came again.

NOW IT'S FIN-ISHED.

She is overcome by emotion and obliquely blames the Palestinian resistance for the destruction wrought by the Israelis.

GOD RID US OF THE PEOPLE WHO ARE UNJUST.

DON'T SAY THAT, HAJJA.

THIS WAS THE WILL OF GOD.

NONE OF US [FIGHTERS] DARED TO COME NEAR YOUR HOUSE.

AND IF SOME-ONE PUT SOMETHING NEAR YOUR HOUSE—

—Khaled means a land mine—

—IT WAS TO [STOP] THOSE WHO CAME TO DE-MOLISH YOUR HOUSE...

NOW BOTH FLOORS ARE ON THE GROUND, BUT PRAISE BE TO GOD.

And then she directs blame elsewhere.

SHARON NEEDS TO DEMOLISH HOUSES.

SHARON NEEDS PEOPLE TO RUN FROM THEIR HOMES.

We walk back up the street to a market place where we find a crowd teasing parts of an Israeli vehicle blown off by a land mine.

A crater near the hospital testifies to the power of the home-made explosives.

Meanwhile, Khaled is getting some funny looks.

I HEARD ON PALESTINIAN TV THAT YOU WERE CAPTURED THE NIGHT THEY ENTERED.

259

J. SACCO 2-08

We walk to the hospital grounds, which were breached by Israeli armor.

Khaled tells me that a boy of eight or nine was killed after the funeral for the two people killed the day before.

He'd gone to throw stones at a military position, and an Israeli soldier shot him in the head, Khaled says.

In fact, here comes a truck blasting the time of the boy's funeral.

DO YOU WANT TO TAKE A PICTURE OF THE MARTYR?

LIKE GO INTO THE MORGUE AND TAKE A PICTURE?

YES.

YOU CAN, IF YOU'D LIKE.

NO, REALLY, THAT'S FINE.

After all, what right do I have to intimacy with the poor kid's corpse? Only time, history, the bone-bleaching years can strip the dead of their privacy and make them sufficiently decent for viewing.

It's time to get back to Rafah and 1956.

J. SACCO 3-08

THE SCHOOLYARD

3:30 p.m.!

School's out!

The boys run into the street through the gate where, on November 12, 1956, the men of Rafah were beaten as they stumbled in the opposite direction over barbed wire and a ditch.

Abed and I enter, too, following the past.

But before we start snooping, we figure we better check in with the present, namely the headmaster of the afternoon primary classes here at El-Ameeriah School.

But the headmaster is otherwise occupied.

After some minutes, the business in the office concluded, the headmaster invites us in.

J. SACCO 3-08

Of course, he says, the boys are taught about The Day of the School. On each anniversary he explains how the men were beaten at the gate.

The headmaster escorts us as I take pictures of the main building and classrooms.

Someone introduces the school gardener, Abdullah.

He was here that day in 1956. He was only 12, he says.

BUT WHY WERE YOU IN THE SCHOOL? YOU WERE BENEATH THE AGE.

I WAS AFRAID TO STAY AT HOME.

He doesn't want to talk about it any more.

He says there are others who remember better than he does.

262

J. SACCO 3-08

THE SEARCH

In the meantime, what was going on outside the school?

We circle around it looking for older ladies who, we hope, can fill us in.

And in one of Shaboura's back alleys, we discover Ra'esa Salim Hassan Kaloob selling sweets at a makeshift stall.

Sure she remembers '56! She was a child, but she says her memory is strong.

She entrusts her goods to some grandkids and takes us to the house of an obliging neighbor.

The women there are cracking up, giggling. We're the most fun they've had in ages. And they're the most fun we've had, too!

Gone are the formalities, the solemnity! In fact, the entire tea-and-coffee-serving spectacle is eliminated because—well, the women are out here with us, not in the kitchen boiling water.

J. SACCO 4.08

Ra'esa says her brother, a Palestinian soldier, went to the school as ordered.

I LEFT THE HOUSE AND NO ONE PREVENTED ME — MY MOTHER WAS A VERY OLD WOMAN, AND I WAS THE OLDEST OF MY SISTERS.

SO I WENT TO THE WALL OF THE SCHOOL.

MAYBE THREE GIRLS WERE WITH ME.

"I saw all the men sitting, their heads down, and the Jews among them walking, going and coming.

"Anyone who moved was beaten.

"They were firing over their heads, and they told them,"

TATA ROSH, IHMAR!*

Soldiers ordered the girls away, but "we came and went many times.

*"IHMAR": YOU DONKEYS

270

J. SACCO 4·08

"The women weren't able to leave their houses at first, but when they saw me running and walking in the streets they became stronger and went out."

I WASN'T AFRAID.

AND I'M [STILL] NOT AFRAID. I'M STRONG.

WERE THERE MANY WOMEN IN THE STREETS?

"Yes, many women, many kids. Holding black flags.

"They ran after their men until they reached this area, screaming and shouting."

A few doors down from Ra'esa's stand, we find Deeba Jamil El-Talili, who also remembers.

MY HUSBAND AND HIS THREE BROTHERS WENT TO THE SCHOOL WHEN THEY HEARD THE LOUDSPEAKERS...

WE STARTED TO SCREAM AND SHOUT AT THE SOLDIERS.

"They pushed us back telling us,

GO HOME! GO HOME!

"[A soldier] pushed us inside and closed the door.

"[Later] we went outside again."

J. SACCO 4-08

Omm Awad El-Najeeli, who lived across Sea Street, tells us—

ALL MY NEIGHBORS, ALL MY DAUGHTERS, ALL OF US, WE WENT OUT.

THEY TOOK OUR MEN SO WE WENT OUT.

"Should we remain in our houses? We were going to die like them!

"We stood at the end of Fatima El-Khateeb Street, and when they shot at us we went up the street and then came back."

WERE THEY SHOOTING AT YOU OR OVER YOUR HEADS?

OVER OUR HEADS.

Soldiers fanned out into Rafah, she says, and the women and children rushed home.

The soldiers entered each house looking for two things: men who had not gone to the designated gathering points and weapons.

WE OPENED THE DOOR FOR THEM AND THEY ENTERED.

FIVE CAME.

JAMILA ISSA SOLAIMAN ABU ZEATER

"Each of them was tall and very strong.

J. SACCO 4.08

272

"They searched all the furniture, the mattresses, the blankets...the dove cage."

"I will not lie. They didn't take anything from our house."

THEY SEARCHED EVERYTHING.

EVERYTHING.

OMM AWAD EL-NAJEELI

"They didn't leave a... chicken. They left nothing. They stole everything."

THEY TOOK ALL MY SEVEN SONS... AND STOOD THEM AGAINST THE WALL ...OPPOSITE MY HOUSE.

TA'AH KHALIL OUTHMAN

"I left the house and followed them screaming and crying."

OKAY YOU ARE CRYING.

TAKE YOUR SONS.

SHUT THE DOOR AND DON'T GO OUT.

J. SACCO 4.08

273

FATIMA EL-KHATEEB: "I remember a terrible scene. One of the soldiers was shouting,

SHOOT HIM! SHOOT HIM!

"He was speaking about my sister's son, who was 15 years old.

NO, THIS IS A YOUNG ONE.

"After they left the house, one soldier came to us.

NO ONE GO OUTSIDE.

ALL OF YOU REMAIN IN YOUR HOUSE.

"I felt that he was a human being.

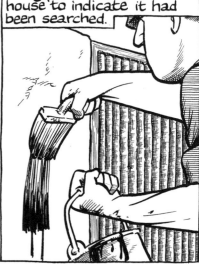

"They put a mark on the house to indicate it had been searched.

"And then a man who was injured, walking on his hands and knees, knocked on our door...

"We all gathered in one room because we were afraid, especially after we received our neighbor...

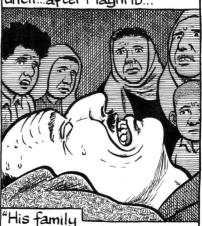

"He remained at our house until...after Maghrib.*...

"His family came to take him...but he died as he got to hospital."

274

* MAGHRIB: EVENING PRAYER

We last left Ghanim Mahmoud Sha'at, who had seen his cousin killed in front of him and who had returned home, lying on his bed, awaiting the soldiers.

Now they were at his door.

STAND UP!

I CAN'T. YESTERDAY I WAS AT THE CLINIC.

Ghanim told the officer he was sick and showed him his UNRWA card.

"They took me from the room.

"And a soldier told me to stand against a wall

"and raise my hands.

HE'S SICK. DON'T SHOOT HIM.

"We walked for awhile...

"One of the soldiers tried to hit me with a heavy stick...

"I fell and it hit me on my back.

"The same officer told the soldiers not to touch me.

"He took me to an area and there were many men...with their faces on the ground. It was an open area...and the soldiers surrounded them.

"All [the prisoners] were old men. I was the youngest among them. I was 21 years old.

"We spent about an hour or an hour and a half.

275

"When they finished searching in the camp, the same officer came back...and they started to ask each of us,

YOUR NAME?

WHERE DO YOU LIVE?

"They were letting the old men leave. Only three of us remained."

Ghanim was taken to one of two alternative gathering points, distinct from the government school, for further screening.

Abed and I hear many stories of men being found in the camp and shot.

For example, Fatima El-Khateeb tells us, "My neighbor, age 55, they took him outside the door and killed him."

Over and over again we are told the story of one Mohammed Thabit, a school teacher discovered hiding at home — some say dressed in women's clothing — and shot by Israeli soldiers.

But his family has emigrated and we cannot properly verify the story.

We also hear of killings of groups of men who left for the school late. But we want an eyewitness.

One man — a young boy at the time — claims to have followed several family members and neighbors from Block O and watched from a distance as they were lined up against a wall and shot.

Others repeat the story, and parts of it are solidly confirmed; indeed, all the men he mentions were killed that day.

But Abed is somewhat skeptical that the man actually witnessed the killings...

and Abed's doubt is as good as a veto.

J. SACCO 5-08

Who decides what is credible and what is not?

Abed and I, that's who, sitting in our room drinking coffee.

We decide.
We edit.
We determine.

In the absence of UNRWA records, of Israeli records —and could we rely on them if we had them?— it's up to us to fill history's glass with as much truthful, cogent testimony as we can.

If some truth spills along the way, we apologize.

Anyway, one day, after we've moved on from this part of the story, we come across four black Palestinians, perhaps the descendants of Turkish slaves, playing a game with stones in the sand.

In passing, one of them tells us he saw seven men gunned down that day in 1956.

When I take out my notepad and ask him to repeat the story, he hesitates.

IT'S SOMETHING DAMAGING TO THE JEWS, AND I DON'T WANT TROUBLE FOR MYSELF.

I tell him I won't name him, and reluctantly he starts again.

"They entered our house and searched it... They said to my grandfather,

YOU ARE YOUNG. WHY DIDN'T YOU GO TO THE SCHOOL?

YOUR ID?

"He looked at the ID and asked the soldiers to take [my grandfather] to the school and check if the age was right or wrong.

"My brother and I secretly followed the soldiers and my grandfather.

J SACCO 5-08

"Near the sanitation department we found seven men lined up against the wall with their hands over their heads.

"My grandfather already had passed that point.

277

"Now we stopped.

"There was an old woman on the street looking for her son, who had gone to the school.

"And the old woman stopped also.

"The woman fell down on the ground to her hands and knees..."

ALL THE PEOPLE KILLED.

ALL THE PEOPLE KILLED.

ALL OF US WENT BACK TO OUR HOUSES.

WE... TOLD THE STORY TO OUR FAMILY.

AFTER HALF AN HOUR MY GRANDFATHER CAME BACK WITH THE SOLDIERS BECAUSE THEY HAD FOUND HE WAS OLDER THAN THE [WANTED] AGE.

Abed and I have to take responsibility for believing or rejecting a witness.

In this case we both trust our instincts and this man's story.

J. SACCO 5-08

He and the others have warmed to us, and they direct us to a woman living nearby.

Her husband, they say, was shot in front of her.

Soon we are sitting with Nasrah Felfel on the same spot she was living with her husband, Salem, all those years ago.

IT WAS HIS FATE TO COME BACK AND TO BE KILLED.

"I told him, ALL THE PEOPLE ARE RUNNING TOWARDS THE SCHOOL, AND YOU SHOULD GO.

"When he went outside he didn't see any people. The men had already gone to the school...

"So he decided to come back...

"Our neighbor [also] left late. They beat our neighbor with the back of their guns, and they took him to the school...

"Suddenly we found them entering the house.

J. SACCO 5.08

"They were searching.

"All of us were afraid and were together in one room.

"They took my husband outside the house.

"[The children] ran after me when I followed their father. They were afraid...and they were screaming and shouting..."

THEY SHOT HIM IN HIS STOMACH, ON THE LEFT SIDE, AND ANOTHER TIME IN HIS HEAD.

YOU SAW THIS, HAJJA?

NEAR THE DOOR OF OUR NEIGHBORS.

J. SACCO 5-08

"I saw it with my eyes.

"And then they shot at us.

"I fell down, and I started to crawl on my hands and knees to get inside the house.

"I tried to go out to see the body many times...but there was a soldier at the end of the street the whole day.

"And my neighbor from time to time shouted to me,"

DON'T GO OUT! HE'LL SHOOT YOU IF YOU LEAVE YOUR HOUSE!

OF COURSE THEY WERE SHOOTING EVERYWHERE,

AND THE BODY REMAINED IN THE STREET IN THE SAME PLACE UNTIL THE NEXT MORNING.

J. SACCO 5·08

While we feverishly dig away at 1956, daily events are shovelled back at us, obscuring our finds, making it that much harder for our subjects to focus on the stratum in question.

100 SHEKELS

She lay buried in the rubble for up to an hour.

I WAS SAYING, 'THERE IS NO GOD BUT GOD.'

That woman we met in the last chapter, for example, 80- or 82-year-old Ta'ah Khalil Outhman... her leg was broken when her house was demolished on top of her a few days before we talked.

Abed and I had already surveyed the apparent Israeli target, a water pumping station across the road, which was heavily damaged.

A second pumping station was completely destroyed the same night.

There was no warning.

Ta'ah awoke when the zinc roof collapsed onto her bed.

THE WHOLE HOUSE FELL DOWN ON ME...

J. SACCO 5-08

282

The whole street, which faces a Jewish settlement across no-man's-land, has been severely shot up and shelled.

It's a wonder that people still patch up their places and remain.

As we turn left onto Sea Street, we come across more unfortunates.

I put money in the hand of the woman, Abed or not.

She gets the dough the other people didn't get.

At least someone is happy.

J. SACCO 5-08

THE MOUTH OF THE LION

Ashraf snatches away Abed's cell phone and a list of names from local historian Owda Ayesh's book.

He's taken over our 1956 project!

WE NEED TO KNOW WHERE SOME OF YOUR FAMILY MEMBERS ARE.

WE HAVE COUPONS FOR THEM.

Coupons?

He means UNRWA chits for extra groceries and provisions.

Of course we have no such thing, but Ashraf waves off our objections.

YOU ARE IN THE MOUTH OF THE LION!

With an efficiency Abed and I have never mustered, The Lion confronts everyone from old men—

NO, THAT FAMILY ALL MOVED TO SINAI.

to kids loitering under a street lamp.

WE'RE LOOKING FOR THESE PEOPLE.

He disappears into a barber shop and then pops out beaming.

I'VE FOUND A '56 STORY FOR YOU.

J. SACCO 5-08

286

He accompanies us on some of our evening interviews and listens closely to old men telling a story he has never heard before.

Ashraf is well known and well liked in Block J, where he seems to have his ear to the ground.

CONGRAT-ULATIONS!

YOUR HOME IS DEMOL-ISHED.

Members of the resistance court Ashraf. Now that he's "abandoned" his home along the border, they want to plant a mine inside for Israeli soldiers.

Ashraf jestfully declines, and refers them to neighbors who also have left their houses.

After the day's interviews, we often hole up in one of the Sea Street restaurants.

We wash down glazed chicken with orange soft drinks and catch up with the saber rattling in Washington.

One night we leave a restaurant as the border erupts with gunfire.

The rounds seem to be smacking into Ashraf's neighborhood.

J. SACCO 5-08

We wait with Ashraf for the shooting to subside.

An ambulance waits with us in case there are casualties.

At one point overhead tracer fire scatters us.

Enough. We tell Ashraf he can sleep at our place tonight.

NO, I WANT TO GO HOME.

His wife and baby are in Block J. His parents, his brothers and sisters, too.

The shooting finally lets up, and Abed and I decide to accompany Ashraf home through the back alleys.

YOU GUYS OUGHT TO WATCH OUT.

WE DON'T WANT TO HAVE TO CARRY YOU.

We don't say much, but Ashraf seems grateful for our company.

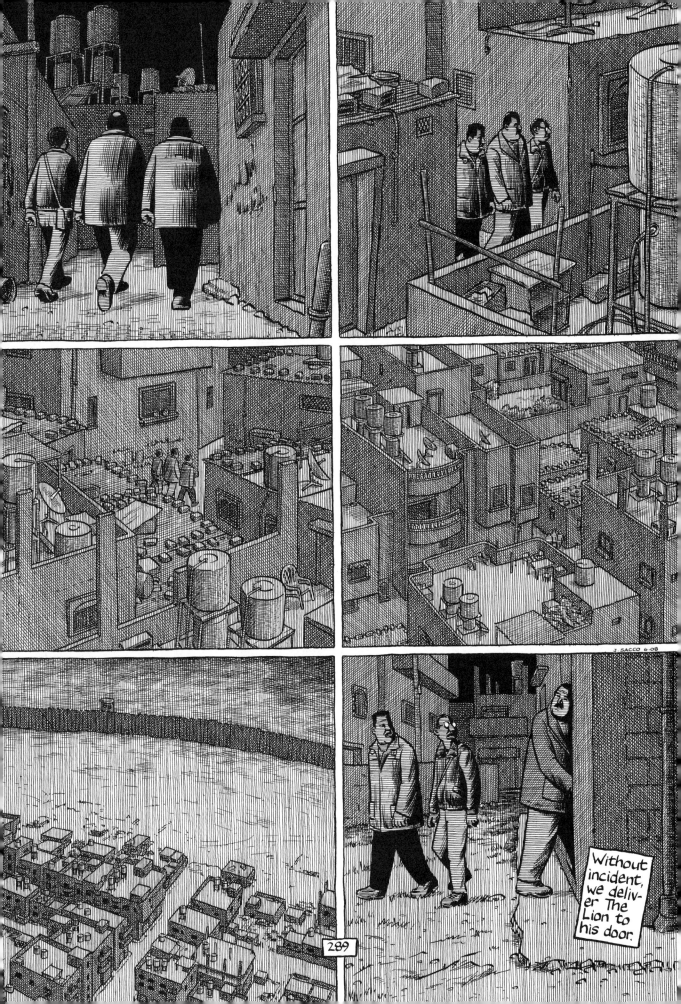

Without incident, we deliver The Lion to his door.

The taxi driver can no longer control himself, not even in front of a foreigner.

LET'S BLOW UP EVERYTHING

WE NEED TWO, THREE OPERATIONS!

BOMBS! BOMBS!

LET'S BLOW UP EVERYTHING, AND IF THAT MEANS WAR, LET THERE BE WAR!

DAILY THEY KILL US, THEY DEMOLISH HOMES, AND MEANWHILE THERE ARE NO OPERATIONS!

SO WE NEED OPERATIONS!

Operations. That's Palestinian-speak for any attacks on Israelis, including suicide bombings.

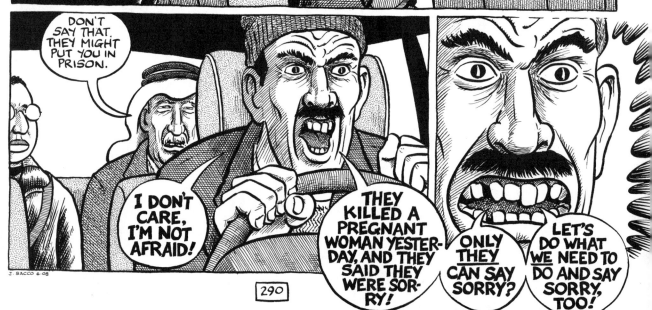

DON'T SAY THAT, THEY MIGHT PUT YOU IN PRISON.

I DON'T CARE, I'M NOT AFRAID!

THEY KILLED A PREGNANT WOMAN YESTERDAY, AND THEY SAID THEY WERE SORRY!

ONLY THEY CAN SAY SORRY?

LET'S DO WHAT WE NEED TO DO AND SAY SORRY, TOO!

J. SACCO 6-08

SHAPES IN

THE DARK

PT.1

We've heard ambulances racing by and one rocket after another hitting Block J.

Abed and I turn off Sea Street to investigate and ask a boy what he knows.

THREE WOMEN WERE WOUNDED DOWN THERE.

BUT DON'T WALK ON THAT SIDE OF THE STREET.

OKAY, GUIDE US.

The boy leads us, and now we can make out dark shapes taking cover behind a corner.

DON'T STOP THERE. RUN ACROSS. THERE'S A TANK UP THE ROAD.

We do as we're told.

The camp ends straight up the street, and beyond that is a deep dark.

If there is a tank there, we cannot see it.

J. SACCO 6·08

One of the guys we're with lives above the general store, which is a few meters from the last detonation.

I start asking:

Who's in there?

How many?

The whole family?

MY FATHER, MY MOTHER, BROTHERS, SISTERS.

WILL YOU CARRY ME THERE?

The next day Abed and I drive to the European Gaza Hospital, which sits off the road to Khan Younis, to visit one of the wounded women.

We've heard her leg was blown off.

The security guard doesn't think it's a good idea to visit her just yet. He's just handed the leg to the family.

SHE'S IN A BAD WAY.

SHE LOSES HER MIND AT TIMES.

SHE'S NOT USED TO THE IDEA THAT HER LEG IS GONE.

294

J. SACCO 6·08

And she's unmarried, he tells us.

Do we understand that?

Do we understand what that does to her prospects?

The other wounded females are laid up at El-Najjar Hospital in Rafah.

Fathia, the older sister, agrees to speak to us.

Her niece, seven-year-old Rola, is knocked out by drugs in the next bed.

Her dressing is soaked in blood.

The doctors won't operate on her badly injured leg until it stops bleeding.

That night, Fathia tells us, they had gone to shop at the market.

BEFORE WE LEFT HOME THERE HAD BEEN SOME...SHOOTING.

BUT IT HAD CALMED DOWN.

As they were returning, a short distance from their house, they found themselves under fire.

"I felt something enter my flesh...

"We stopped and ran back to the nearest door.

"I was in front, and now they started shelling.

"Uncountable shells!

HELP ME, AUNTIE!

HELP ME!

295

"I looked back

"and I saw her covered in blood.

"I saw my sister on the ground.

I'VE LOST MY LEG!

"She was five or six meters away but I couldn't reach her.

"The shelling was heavy.

"Everyone who showed his head to help my sister was shelled."

Finally, she says, a brave neighbor pulled her sister into his building, and medics evacuated them over a wall to avoid the rockets, which were still crashing in the street.

I have to ask: Why are you living along the border in such a dangerous area?

She says their home in Block J was demolished two months ago.

They then rented in the Tal El-Sultan neighborhood, but the Israelis damaged their new apartment and destroyed their car while demolishing the home of a neighbor.

With so many people made homeless by the demolitions, there was no other place to rent but back in Block J.

NOW WE'VE ALREADY PAID RENT FOR THE MONTH.

WHERE ELSE ARE WE GOING TO GO?

J. SACCO 7·08

This is the part of the story that wobbles and strains.

THE SCREENING

Because while anyone would remember a two-second flurry of clubs rising and falling onto skulls and flesh...

and the continuous gunfire as the school-yard filled up...

what about the next eight- or ten-hour stretch when the gears shifted down to the slow, bitter, but relatively systematic sifting of men?

But many interviewees agreed on certain component elements of the next few hours, starting with the arrival of the officers.

THE OFFICER OR OFFICERS

AFTER 12 O'CLOCK, MAYBE, WHILE ALL THE PEOPLE HAD THEIR HEADS ON THE GROUND...

MAHMOUD SALMAN QISHTAH

...A JEEP ENTERED.

ZAKI HASSAN EDWAN

A JEEP CAME WITH TWO SOLDIERS INSIDE, ONE OF THEM SHORT, ONE OF THEM TALL.

AWAD MOHAMMED AHMED

MOHAMMED ZIDAN: "In the afternoon two cars entered. It seemed that inside the two cars were officials of high rank."

J. SACCO 9·08

...AN INTER-NATIONAL ONE CAME. MAYBE HE WAS ISRAELI, BUT I DON'T KNOW WHERE HE CAME FROM.

MOHAMMED HASSAN MOHAMMED

I DON'T KNOW WHETHER HE WAS A HIGH-RANKING JEWISH OR BRITISH ONE...

IBRAHIM SAKER

...I THINK HE WAS HIGH-RANKING IN THE UNITED NATIONS.

MOHAMMED JUMA' EL-GHOUL

A FOR-EIGNER, MAY-BE A BRITISH ONE ...BESIDE HIM A TRANSLATOR WHO KNEW ARA-BIC.

ANONYMOUS 1

WHO THEY WERE, WE DON'T KNOW, BUT WE HEARD THAT THEY WERE BRITISH AND FRENCH.

AYESH ABDEL-KHALIK YOUNIS

With the presence of this officer or these officers, most agree that the situation eased.

MOHAMMED ZIDAN: "Because immediately, by a sign of his hand... the firing stopped."

"He talked directly to the people and asked them to raise their heads."

301

"And he started shouting to the people, RAISE YOUR HEADS!

"He stood in the middle and stopped the firing."

THE LEGEND OF THE DOVES

HE WAS NOT A JEW. MAYBE HE WAS BRITISH OR A FOREIGNER...

ABDELWAHAB MAHMOUD ABDELWAHAB EL-ASMAR

"and a dove came and stood on his shoulder."

I SAW THREE DOVES FLY UP AND FLY DOWN VERY CLOSE TO US...

SALEH MEHI ELDIN EL-ARGAN

"I said, THESE ARE MERCIFUL ANGELS WHO'VE COME TO US.

"The one who was sitting beside me said,"

WHERE ARE THOSE ANGELS?

THERE IS NO MERCY HERE.

303

J. SACCO 7-08

THEY SELECTED TWO COLLABORATORS...WHO THEY KNEW WERE SOLDIERS AND ASKED THEM TO POINT TO THEIR COLLEAGUES.

SO EVERY SOLDIER WHO KNEW HE WOULD BE SELECTED TRIED TO HIDE HIS FACE.

ANONYMOUS 1

...AND THE ONES WHO [TRIED] TO HIDE THEMSELVES THEY TOOK.

ABDUL-MALIK MOHAMMED KULLAB

AT THE END, WHEN SOME SOLDIERS REFUSED TO SHOW THEMSELVES, THE ISRAELIS DECIDED TO COME AND SELECT PEOPLE.

YOU, STAND UP!

YOU, STAND UP!

YOU, STAND UP!

"They selected people who were not soldiers."

MOHAMMED YOUSEF SHAKER MOUSA

'HEY, YOU, COME HERE!'

THEY WOULD TAKE HIM AND...SHOOT HIM.

"This happened. We know. Everybody was trying to hide his face. So they wouldn't shoot him."

MOHAMMED JUMA' EL-GHOUL

J. SACCO 8-08

306

THEY WOULD COME AMONG US AND SELECT ONE, TWO, THREE.

'STAND UP! 'STAND UP!'

"They took them behind a wall. The western wall.

"And then shot them."

MOHI ELDIN IBRAHIM LAFI

Despite these allegations and others to follow, we find no credible eyewitness account of any shootings in the schoolyard itself.

The Israelis were gathering the Palestinian soldiers and other suspects netted in the screening in a separate holding area.

THE CAFE OWNER

One often repeated story, which demonstrates just how disparate some recollections are, concerns an alleged Israeli spy who had lived in Rafah and held a grudge against a cafe owner named Ihdayhee.

IHDAYHEE WAS SITTING AMONG US. THE SPY CAME AND SAID, 'IHDAYHEE, COME OUT.'

ISMAEL IBRAHIM YOUSEF

"So Ihdayhee went, but none of the people sitting saw him killed. But we heard the shooting. I don't know where.

"We didn't dare to raise our heads."

307

SUDDENLY I HEARD A VOICE CALLING ZAKI IHDAYHEE. ZAKI IHDAYHEE APPEARED AND HE NEVER RETURNED.

AYESH ABDEL-KHALIK YOUNIS

THIS SPY CALLED HIM, SELECTED HIM, AND SHOT HIM... THEY TOOK HIM AND SHOT HIM BEHIND THE BUILDING.

AHMED HASSAN EDWAN

THEY CALLED HIS NAME FROM THE LOUDSPEAKER INSIDE THE SCHOOL. THEY TOOK HIM BEHIND THE BUILDING, AND WE HEARD SHOOTING.

MOHAMMED ISMAEL EL-SBAKHI

308

MOHAMMED ZIDAN:
"Through the loudspeaker they called for Ihdayhee and his sons. Of course, he wasn't there...

"The next day we heard that Ihdayhee had been killed inside his house or in the streets."

MOHAMMED HASHIM IBRAHIM ABU TALIB

[IHDAYHEE WAS] KILLED IN THE STREET... I SAW THE BLOOD RUNNING FROM HIS BODY.

THE LINES

Not satisfied they had discovered all the soldiers in the schoolyard, the Israelis next attempted to enlist the aid of local notables.

THEY ASKED EACH MUKHTAR TO COME AND SELECT THE SOLDIERS FROM HIS VILLAGE.

MOHAMMED YOUSEF SHAKER MOUSA

"They lined the mukhtars in one area.

"Most of the mukhtars didn't go up. And some...went just to save the lives of the people.

"Maybe the mukhtars said,

ANYONE WHO IS A SOLDIER, COME HERE.

[THE ISRAELIS] ASKED THE PEOPLE TO STAND IN ONE LINE AND WALK IN FRONT OF THE MUKHTARS.

ANONYMOUS 1

"They didn't insist, and they didn't mention anyone by name."

"The mukhtars looked at us and never selected anyone...

"When I finished my turn and was going back, the soldier who guarded the selected area told me,

YOU! COME HERE!

"All the mukhtars ...shouted,

THIS IS THE PHOTOGRAPHER WHO MAKES THE IDENTITY CARDS FOR THE PEOPLE!

"So I went back to my place."

Awadallah Ahmed Awadallah, one of the mukhtars who had come forward, drives home the point. "We didn't identify anyone," he tells us.

"You have to understand this."

J. SACCO 8-08

WE HAD TO STAND IN FRONT OF THE JEEP FOR AWHILE... AND THEN KEEP WALKING.

ABDULLAH HASSAN KHADER EL-MOGHAIYER

The men were led to a group of tables where they were questioned individually.

MANY SOLDIERS WERE LINING THE PEOPLE.

THE QUESTIONING PROCESS WAS VERY SLOW.

AYESH ABDEL-KHALIK YOUNIS

AND THEY TOOK WHO THEY WANTED

"They stopped me and asked,

WHAT'S YOUR WORK?

TEACHER.

"So they left me..."

WHEN MY TURN CAME THEY ASKED,

WHERE DO YOU LIVE? WHAT'S THE NATURE OF YOUR WORK?

I'M A POLICE-MAN.

ANONYMOUS 2

"Questions of this kind. I passed through without any problem."

JUST ONE QUES-TION AND ONE AN-SWER,

AWAD MOHAM-MED AHMED

"and then go."

311

IT WAS ONLY TEN DAYS SINCE I'D LEFT THE ARMY... I HAD A CIVILIAN [IDENTITY] CARD.

ABDULLAH HASSAN KHADER EL-MOGHAIYER

"There was a colleague of mine whose personality was very very weak, and when they took him in the morning he gave all the information and all the names, and he stood... with them at the tables.

"When I came and showed them my identity card, they let me go."

"After five minutes...a soldier caught me by the collar..."

YOUR COLLEAGUE TOLD ME YOU'RE A SOLDIER.

I'M NOT A SOLDIER!

YOUR FRIEND TOLD ME: YOU'RE A DRIVER FOR A MAJOR!

THE SPEED UP

At some point the Israelis must have realized they might not finish screening all the men before sundown.

WHEN IT WAS ABOUT 4 O'CLOCK THEY STARTED TO MAKE THE PEOPLE STAND UP 30 AT A TIME.

ISMAEL ABDULLAH FARAHAT

MOHAMMED ZIDAN: "The people were many and the investigation rooms were few. It was near sunset and they started to hurry up the process...

"There was no time. They would take ten people at a time, but there was no time."

THEY DIDN'T CARE WHETHER WE WERE SOLDIERS OR NOT.

MOSA ABDULLAH EL-HAJJ MOHAMMED

THEY SELECTED THE HANDSOME GUYS, THE WELL-BUILT GUYS.

"We reached the desks and they selected us with their eyes."

THEY DIDN'T ASK YOU ANY QUESTIONS?

NO, THEY DIDN'T.

THEY JUST SAW US AND SELECTED US.

YOU GO THERE! YOU GO THERE!

SIT THERE!

MOHAMMED ZIDAN: "My turn hadn't come up...

"I was just sitting, watching."

THE BUSES

As the screening wrapped up, the suspected combatants were led to a number of buses waiting outside the school gate.

ALI SOLAIMAN SHA'AT: "They made us walk in groups of five."

WHILE WE WERE WALKING THEY HIT US.

MOSA AHMED EL-QEESI

"We entered the buses."

THREE IN EVERY SEAT.

AND WE SAT LIKE THIS.

THE ONE WHO RAISED HIS HEAD, THEY HIT.

J. SACCO 9-08

GHANIM MAHMOUD SHA'AT: "They made us sit on top of each other between the seats..."

"The soldiers climbed over the people to beat them."

ONE OF THE SOLDIERS —THROUGH THE WINDOW— HIT ME ON MY LEFT SIDE...

MOSA ABDULLAH EL-HAJJ MOHAMMED

THERE WAS ONE WHO REFUSED TO ENTER THE BUS. THE SOLDIER ASKED HIM TO WALK, AND HE DIDN'T WANT TO WALK.

ABDULLAH HASSAN KHADER EL-MOGHAIYER

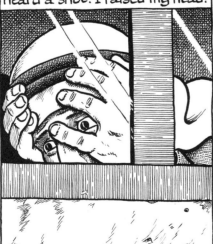

"When I entered the bus, I heard a shot. I raised my head.

"I saw him dead, [being] pulled and hidden behind the cactus trees."

J. SACCO 9-08

The suspects taken from the government school and the other gathering points were briefly incarcerated in Gaza City and elsewhere and then transferred to Atlit prison in northern Israel.

There, with thousands of other prisoners of war, they awaited repatriation.

THE RELEASE

NOW IT'S ABOUT SUNSET...

WE HEARD THE WOMEN SHOUTING FROM OUTSIDE.

ALL THE WOMEN CAME TO THE SCHOOL AT THAT MOMENT.

AWAD MOHAMMED AHMED

[WE] HEARD THE WOMEN OUTSIDE SCREAMING AND SHOUTING.

OH, THEY'VE KILLED THE PEOPLE!

THEY'VE KILLED THE PEOPLE!

ZAKI HASSAN EDWAN

THERE WAS ONLY ONE HOUSE BETWEEN US AND THE SCHOOL. WE'D HEARD EVERYTHING.

"I went outside.

HOSSON SALAMA BADWAN

"Many many women were waiting to learn the fate of their men."

316

J. SACCO P-08

ALL THE KIDS, ALL THE WOMEN WERE IN THIS AREA WAITING FOR THEIR MEN, AND THEY MADE MALTAMAH.*

RA'ESA SALIM HASSAN KALOOB

*MALTAMAH: A DEMONSTRATIVE FORM OF GRIEF

AND WE [BECAME] NOISY WHEN WE HEARD THE WOMEN SCREAMING.

"We thought they were being attacked by the Israeli soldiers.

ABDUL-MALIK MOHAMMED KULLAB

"So they started shooting over our heads."

THE GOOD THING IS THAT THEY DIDN'T ATTACK OUR HONOR.

MOHI ELDIN IBRAHIM LAFI

OUR WHAT?

HE MEANS THE WOMEN.

DEATH AND MONEY ARE NOTHING.

THE IMPORTANT THING IS OUR HONOR.

J. SACCO 9-08

NO ONE WENT THROUGH THE GATE...

ANONYMOUS 4

"We were afraid to go to the main street. We were very afraid.

"Because we'd seen all the people who had been killed [there]..."

THE PEOPLE WERE AFRAID TO GO THROUGH THE GATE.

MOHAMMED YOUSEF SHAKER MOUSA

"They thought ...that leaving the school would be the same as entering the school.

"I jumped the wall...opposite my shop,

"and I came back through the same [path] I had used to go to the school."

J. SACCO 9-08

WHEN WE CAME OUT WE FOUND THE WOMEN SCREAMING.

AHMED KHALIL EL-BAWAB

[MY HUSBAND] JUMPED OVER THE WALL...

HOSSON SALAMA BADWAN

"He was jumping and running,

"looking to hide in the house."

AT MY HOUSE I HEARD THE NEWS THAT I'D BEEN KILLED.

AWAD MOHAMMED AHMED

AFTER SUNSET... MY FATHER AND BROTHERS CAME BACK AND TOLD US WHAT HAPPENED.

ANONYMOUS 3

"One after another they returned.

"My father was last because he was an old man.

"From houses that had lost [someone] you could hear the shouting, the screaming and crying.

"You know how women behave.

"They tore their clothes.

"Screaming and crying."

Perhaps, you are thinking, the curtain has come down on the story about the Israeli screening operation in Rafah on November 12, 1956.

After all, the surviving men have either escaped the school and are back at home or are on buses headed into confinement.

THE MOUTH OF THE LION
PT. 2

But what of that third group, the dead?

To find out their story we need to locate their relatives.

Ashraf takes charge!

Waving the list from Owda Ayesh's book, he marches into a general store and accosts the first person he sees.

DO YOU KNOW ANY OF THESE FAMILIES?

ANY OF THEM LIVE AROUND HERE?

NO. I DON'T KNOW ANY OF THEM.

WHY DO YOU WANT TO KNOW?

YOU DON'T KNOW ANY OF THEM BUT YOU WANT TO KNOW WHY?

ENOUGH!

327

But the Lion isn't always charging, and he isn't always roaring.

One night, before setting out for another interview, he takes out a $100 bill.

He caresses Benjamin Franklin's face.

THIS IS GOING TO PAY THE RENT THIS MONTH.

I HAD TO ASK FOR THIS MONTH'S PAY IN ADVANCE.

UNRWA IS TELLING US THEY WILL GIVE US TWO HOUSES...

ONE FOR MY FATHER AND ONE FOR ME.

BUT WE ARE FOUR BROTHERS.

His brothers are unmarried, and only heads of households are eligible for the housing units UNRWA is slowly building to replace the homes the Israelis have bulldozed.

Ashraf is case number 710.

His father is case number 711.

There are hundreds of refugee families on the waiting list.

As one UNRWA representative in Gaza City told me, "First demolished, first served."

Ashraf estimates he won't move into new UNRWA housing for two years.

WHAT ABOUT BETWEEN NOW AND THEN?

J. SACCO 10-08

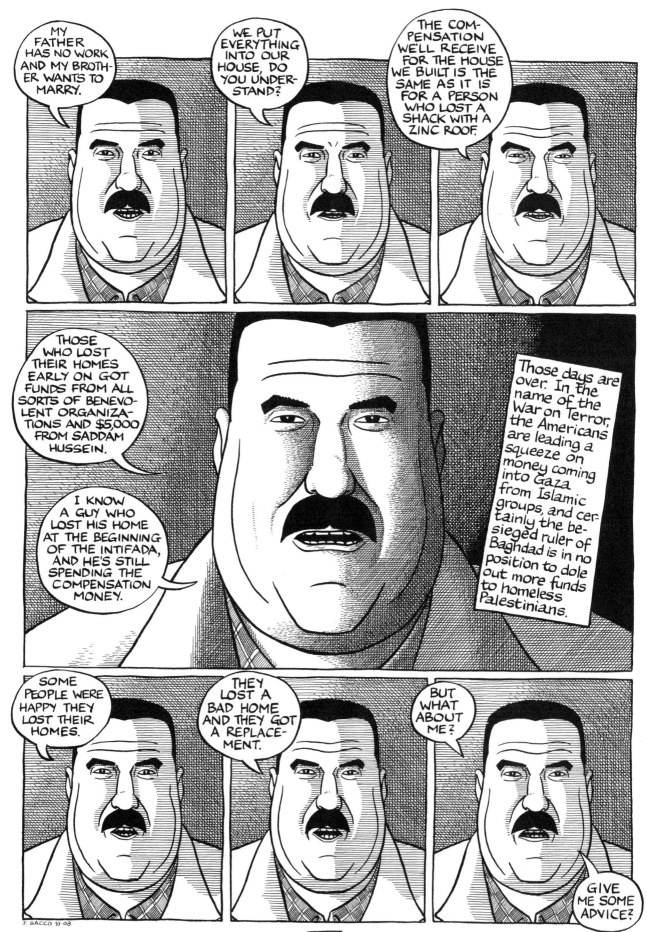

MY FATHER HAS NO WORK AND MY BROTHER WANTS TO MARRY.

WE PUT EVERYTHING INTO OUR HOUSE, DO YOU UNDERSTAND?

THE COMPENSATION WE'LL RECEIVE FOR THE HOUSE WE BUILT IS THE SAME AS IT IS FOR A PERSON WHO LOST A SHACK WITH A ZINC ROOF.

THOSE WHO LOST THEIR HOMES EARLY ON GOT FUNDS FROM ALL SORTS OF BENEVOLENT ORGANIZATIONS AND $5,000 FROM SADDAM HUSSEIN.

I KNOW A GUY WHO LOST HIS HOME AT THE BEGINNING OF THE INTIFADA, AND HE'S STILL SPENDING THE COMPENSATION MONEY.

Those days are over. In the name of the War on Terror, the Americans are leading a squeeze on money coming into Gaza from Islamic groups, and certainly the besieged ruler of Baghdad is in no position to dole out more funds to homeless Palestinians.

SOME PEOPLE WERE HAPPY THEY LOST THEIR HOMES.

THEY LOST A BAD HOME AND THEY GOT A REPLACEMENT.

BUT WHAT ABOUT ME?

GIVE ME SOME ADVICE?

J. SACCO 10·08

I still have none to offer.

IT DEPRESSES ME TALKING TO YOU.

YOU REMIND ME OF MY PROBLEMS.

I search for something to say.

... AND THE HOUSES ARE BEING BUILT IN A WAY SO YOU COULD ADD ANOTHER FLOOR.

I recall an UNRWA official telling me about a new development that will go up near Tal El-Sultan.

YOU COULD BUILD UP AND HAVE ROOM FOR YOUR BROTHERS.

I'm not sure whether I've mollified Ashraf or he's exhausted himself.

IT WILL TAKE ME TEN YEARS TO GET THROUGH THIS.

IN TEN YEARS I'LL CALL YOU UP AND TELL YOU I'M ON MY FEET AGAIN.

WHAT'S YOUR PHONE NUMBER?

Finally, we have a laugh.

Fifteen minutes later we're on our way to hear about the victims of 1956.

But in the dark, the Lion regains his focus.

I ASKED FOR YOUR ADVICE AND HELP, AND YOU DIDN'T HAVE ANY.

331

The bodies...

We want to understand how most of them got from the streets and alleys of Rafah to here, a clay area called "matianah" in the Tal Zorob neighborhood on the western side.

CLEANING UP

Even before the screening operation was over, the process of clearing away the dead had begun.

I HEARD A GIRL SCREAMING,

ANONYMOUS 3

THE JEWS HAVE KILLED... OUR MEN AND BURIED THEM WEST OF RAFAH!

THEY KILLED OUR MEN!

"Repeating this over and over.

"And I went out with the children, crying... without caring about anything.

"Then I saw a blue pick-up with a green covering... a civilian truck driven by soldiers.

J. SACCO 11-08

332

"I saw the bodies stacked on top of each other, and their legs hung out of the end of the truck.

"I saw only one car... Many cars had already passed.

"I turned back to my home crying and fearful. We started to hit our faces with our hands.

"We thought they'd killed *all* the men."

One man held at a secondary gathering point, an UNRWA school on Sea Street to the west of town, told us that as he and the others were being released—

—WE SAW ONE OR TWO CARS CARRYING BODIES.

ANONYMOUS 5

"What I saw is—this is certified—we should be honest when we are telling the story...

"I saw one car actually.

"The car was moving and we were leaving the school, that's all."

Owda Abdullah Hejazi, who had been released from the government school, arrived home in Tal Zorob where he had a clear view toward the west.

THE LAND AT THAT TIME WAS EMPTY... WITHOUT BUILDINGS, WITHOUT HOUSES.

"I saw the trucks carrying the bodies...

"About four trucks ...one by one...

"A few minutes before Maghrib [prayer].

J. SACCO 17-08

"They...threw the bodies out and went back.

"I couldn't see who was taking out the bodies."

There is at least one man who can shed light on "who"—Mohammed Atwa El-Najeeli, left for dead near the UNRWA distribution center, bleeding from his many wounds.

IN THE AFTERNOON, AFTER THE ASR [PRAYER], I HEARD.. THE SOUND OF A VEHICLE COMING TO GET THE BODIES.

"I saw it was full of youths... and all of them with their tongues out.

"They were dead.

"Like fish.

"Like fish.

"On top of each other.

"The vehicle came with two soldiers, and two Palestinians came toward me.

"They took the bodies, all the bodies.

"I was the last.

334

"They took me by my legs.

"When I realized they were Arabs, I told them I'm still alive.

ARE YOU STILL ALIVE?

YES.

SO SHUT UP.

OKAY, LET'S GO. WE'RE FINISHED HERE.

"They went. I was the only one in the street... Only me.

"It became cold.

"Now the people left the school. I heard them... and heard shooting also.

"I began to tell myself, 'Maybe someone will come and find me.'

"No one came except one of my dearest neighbors.

ARE YOU MOHAMMED?

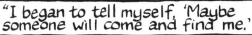

In a second discussion, when I ask Mohammed more closely about the Palestinians who were gathering the bodies, he says,

IT WAS THE POLICEMEN WHO TOOK ME.

[IN] THEIR UNIFORMS.

Who then were these men who removed the dead from the streets?

What happened to them?

One story is repeated to us over and over.

THEY TOOK THE BODIES BY CARS ...AND KILLED THE ONES THAT DUG THE GRAVES.

ABDEL HADI MOHAMMED LAFI

...THEY BURIED THE BODIES AFTER KILLING THE PEOPLE WHO DUG THE HOLES.

MOHAMMED YOUSEF SHAKER MOUSA

THEY SHOT THE ONES WHO BURIED THE BODIES AND BURIED THEM.

AHMED HASSAN EDWAN

Without corroboration, Abed and I are about to file this story under "legend" until, one day, someone tells us he had heard that the Israelis forced the director of the UN sanitation center to pick some workers to collect the bodies.

The director has since died...

But after a few phone calls, we're sitting with his son, who also works at the sanitation center.

Yes yes, he knows the story. He heard it from his father.

A day or two later we're in his car looking for Ibrahim Saker, a former employee of his father's who apparently was one of those tasked with picking up the bodies.

And here he is in the streets of Yibna!

Hey! Hey! Do you remember me? Do you remember my father?

Of course! Of course!

Get in the car! We need to talk to you!

But I'm going to play dominoes!

Get in the car!

337

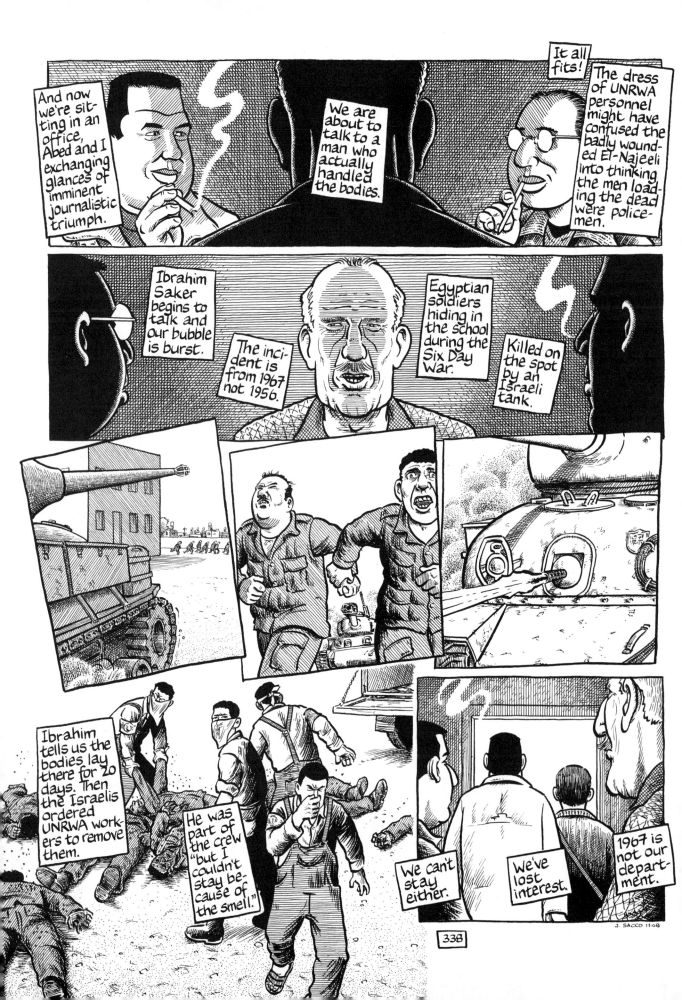

THE LIST

Ashraf is blunt:

THE GOAL IS TO FIND A FATHER WHO BURIED HIS SON.

I wish he'd put it more delicately, but neither he nor Abed thinks I need worry about anyone's sensibilities.

PALESTINIANS ARE LIKE IRON.

We walk the alleys of the refugee camp armed with Owda Ayesh's list of Rafah's dead.

Our method is simple.

We pick out a name, find the neighborhood where his extended family is supposed to live, and begin knocking on doors.

"Does anyone here remember the, er, martyr?"

Our method soon hits some snags.

We sit with one very elderly man whose son was killed in '56 all right but in Khan Younis.

He doesn't know where his son is buried, and now he's crying.

This woman's father was taken and killed, yes, but in March '57, when the Israelis were withdrawing.

It turns out Owda Ayesh's list contains not just the names of everyone killed on November 12, 1956, but everyone from Rafah killed during the general period, soldiers included, even if he was killed elsewhere.

J. SACCO 11-08

339

One night in Shaboura we consult a few guys who hold the list up to a street lamp,

and then send us down a dark passageway.

Abed flicks on his lighter to remind himself of the name of the deceased.

Ramadan Mohammed El-Modalel.

Ramadan Mohammed El-Modalel.

Abed handles the introductions.

OUR FRIEND JOE IS WRITING A BOOK ABOUT WHAT HAPPENED IN RAFAH AND KHAN YOUNIS IN 1956.

WE HAVE A LIST OF THE MARTYRS FROM OWDA AYESH'S BOOK.

WE READ THAT SOMEONE FROM THE MODALEL FAMILY WAS KILLED, AND WE CAME TO SEE IF WE COULD FIND SOMEONE FROM HIS FAMILY.

J. SACCO 11-08

This guy has just woken up, and he doesn't know what we're talking about.

GO INSIDE AND ASK THE OLD WOMEN AND THE OLD MEN.

THEY MIGHT KNOW ABOUT HIM.

The young man's grandmother appears at the door.

WE WOULD LIKE TO ASK YOU, HAJJA, ABOUT RAMADAN MOHAMMED EL-MODALEL, WHO DIED IN '56.

EH ?!

YOU FOUND HIM ?!

J. SACCO 11-08

WE ARE HIS FAMILY.

HE'S THE COUSIN OF MY HUS-BAND.

WE DON'T KNOW WHERE HE IS.

RAMADAN MOHAMMED EL-MODALEL

HE WAS IN THE ARMY, AND HE ESCAPED TO THE SEA, AND HE NEVER CAME BACK. HE WAS IN KHAN YOUNIS.

HE GOT MARRIED TO A CITY WOMAN, FROM JAFFA, AND SHE WENT TO AMMAN, AND HE CAME BACK HERE.

HIS MOTHER DIED WHEN HE WAS SIX MONTHS OLD, AND WE HAD TO SEND HIM TO OUR NEIGHBORS TO SUCKLE HIM. MANY NEIGHBORS.

J. SACCO 12·08

HE WAS HIS FATHER'S ONLY CHILD,

BUT HE LOST HIM.

COME IN!

I'LL SERVE YOU CAKE AND MAKE TEA FOR YOU.

We excuse ourselves. We're pressed for time. We say goodbye.

IT'S NOT RIGHT!

COME IN!

J. SACCO 12-08

I THOUGHT YOU'D FOUND HIM.

That old woman has lived with her uncertainty for almost 50 years. On the evening of November 12, 1956, perhaps hundreds of uncertainties flared over the fates of loved ones in Rafah.

As Mohammed Juma' El-Ghoul told us,

WHOEVER DIDN'T COME BACK TO HIS HOUSE...

WAS DEAD OR A PRISONER.

THE BURIALS

Abdelwahab Mahmoud Abdelwahab El-Asmar awaited word about his brother and nephew.

THEY DIDN'T COME BACK THAT NIGHT SO WE BEGAN TO THINK THEY HAD BEEN SHOT.

Latifa El-Qeesi wondered about her missing husband.

MY FATHER ARRIVED FROM THE SCHOOL. I ASKED HIM, 'DID YOU SEE MOSA?'

YES, I SAW HIM WHEN I REACHED THE SCHOOL, BUT LATER I DIDN'T.

DID YOU SEE HIM ON THE BUSES?

NO.

"We spent all night crying because [we] thought he was among the people who had been killed.

"We didn't sleep."

J·SACCO 12·08

"I went to the first one...near the cactus tree. Near him [another]. And the third at the door of my parents' home, and another one near to him. Four.

"I didn't find my husband among them.

"[Then] shooting started.

"I was pregnant at that time, five months.

"I wasn't able to run so they left me, and I stayed at my parents.'"

News was beginning to spread about the bodies that had been dumped on the matianah in the Tal Zorob neighborhood.

Among the first to go to the site was Owda Abdullah Hejazi, who had seen the trucks taking the dead there.

SOMEONE FROM OUR FAMILY WAS MISSING... AND HIS FATHER TOLD US, 'LET'S GO FIND HIM.'

J SACCO 12.08

"There were many, many, many people.

"Mostly women, but men also...

"turning the bodies to look at the faces.

"They didn't stay for long.

"If they found their dead, they took them and went. Using blankets.

J. SACCO 12·08

"It was horrible...

"The people were afraid.

"There was no shouting there. No screaming.

347

"It was slightly like thieving."

WE DIDN'T FIND HIS BODY AND WE WENT BACK.

Owda's relation, it turned out, was away in Egypt.

Ahmed No'man Zorob also came to look for missing relatives that night.

THE PEOPLE [WERE] HIDING BECAUSE THEY DIDN'T WANT TO BE SEEN BY THE JEWS.

IT WAS DARK AND THEY HID THEMSELVES AMONG THE CACTUS.

"We reached the matianah area...

"There were many bodies, many groups of bodies.

"Here a group, there a group, wherever the truck left the bodies...

WE DIDN'T FIND THEM.

WE FOUND OUT OUR FAMILY MEMBERS HAD BEEN TAKEN PRISONER.

"They...put them like fish."

350

We're directed to Block O to meet a man named Abdullah Abdelrahim Ghanim, who lost a number of relatives that day in 1956.

Perhaps catastrophe follows Abdullah around.

The Israelis have recently demolished his three-story home, which was shared by four related families.

Now the lot of them, 24 people in all, are crammed into the back of a decrepit, empty shop.

His sons would rather talk about the here and now, their destroyed house, not the long-ago event we're hosing off for reconsideration.

THE FLIES WERE ON THE WALLS BECAUSE THEY'D DEMOLISHED THE SEWAGE SYSTEM.

WE KEPT OURSELVES IN THE HOUSE TO THE LAST BECAUSE WE HAD NO OPTIONS, NO OPTIONS.

But Abdullah, who has heart problems and has not worked in 20 years, graciously obliges our inquiries into the past.

He was a teenager when he went to look for his brother Ismael Abdelrahim Ghanim, his uncle, Yousef Khalil Ghanim, and his cousin, Issa Mustafa Ghanim.

THE PEOPLE TOLD US THEY'D THROWN THEM NEAR TAL ZOROB

MY COUSINS, MY BROTHERS, THEIR WIVES... ALL THE WOMEN OF THE NEIGHBORHOOD, WE WENT RUNNING.

J SACCO 12-08

"I found my relatives thrown on the ground.

"But some other bodies were in a trench. Not completely buried. Just a bit of sand."

And the number of bodies?

I DIDN'T COUNT THEM, [BUT] MORE THAN 50, 60.

AND THE REST IN THE TRENCH.

"The people dug them out.

"At the time you want to take your body and go, that's all. You may help with other bodies if you know them, but the main thing is to get your dead.

"We took all the bodies and buried them in the Tal Zorob cemetery, the western cemetery of Rafah."

J. SACCO 1-09

352

Early in the morning the furtive search for the missing continued.

Latifa El-Qeesi looked in the streets for her husband with her mother.

WHENEVER WE HEARD THE JEEPS AND VEHICLES COMING, WE HID OURSELVES AMONG THE HOUSES.

Finally, Latifa met a relative who gave her the news that her husband had been taken prisoner.

DON'T WORRY, THEY TOOK THEM... ON THE BUSES.

Later that morning, the Israelis officially lifted the curfew for a short time, allowing the wounded to seek care and others to gather and bury the remaining bodies.

Mariam El-Najeeli learned that her husband was alive and in the UNRWA clinic.

MANY PEOPLE CAME FROM ALL OVER TO SEE THEIR RELATIVES.

MANY, MANY, MANY PEOPLE.

J. SACCO 1-09

"The soldiers were at the door and prevented us from going inside.

"If I had entered, I would have screamed and made a great [scene].

354

"But thank God I didn't see [him]."

Bodies were collected from the side streets where they had lain overnight. Some were not immediately identified.

MOHAMMED YOUSEF SHAKER MOUSA

[A MAN FROM THE NEIGHBORHOOD] WAS SHOT... SOME PEOPLE TOOK HIM INTO THEIR HOUSE AND HE DIED [THERE].

"My father and uncle carried him, wrapped in a blanket... to the street and removed the cover from his face to allow the people to see him.

"His family came and recognized him and took him."

Nasrah Felfel's husband had been lying a few meters from her front door since he'd been shot the morning before.

NOW I NEEDED PEOPLE TO HELP ME BURY THE BODY.

"One of his relatives was killed in another area, and they brought his body on a donkey cart and came here...

"I went with them to the eastern cemetery."

Meanwhile, people rushed to Tal Zorob's matianah where many bodies remained.

I express doubt, but Abdelwahab Mahmoud Abdelwahab El-Asmar insists that while searching for his brother and nephew he counted 133 bodies in two separate groups of dead.

I COUNTED THEM ONE BY ONE.

"At the third group [my brother's] daughter ...found them.

HERE IS MY FATHER!

COME!

"We covered them with blankets and we buried them [near] the main road... We didn't have time to bury them in another area..."

THIRTY DAYS LATER THERE WERE NO CURFEWS, IT WASN'T TENSE. I WENT THERE AND DUG [UP] AND TOOK THE BODIES.

Abdelwahab reinterred his relatives in the Tal Zorob cemetery.

J. SACCO 1-09

*SEE P. 242

357

"The people hurried, trying within two hours to take the bodies to a fusgeya in the cemetery...

"We carried him with our hands.

"Some people dragged the bodies on the ground.

"We mixed all the people.

"We put four or five bodies inside one fusgeya... [on top of] each other."

J. SACCO 1-09

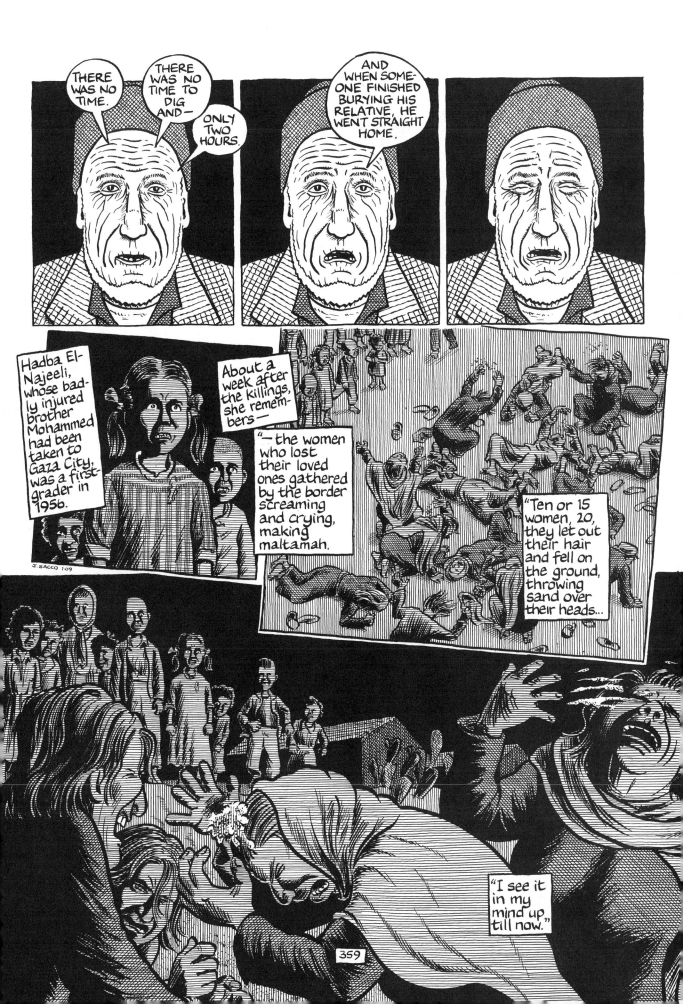

Amplified orators shatter our eardrums with garbled denunciations of the imminent attack on Iraq, but Hani, who helped organize this demonstration, will not be one of them.

Alas, his prepared invective has been bumped.

A mock tank and a mock warplane are set alight, and when the bonfires of wishful thinking have died down, the show comes to a close.

The Hamas men march away smartly up Sea Street, and the schoolboys, weighed down by their books, can barely keep up.

J. SACCO 1-09

One afternoon, Sameh, the landlord's son, brings us a bottle of fresh water and news.

DEATH

An American woman, one of the International Solidarity Movement activists protesting the demolition of homes in Rafah, has been run over by an Israeli bulldozer.

Abed makes some calls.

The American woman is dead.

Her body is at El-Najjar hospital.

Rafah is one of the most dangerous places in the Palestinian territories.

But while the rest of Gaza has been bursting with violence, Rafah has been relatively quiet in my weeks here.

Only three people have been killed: two Islamic Jihad members in a tunnel the Israelis destroyed; and the boy whose funeral we watched from our balcony.

At the hospital I talk to one of the activists who witnessed the death of his colleague.

Rachel Corrie, 23, from Olympia, Washington, was among a group of foreign nationals determined to prevent the demolition of a home in the El-Salam neighborhood.

J. SACCO 2-09

Apparently Corrie slipped on a mound of earth being pushed up by a bulldozer

and was crushed as the driver continued over her,

with blade lowered,

and backed up.

But Death is not finished with Rafah today.

A Red Crescent ambulance rushes in,

and another casualty is propelled into emergency.

Ahmed El-Najjar, 49, who lives in Rafah's Tal El-Sultan neighbor-hood, was shot by Israeli forces in the head, the chest, and the leg, reportedly while standing in his doorway. In a few min-utes he is dead.

His wailing, blood-stained relatives take pos-session of the body.

But if, like Corrie's friends, they are in shock, there is nothing shock-ing about what has happened to their kin.

The killing of a Pales-tinian in Gaza is a routine occur-rence. His loss will cause not a ripple outside of his imme-diate circle of family, friends, and neighbors.

The killing of an Amer-ican, how-ever—

363

Abed and I make our way to the adjacent morgue.

The crowd parts way and lets us through.

Corrie's friends stand around in disbelief;

my pal Asim, the photographer, sits dazed against a wall;

local photojournalists, stringers for Western wire services, go about their business-as-usual.

Two hours ago Rachel Corrie, an American, was killed by an Israeli bulldozer as she attempted to defend a Palestinian home.

She is about to enter the realm of iconography.

But the hospital staff isn't thinking about that.

Right now Corrie is a body that must be tended to.

They plead with everyone to clear out of the room and let them get on with it.

J. SACCO 2-09

SHAPES IN THE DARK PT.2

The squeaking sound of armored vehicles, passing endlessly on the Philadelphi Route a few dozen meters from Fuad's place, bounces off the buildings around us.

Fuad keeps the windows slightly open so they won't shatter if there's a blast, and he has long mapped out his avenues of escape.

OUT THE DOOR IF THEY COME FROM THIS SIDE...

OUT THE WINDOW IF THEY COME FROM THIS SIDE.

Tonight is the night everyone expects the war against Iraq to begin, and Rafah is bracing for a possible Israeli attack under its cover.

Fuad's parents have pressured him to leave the house, which he watches over, at least during these critical hours, and he has agreed to sleep at our place tonight.

J. SACCO 3-09

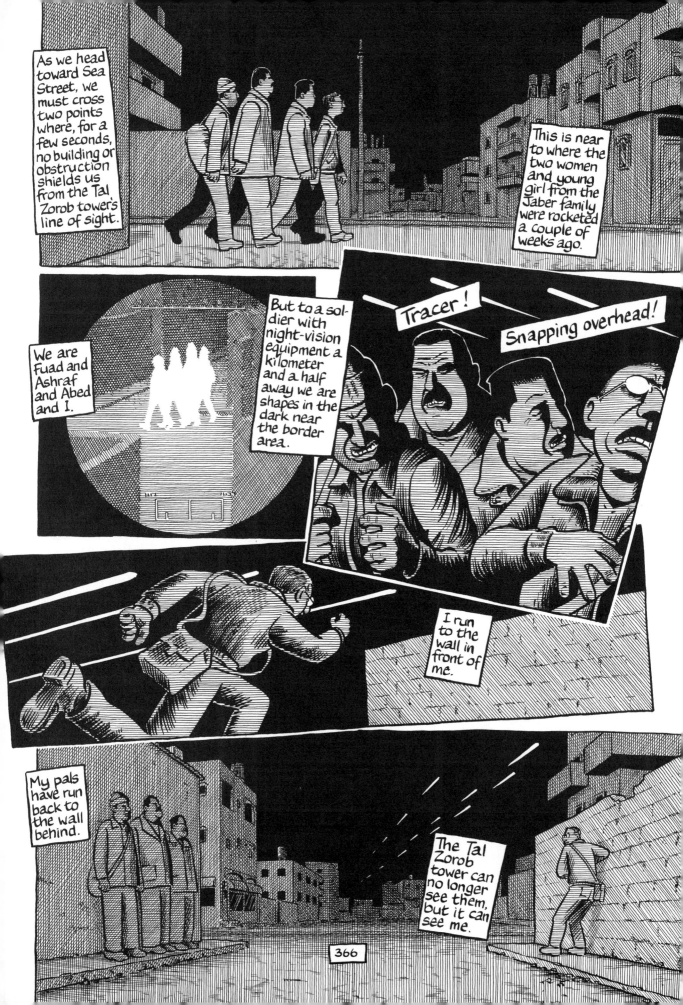

As we head toward Sea Street, we must cross two points where, for a few seconds, no building or obstruction shields us from the Tal Zorob tower's line of sight.

This is near to where the two women and young girl from the Jaber family were rocketed a couple of weeks ago.

We are Fuad and Ashraf and Abed and I.

But to a soldier with night-vision equipment a kilometer and a half away we are shapes in the dark near the border area.

Tracer!

Snapping overhead!

I run to the wall in front of me.

My pals have run back to the wall behind.

The Tal Zorob tower can no longer see them, but it can see me.

DID YOU SEE THEM?

On the first Friday of the Iraq war, over all the other sermons blaring from Rafah's minarets, we strain to catch our own neighborhood imam's ear-splitting fulminations.

ISRAEL, AMERICA, AND BRITAIN: THE THREE PILLARS OF EVIL!

MY BROTHER MUSLIMS SHOULD REALIZE THAT THE FUTURE IS ISLAM'S, BUT FOR THAT WE MUST PAY THE PRICE!

AND PALESTINIANS AND IRAQIS ARE PAYING THE PRICE!

War!

And all the dread of its build-up is now replaced by desire as Palestinians wait and pray for the anti-aircraft fire streaming into the Baghdad night to tear an American bomber from the sky.

Praise be to God, the first victories come!

Two enemy helicopters have collided and their occupants are killed.

The owner of the appliance store, where we stop by to do a little shopping, cannot tear his eyes from the television.

I HOPE THEIR BODIES WERE CUT TO PIECES AND MIXED TOGETHER.

J. SACCO 3·09

The next day the Iraqis deliver on a promise to show captured Americans.

Look at them shake with fear!

And here are American dead on display

and close-ups of their wounds.

I balk

The footage of the bodies disturbs me.

THEY ARE SOLDIERS, JOE.

SOLDIERS.

THEY CAME TO KILL.

IF AMERICA WINS THIS WAR, PALESTINIANS WILL BE THE FIRST LOSERS.

And that, in their minds, is what's at stake: An American victory would assure Israel of its never-ending supremacy.

Geo-strategic considerations aside, they enjoy the moment.

DID YOU SEE THEM?

J. SACCO 3·09

And so it goes over the next few days as reports come in of more helicopters falling, of dozens of tanks burning.

DID YOU SEE HOW THE OLD MAN SHOT DOWN AN APACHE?

DID YOU SEE IT?

SADDAM HUSSEIN 100 PERCENT!

But not everyone is so caught up in the cheap propaganda and the minor American setbacks to expect Iraq to prevail.

Khaled's view is the most philosophical.

It is stripped of illusion and seems somehow self-reflective.

IT'S NOT A MATTER OF VICTORY.

IT'S A MATTER OF RESISTING TILL THE END.

The Israelis, who had conquered the Sinai peninsula during the war, began to withdraw, too, in fits and starts, though Ben-Gurion vowed to hang on to the Gaza Strip.

An impatient Washington threatened to back economic sanctions on Israel at the U.N.

Ben-Gurion bowed to the inevitable, and the IDF completed its pullout, including from the Gaza Strip, on March 16, 1957.

But questions had already begun to arise about Israeli behavior in Gaza in general and in Rafah specifically.

For weeks Israel had prevented the handful of U.N. observers based in Gaza City, commanded by U.S. Army Lt. Col. R.F. Bayard, from moving around the occupied territory freely.

On November 13, 1956, Bayard wrote to his superior, "It is quite evident that the Israelis do not wish to have United Nations Observers...reporting upon the actions they are taking against the civilian populace.

"From the reports we receive from UNRWA personnel and from the very few incidents that have been witnessed by Observers, I have come to the conclusion that the treatment of civilians is unwarrantly rough and that a good number of persons have been shot down in cold blood for no apparent reason."

J. SACCO 4.09

373

Press accounts began to refer to an incident in Rafah in which some 50 Arabs were killed, and U.N. Secretary General Dag Hammarskjold wrote to Israeli Foreign Minister Golda Meir on November 21 expressing "great concern" about the "situation in the Gaza Strip, in particular Rafah..."

Meir answered that, regarding Rafah, "complete tranquility prevails in the whole area, and relations between the local population and the authorities are amicable."

As to reports of widespread killings by Israeli soldiers, Meir wrote that "rioting instigated by Egyptian agents took place in Rafah on 10 and 12 November.

"During the disorders the UNRWA Food Depot in the town was attacked by an unruly mob and the Israel authorities were compelled to take action to prevent large scale looting and destruction.

"Order was restored with some difficulty and, regrettably, there were casualties among the mob."

On November 23, the 13 Knesset members of the Foreign Affairs and Defense Committee had their own questions for IDF Chief of Staff Dayan about the conduct of Israeli forces in Gaza. In a closed door session he assured them that while in "borderline" circumstances some units may have fired on those who might otherwise have been captured,

...I DON'T KNOW OF ANY INSTANCE WHERE THEY STOOD PRISONERS IN A ROW AND KILLED THEM.

MK* Moshe Aram wanted to know, "What exactly happened in Rafah?"

IN RAFAH THERE WAS A BIT OF AN UNFORTUNATE CONVERGENCE OF EVENTS, AND THE ARABS THERE HAD A NEGATIVE DISPOSITION...

*MK: MEMBER OF THE KNESSET

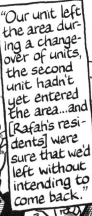
"Our unit left the area during a change-over of units, the second unit hadn't yet entered the area...and [Rafah's residents] were sure that we'd left without intending to come back."

The second unit, Dayan explained, entered the next day to search for arms and Egyptian soldiers.

...THEY ANNOUNCED A CURFEW ON THE LOUDSPEAKERS AND THAT ALL THE MEN HAD TO ASSEMBLE, AND NOT ONLY DID THEY NOT SHOW UP BUT THEY PAID NO ATTENTION TO THE CURFEW INSTRUCTIONS.

"There were a lot of Egyptian soldiers and a lot of arms among this big group of Arabs who weren't listening to the instructions, which is why I said a certain disposition was involved."

SO THE UNIT OPENED FIRE. I DON'T KNOW WHERE THEY FIRED AND WHETHER THE ARABS FIRED...

ABOUT 40 PEOPLE WERE KILLED...

...BUT IF THERE ARE 200 SOLDIERS IN THE HOUSES WHO DON'T WANT TO HAND THEMSELVES OVER AND ARE INCITING OTHERS NOT TO IDENTIFY THEMSELVES, THEN THE UNIT COMMANDER WAS ABSOLUTELY RIGHT WHEN HE OPENED FIRE.

Ultimately, Dayan said, the Arabs "responded to the order to come for identification, and then 200 Egyptian soldiers were found..."

J. SACCO 4.09

On November 28, Ben-Gurion rejected a proposal to debate the Rafah incident in the Knesset but offered an explanation that combined and added to elements of Meir's and Dayan's accounts.

U.N. stores were looted, he said, and rioting continued during a replacement of units.

Israeli soldiers imposed a curfew and began a search for arms.

A NUMBER OF PEOPLE IN THE TOWN VIOLATED THE CURFEW AND SOME OPENED FIRE ON OUR FORCES.

AFTER FIRING A NUMBER OF WARNING SHOTS IN THE AIR, OUR SOLDIERS WERE FORCED TO OPEN FIRE ON THE RIOTERS AND 48 OF THEM WERE KILLED AND A NUMBER WERE WOUNDED.

In the same Special Report for the U.N. General Assembly which outlined the killings in Khan Younis,* UNRWA navigated between the competing claims about what had happened in Rafah.

designated hour. In the confusion, a of refugees ran toward the screening of being late, and some Israel soldiers ked and opened fire on this running

"The Israel authorities in Gaza state that the attitude of the refugees in Rafah camp was hostile and that there was some resistance to the screening operation, during which the casualties occurred.

"The refugees deny any such resistance."

The "facts appear to be," UNRWA concluded, that some refugees did not hear the loudspeakers calling on them to gather and that not enough time was allowed for the men to reach the designated screening sites.

tor ived from sources which ustworthy lists of names of person legedly killed at Rafah on 12 November, numbering

*SEE P. 117

"In the confusion, a large number of refugees ran toward the screening points for fear of being late, and some Israeli soldiers apparently panicked and opened fire on this running crowd."

376

According to sources UNRWA's director deemed "trustworthy," 111 persons were allegedly killed in Rafah on November 12, 1956, of whom 103 were refugees, seven local ("original") residents, and one Egyptian.

RETURN

The Israelis and the Egyptians eventually exchanged prisoners, and those bussed from Rafah to Atlit prison in Israel came home.

Mohammed Atwa El-Najeeli, badly wounded on November 12, 1956, remained in Gaza City hospitals for some three months.

Now he laughs about the experience.

MY FRIEND CAME TO SEE ME AFTER TEN DAYS.

HE WALKED ALL THE WAY FROM RAFAH TO GAZA CITY ALONG THE BEACH TO FIND ME.

"He told me,"

ARE YOU OKAY, MOHAMMED?

AM I OKAY?

WHAT ARE YOU SAYING?

I ask his wife, Mariam, about her feelings while Mohammed was away.

I WAS PREGNANT.

I WAS NOT ABLE TO WALK FROM HERE TO GAZA CITY.

BUT I USED TO SEND FOOD FOR HIM WITH THE AMBULANCES.

AND CLOTHES.

THE AMBULANCES BROUGHT ME THE CLOTHES [IN WHICH] HE WAS SHOT.

THEY HAD BEEN CUT BY SCISSORS.

HIS LONG UNDERWEAR WAS FULL OF BLOOD.

"I washed all those clothes and his underwear.

"What was in my mind?

"I was crazy.

"I was mad.

"I was crazy seeing that this happened to my husband,"

MY LOVER.

377

J. SACCO 4·09

They have blocked up the windows and doors with bricks and corrugated metal to keep out unwanted guests, particularly militants.

We enter through what Ashraf calls a "secret door," a hatch set above ground level.

It's a mess inside.

The birds have taken over in here, too, and the floor is stained in places by fallen eggs.

We want to take a look from the roof, but—

STOP!

—an AFV on a rise has the whole thing covered.

We are not going to risk showing ourselves on top of an "abandoned" structure.

We move to a safer balcony that overlooks a long stretch of houses that, too, are mostly empty.

J. SACCO 4.09

In the other direction Fuad calls out to the Egyptian soldiers across the border who are checking us out with binoculars.

They do not return the greeting.

Okay, that's that.

I say farewell to Fuad.

Then I say goodbye to Ashraf,

and as we embrace

a machine-gun opens up!

BAP BAP BAP

A horse hitched to a cart bolts past us,

and so we have our last laugh.

Abed and I came here to find out what happened on November 12, 1956, and now, arguably, we are the world's foremost experts.

How often we forced the old men of Rafah back down this road lined with soldiers and strewn with shoes.

How often we shoved the old men between the soldiers with sticks and through that gate.

How often we made them sit with their heads down and piss on themselves.

In the end, when we'd finished with them, we let them break down the wall and run home.

As we negotiate the traffic, I recall one of our final interviews. It was with the grandfather of one of Abed's pals.

Abu Juhish was clubbed on his head as he entered the school, and his friends had tried to staunch the bleeding with sand.

*SEE P. 266

383

J. SACCO 4.09

Abu Juhish had health problems, and our meeting with him was put off a number of times.

Finally his grandson Belal took us to see him.

Abu Juhish clearly strained to tell us even sketchy details of his story.

Soon he was crying.

It wasn't the first time one of the old men had cried in front of us, and I knew how to handle it.

I assured him it was okay, that he needn't continue, that—

BE STRONG, MY GRANDFATHER.

NOW TRY TO TALK FROM YOUR MIND, NOT WITH PASSION.

TRY TO REMEMBER.

And so Abu Juhish continued fitfully until Belal interrupted to cut to the chase.

WHAT IS THE WORST THING YOU REMEMBER FROM THAT DAY?

FEAR.

FEAR.

Suddenly I felt ashamed of myself for losing something along the way as I collected my evidence, disentangled it, dissected it, indexed it, and logged it onto my chart.

384

J. SACCO 4·09

And I remembered how often I sat with old men who tried my patience, who rambled on, who got things mixed up, who skipped ahead,

who didn't remember the barbed wire at the gate or when the mukhtars stood up or where the jeeps were parked,

how often I sighed and mentally rolled my eyes

because I knew more about that day than they did.

J. SACCO 4.09

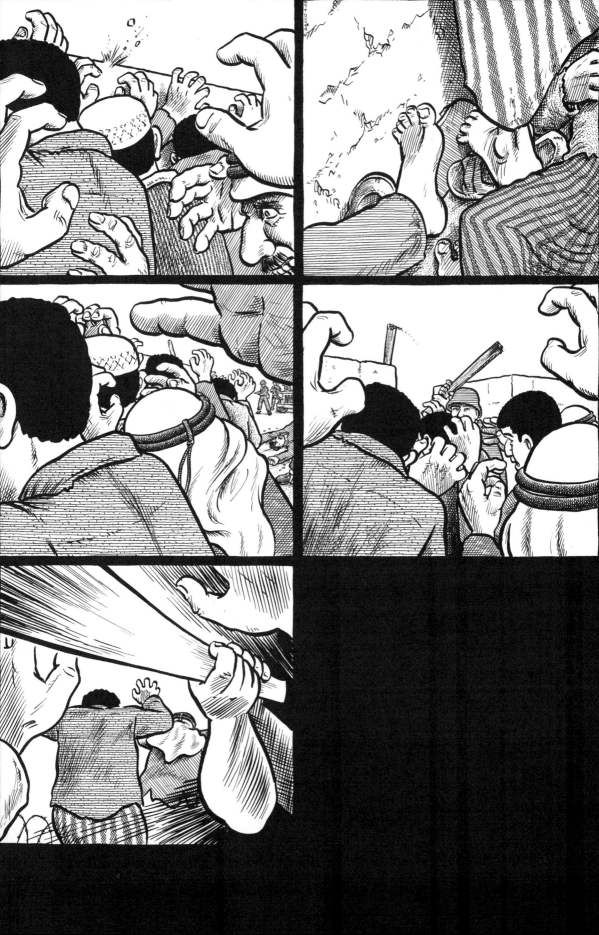

APPENDIX 1

DOCUMENTS AND SOURCES, 1956

A historical investigation into any particular incident can seldom ever be truly complete. Scratching further might uncover something new and significant—an unopened file or a long-lost letter, for example. This book is chiefly dependent on the oral testimony of Palestinians asked to recall the tragic events in Khan Younis and Rafah in November 1956. As much as possible I have tried to present the available documentary evidence to supplement these personal accounts. I visited the U.N.'s archives in New York a number of times and contracted two Israeli researchers to dig through Israeli archives as well.

Below, I present extended cullings from some of the documents I quoted in the book to provide more context for the interested reader. Also included are selected newspaper reports from the period (many of which provide much misinformation), as well as additional comments by Mordechai Bar-On, chef de bureau to IDF chief of staff Moshe Dayan in 1956, whose knowledge of the Israeli perspective is intimate. My brief commentaries follow when appropriate. Readers are alerted in those cases where words on old, photocopied documents were difficult to read.

Letter from Lieutenant Colonel (U.S. Army) R. F. Bayard, chairman of the Egyptian-Israeli Mixed Armistice Commission [U.N. observers] to Colonel Leary, acting chief of staff of the United Nations Truce Supervision Organization (UNTSO), November 13, 1956 (see p. 373):

Dear Colonel Leary,

I felt that it is about time I got a letter off to you in order to keep you informed of conditions in general in the Gaza Strip as we see it. It is quite evident that the Israelis do not wish to have United Nations Observers circulating in the Strip and reporting upon the actions they are taking against the civilian populace. From the reports we receive from UNRWA personnel and from the very few incidents that have been witnessed by Observers, I have come to the conclusion that the treatment of civilians is unwarrantly rough and that a good number of persons have been shot down in cold blood for no apparent reason. It seems to me that representatives of the International Red Cross should be present on the scene. Of course, we hear many rumours of atrocities, much of which we can discount, but a small percentage are probably factual. No doubt it would be quite embarrassing to the Israelis if we could circulate freely and report upon these incidents. We will keep a written record of those incidents reported to us by UNRWA personnel. Mr. [Thomas] Jamieson [an UNRWA official] states that many key

UNRWA native personnel are missing from the camps and are believed to have been executed by the Israelis. . . .

Many Israeli soldiers have robbed civilians, taking watches, rings, fountain pens, etc. away from the Arabs either in their homes or on the streets. Every vehicle and every bicycle [in Gaza City] has been confiscated. Private workshops and machine shops have been stripped of all mechanical tools. Many mules and horses have been taken and cloth has been taken from the stores.

I have been visited on several occasions by the more prominent Palestinians with a request for assistance. The Palestinians begged us, the UNTSO, not to leave and state that as long as we remain the people have some hope and confidence in the future....

Life here is very easy as far as we of the UNTSO are concerned. However, it is unpleasant to witness the treatment of the local populace and particularly to note the indignities directed upon personnel friends....

Best regards,

R. F. Bayard
Lt. Col. US Army
Chairman

On November 18, 1956, the IDF Southern Command Headquarters sent a top-secret communiqué tasking two officers with investigating the "Rafah incident."

Re: Appointment of an inquiry commission into a search in RAFAH 12/11/1956 in which 40 [or 60—original unclear] were killed and 20 injured

1. In light of my authority, according to High Command regulations (1955), I, General Haim Laskov, Chief of the Southern Command, hereby appoint you:

    Colonel Arieh Reiss, chairman
    Captain Herzl Golan, member

    members in the above mentioned inquiry commission.
    . . .
3. To receive first-hand details, you will approach the military governor of Gaza.
4. The inquiry report original with 3 copies will be personally handed by you to the Command adjutant administrative officer no later than the 25th of Nov. 56.

Whatever report Colonel Reiss and Captain Golan submitted could not be found in the IDF archive by my researcher.

A five-page classified IDF report, dated November 25, 1956, entitled "Problems in the Gaza Strip and Outlines for Intelligence Activity," and signed by Officer Avshalom Shmueli, notes:

8. Searches and operations by our forces:

E. During searches the governor's loudspeakers were used. It was recently agreed that the governor is responsible for detailed orders regarding search procedures. This after exposure of a search in Rafah in which tens of Arabs were killed. According to a rumor, the leak to the press, in this case, came from the governor's circles.

Article from the *Times* (London), dateline Tel Aviv, November 18, 1956, by "Our Correspondent":

REPORTS OF SHOOTING OF ARABS

Reports of indiscriminate shooting of Arabs by Israel troops occupying the Gaza strip [*sic*] continue to circulate here and are causing the Government much concern. . . .

The worst of these unfortunate shooting incidents, which seem to have gone on at intervals all last week, took place at the refugee camp of Rafah last Tuesday [*sic*: it was a Monday]. According to an U.N.R.W.A. field director, Mr. T. Jameson [*sic*: Thomas Jamieson], at least 60 refugees were killed and 30 were seriously wounded when fire was opened by an Israel unit which, as it approached Rafah camp, saw what its officer took to be an organized attempt by some thousands of refugees to break out and loot U.N.R.W.A. stores. Arab sources at Rafah put the dead at a much higher figure.

The commander of the Israel forces in the Gaza area, Colonel Chaim Gaon [*sic*: Haim Gaon], says that 12 men of Rafah camp "may have been killed" and their bodies taken away by members of their families who, in refugee-fashion, are reluctant to admit their dead and so lose a part of their U.N.R.W.A. rations, which are drawn by heads of families only.

A MISUNDERSTANDING

The Rafah incident seems to have had its origin in a mishap which reflects upon the military organization of the district. Apparently an Israel unit which had been on guard at the camp and had taken part in the screening of refugees withdrew from the camp—which is sprawled over and around Rafah township—before its relief had arrived. The refugees, many of whom had been standing about in a big enclosure waiting to be screened, are thought then to have assumed that the Israel Army was withdrawing behind the old armistice lines and to have taken what must have seemed a heaven-sent opportunity to loot U.N.R.W.A. stores.

According to U.N.R.W.A. field officers, however, the amount of looting was negligible. It is probable that the Israel relieving unit, faced by some thousands of Arabs who looked as if they might be in a riotous mood, lost its nerve. There is no doubt that the Arabs, caught out of bounds and probably up to mischief lost their nerves when they caught sight of the approaching Israel soldiers. The result was the unnecessarily bloody episode of the kind Israel's enemies are likely to turn to damaging account against her.

Officials of the U.N.R.W.A. and other observers who have been trying to get at the real truth of the Rafah shooting and other incidents of last week do not accuse Israelis of any deliberate brutality. On the whole Israel soldiers have behaved well....

The Israeli newspaper *Kol Ha'am* reported the following on November 20, 1956:

SECURITY COUNCIL CALLED ON TO PREVENT FURTHER MASSACRE OF
ARABS IN THE GAZA STRIP

(U.N. Headquarters; UP service) Today the director of the office for Palestinian refugees in New York, Dr. Issam Tanum [or Tanus—original unclear], in a memo to the Security Council, accused Israeli forces in the Gaza Strip of preparing for "genocide"—mass destruction—among the refugees.

[Tanum/s] demanded that the council take immediate steps to prevent further slaughter. He claimed that 50 refugees have been murdered in cold blood.

THE BRITISH PRESS ON THE DISTURBANCES

London: Today the press has published many accounts of the incidents in the Gaza Strip which involved Arab refugees and Israeli soldiers. A writer for the *Daily Express*, Donald Wise, reported that Israeli soldiers had leaped from trucks to beat citizens, and he quoted a UN spokesman who claimed that 59 Arabs had died in the recent incidents.

A writer for the *New Chronicle* reports an Arab account from Gaza which said, "If Colonel Bayard, head of the UN in Gaza, hadn't remained here, I'm sure that thousands of refugees in Gaza and the surroundings would have been killed. Anyone who sets out on the path of slaughter and destruction in cold blood, whether he's Arab or Israeli, doesn't want UN witnesses." Reporter Peter Vane [name unclear] writes that the Israelis have tried their hardest to remove Bayard from the area.

The *Times* reporter in Tel Aviv has also written about the events in Rafah.

ance Ha'am reported the following on November 21, 1956:

THE OFFICIAL VERSION

In relation to the events in Rafah, the military commander of the Gaza Strip, Lt. Colonel Haim Gaon, gave the following version to representatives of the press who were touring the area on November 18:

On the tenth of November IDF forces in Rafah were replaced. The residents, who assumed that the IDF was leaving the town, began looting UNRWA warehouses and protesting at the military command headquarters. According to the military commander, they fired at the headquarters and at vehicles on the roads. The rioting continued through the next day, November 11. The IDF sealed the town and on the following day, November 12, imposed a curfew and carried out searches. The residents of Rafah were ordered to show some identification. They displayed passive resistance and in some cases active resistance. One sergeant was injured by their shooting. The army was given orders to bring the men out of their houses by force. Some began fleeing toward the sand dunes, according to Lt. Colonel Gaon, but steps were taken to prevent their escape. During the operation there were 30 casualties, including both dead and wounded. The military commander reported that the searches resulted in the arrest of 200 Egyptian soldiers, 150 Palestinian soldiers, a few suspected Fedayeen and many other suspects.

The residents of occupied Rafah are still in shock from the terrible events of the past week. They are also full of rage [blank—censored].

The military commander of the Gaza Strip published orders for anyone traveling in Gaza in which he declared that the population is hostile and forbade visitors from making contact with residents.

Letter from U.N. Secretary General Dag Hammarskjold to Israeli Foreign Minister Golda Meir, November 21, 1956 (see p. 374):

According to information received which I must consider as reliable, the situation in the Gaza Strip, in particular Rafah, has been one giving rise to great concern. I will not here go into the question of the reasons for this unrest, nor into the information we have on the casualties ensuing. I hope that the situation has improved, and I gather from you that according to your information that is the case. However, the situation remains one which I cannot disregard in the execution of my obligations under the relevant General Assembly Resolutions. The other day I addressed to you a request that observers from the United Nations Emergency Force be permitted to enter to be stationed and to function within the Gaza area. I now wish to repeat this request....

Letter in reply from Foreign Minister Meir, November 21, 1956 (see p. 374):

I refer to your letter of 21 November on the situation in the Gaza Strip. As I informed you on the same day, rioting, instigated by Egyptian agents, took place in Rafah on 10 and 12 November. During the disorders the UNRWA Food Depot in the town was attacked by an unruly mob and the Israel authorities were compelled to take action to prevent large scale looting and destruction. Order was restored with some difficulty and, regrettably, there were casualties among the mob. Since then, however, complete tranquility prevails in the whole area, and relations between the local population and the authorities are amicable. . . .
In view, however, of your desire for direct information [about the situation in Gaza], the Government of Israel would welcome the visit of your personal representative who will be given all facilities to investigate and report on the situation in the area.

On November 23, 1956, the Israeli Knesset's Foreign Affairs and Defense Committee met with IDF chief of staff Moshe Dayan to discuss the war and its conduct (see pp. 374–75). This is the relevant part of the transcript:

MK Yaakov Hazan: What about the treatment of prisoners? I don't mean those prisoners who are already in our hands. I don't believe in stories that someone heard from someone, but if someone comes to me and says that he himself saw something, then I have to believe him. I heard different stories about units that behaved humanely toward prisoners when they captured them, but I've also heard about brutal and inhumane treatment of prisoners in other units. Is anything known about this, and what is the army thinking of doing?
. . .

Chief of Staff Moshe Dayan: . . . I haven't heard any specific complaints about the treatment of prisoners after they were captured. Perhaps there were a few such incidents, I'll put the question to the head of [. . .] maybe he has information about complaints. They didn't reach me, but that doesn't mean it didn't happen.

. . .

Regarding Knesset Member Hazan's question about whether different units behaved differently toward prisoners—there was different treatment, I know about certain units in their encounters with prisoners in certain places or with fleeing Egyptians—I don't know of any instance where they stood prisoners in a row and killed them—killing them instead of taking them prisoner. I imagine that there were borderline cases, where the people could have been captured or killed and it depended on the particular inclination of the specific unit. In one unit they told them to line up, seized their weapons, and then took the people prisoner, and in another unit they opened fire on people when it was possible either to capture them or kill them.

MK Moshe Aram: . . . Knesset Member Hazan spoke about the handling of prisoners at the time they were taken. I'm sorry to say that I heard about the handling of prisoners during the time they were in the camps. I heard something very grave, that even now they're being beaten, and sometimes they're being abused in other ways. I see this as a political question, not a military one. Is there any kind of treatment being given to the prisoners beyond handing out their food rations? Is there any kind of spiritual treatment, because one of these days these people will go back to their countries. Is there any kind of treatment that will show them what kind of country this is, what kind of army, what this community is that they've fallen into?

. . .

What was the point of making it public that tear gas was sent to Rafah? It was even said somewhere that poison gas was sent, although Soviet channels immediately denied that voluntarily, but how and why was that made public?

What exactly happened in Rafah?

. . .

Chief of Staff M. Dayan: . . . I don't know of disturbances in Gaza and in the Strip. I think there's absolute quiet. I include Rafah in this, apart from the one incident. As long as the Egyptians were fighting there, they fought too. Once the matter was over, they quickly stopped fighting as well. The residents haven't shown any signs of resistance or lack of cooperation. I don't think they're planning any act of protest or physical resistance to our presence there.

I'm sure if the U.N. comes and asks them who they'd rather have there, they'd choose Arabs, but there's no physical expression of this. In Rafah there was a bit of an unfortunate convergence of events and the Arabs there had a negative disposition. The convergence was this: Our unit left the area during a changeover of units, the second unit hadn't yet entered the area. At the same time, the prime minister here was giving a speech about his answer to the U.N.'s demand for a withdrawal, and there they were sure that we'd left without intending to come back. The second unit entered the next day and imposed a curfew and had to search the arms caches and the Egyptian soldiers who were still there. This had been done in other parts of Gaza, and until it was done neither the arms nor the Egyptian soldiers were handed over. Once the search took place, both the Egyptian soldiers and the arms were found. So we went from one area to the next until it was Rafah's turn.

MK Menachem Begin: How much time passed between the one unit leaving and the other coming in?

Chief of Staff Moshe Dayan: A night or a day. Basically, the clash didn't happen with the arrival of the second unit. Afterward, they announced a curfew on the loudspeakers and that all the men had to assemble at a specific place for identification. They ignored the curfew and no one came. The loudspeakers went around and announced the curfew and that the men had to assemble, and not only did they not show up but they paid no attention to the curfew instructions. There were a lot of Egyptian soldiers and a lot of arms among this big group of Arabs who weren't listening to the instructions, which is why I said that there was a certain disposition involved. So the unit opened fire. I don't know where they fired and whether the Arabs fired. I don't know the general picture. After the shooting started in a few places, the Arabs went into their homes and after that they responded to the order to come for identification, and then 200 Egyptian soldiers were found. About 40 people were killed. I'm sure that many hundreds of Egyptian soldiers could hide in the sands between Gaza [City] and Rafah, but if there are 200 soldiers in the houses who don't want to hand themselves over and are inciting the others not to identify themselves, then the unit commander was absolutely right when he opened fire. It's unacceptable that the army declares a curfew and people go on wandering in the streets.

MK Moshe Aram: Were those killed all soldiers?

Chief of Staff M. Dayan: I think one boy was injured, there were no women, only men. During the identification, the [Egyptian] soldiers weren't wearing uniforms, but when they were asked for their papers it became clear that they were soldiers.

The problem with the Arab population is external and political, not local. There are plenty of informers there. In Gaza and El-Arish there are also Egyptian agents and soldiers and Fedayeen who want to take action, but the others hand them over, not because of loyalty but because of the informers.

Minutes of the debate in the Knesset, November 28, 1956. Proposal by Knesset Member Esther Vilenska (Israeli Communist Party) to debate the events in the Gaza Strip.

We propose a debate in the Knesset plenum on the events that occurred in the Gaza Strip. Information has reached us from soldiers and residents in the Gaza Strip about looting, humiliation, and killings of the Arab population in different parts of the Gaza Strip. There has been extremely disturbing information that after Gaza was occupied, tens of residents were taken from their houses and shot without cause. Even the meager information that the censor has allowed the Israeli press to publish shows that dreadful acts have been carried out in Gaza, acts which any person of conscience, regardless of party affiliation, cannot fail to condemn.

Today's *Ha'aretz* includes an article from *Ha'olam Hazeh*, which says, among other things, "Two weeks ago an event occurred in occupied Rafah, which, according to the international press, ended with the killing of more than fifty Arabs. With unsurpassable stupidity, this apparatus thinks that it's possible to silence such an event at a time like this in the most sensitive place on earth. That's why the first piece of information came from the UNRWA people who are there, who spoke of a horrific massacre. To the whole world Israel's silencing looks like an expression of bad conscience." That's from *Ha'olam Hazeh*.

The whole country has heard and is talking about these things. The Israeli public is ashamed of these acts and wants an immediate stop to them. There's no excusing these murderous acts in that they occurred during a time of war. These things were done after the occupation, to a peaceful population, just as on October 29 similar criminal acts were done to 49 peaceful residents of Kafr Kassem, acts that two weeks ago in the Knesset MK Schocken called "worse than treason."

[Just days before the Sinai war started, Kafr Kassem, a village of Arabs living inside Israel near Tel Aviv, was put under curfew by the Israel Border Police. Villagers returning home from their fields and neighboring areas, unaware that a curfew had been imposed, were stopped at the police roadblocks and killed.]

We protest these crimes not just from a general democratic standpoint but to an equal degree out of love for our people, out of a desire to erase a stain from our people. The government is responsible for these crimes just as it is responsible for its aggressive policy toward Egypt and its repressive policies toward the Arab population in Israel.

We propose a debate on the events in the Gaza Strip in order that the Knesset will decide 1) to condemn the acts of looting and murder that have been carried out by Israeli rule in the Gaza Strip; 2) to immediately halt these criminal acts; 3) to bring those who committed such acts to trial; 4) to carry out the United Nations' emergency decree to pull out IDF troops from all the occupied territory, including the Gaza Strip.

Prime Minister and Defense Minister David Ben-Gurion's reply (see p. 376):

I shall not debate with the two previous speakers [other speaker not identified]. It is not for them to talk of conscience, murder or robbery. I wish to report to the Knesset on the events which took place. The matter has already been discussed in the Knesset Foreign Affairs and Defense Committee, and a report has been sent to the Secretary General of the United Nations.

The following events took place at Rafah where there are both local residents and a number of refugees. Rafah was liberated by the Israel Defense Army which drove out the Egyptian invader—and I hope he will never return there.

On the day after my broadcast to the nation, on the evening of 11 November, Rafah had the mistaken impression that the Israel Defense Army was about to withdraw from the town. Whether this false report was spread by the agents of these two speakers or others, I do not know—but that was the impression created. As a result, disturbances took place, UNRWA stores were looted, and shots were fired by the rioters. On the following day, during which the unit stationed in the town was due to be relieved—by another unit which was late in arriving—the disturbances began again. They did so after the unit stationed in the town had left. One officer and three soldiers who remained fired in the air and succeeded in dispersing the rioters. Later, the relieving unit arrived and imposed a curfew to carry out a weapons search, for we had information—and we still have information to this effect—that there were numerous Egyptian soldiers and Fedayeen in disguise still in the Gaza Strip, murderers sent there by the Egyptian dictator.

A number of people in the town violated the curfew and some opened fire on our forces. After firing a number of warning shots in the air, our soldiers were forced to open fire on the rioters and 48 of them were killed and a number were wounded. Searches were made and, as a result, 250 Egyptian soldiers and a large quantity of arms were discovered.

Since this incident, quiet has reigned in Rafah and in the whole of the Gaza area. Efforts have been made by the Israel Defense Army to restore normal life. Local councils have reopened, medical assistance has been provided, postal and telegraphic services and transport restored. Two representatives especially sent by the Secretary General of the United Nations visited Gaza yesterday and they will also visit other places. They were astonished that in a few days after the occupation such tranquility and normalcy prevail in the area.

On this occasion, I must refute the disgraceful slander being spread by Nasser's agents in Israel—they are also the agents of certain others, whose names I don't wish to mention for reasons sufficient for me—that the Government is preparing to do to the Arabs in Israel what Egypt is doing to the Jews in Egypt. This is a vile calumny and incitement of the worst possible kind, which only traitors and enemy agents could disseminate.

I wish to state here, if any need exists to make such a statement, that the Arab citizens of Israel enjoy full equality of civic rights. They are treated exactly like Jewish citizens, and none of us considers them responsible for the criminal misdeeds of the Arab rulers. The Government will take stringent legal measures against those who spread the slander, the purpose of which is to stir up unrest in this country. The Egyptian atrocities will not take place in Israel, and if any act of murder does take place, the murderers are handed over to the law and tried as though they had murdered Jews. For Israeli justice makes no distinction between Jewish and Arab murderers. Only foreign agents and traitors could spread such calumnies. I propose to remove this matter from the agenda.
[62 voted in favor of removing the matter from the agenda, 3 against.]

Ben-Gurion's reference to two U.N. representatives (Colonel K. Nelson and Captain G. Svedlund) being "astonished" at the level of "tranquility and normalcy" in Gaza raised eyebrows at U.N. headquarters. In a cable to UNTSO acting chief of staff Colonel Leary on November 28, 1956, Colonel Nelson wrote, "I made no specific or categorical statement to the effect that everything was OK in Gaza Strip. Yesterday I toured Gaza town only repeat only. The Israelis may have concluded that my impression was that 'everything seems OK in Gaza' but I could not have said that everything was OK in Gaza Strip since I did not leave Gaza town. . . . The basis of Ben-Gurion's alleged statement is no categorical [sic] quoted from me. . . ." In a communication to the U.N. secretary general on December 1, 1956, after finally traveling around the Gaza Strip, Colonel Nelson was able to report, "Conditions throughout the area can be classified as progressively normal." Day-to-day life was "being restored under an orderly plan of Israeli authorities. . . . Method of Israeli [sic] may be strong arm but there is evidence of control of population and stability. . . . Situation in Rafia [sic] is calm for both refugee and local inhabitants."

The foundation for any historical account of the Khan Younis and Rafah killings is the "Special Report of the Director of the United Nations Relief and Works Agency for Palestine Refugees in the Near East (Covering the period 1 November 1956 to mid-December 1956)," presented to the General Assembly (Official Records: Eleventh Session, Supplement No. 14A A/3212/Add.1), New York, 1957 (see pp. 116–17 and 376).

Paragraphs 20 through 30, under the heading "Effects of Military Operations on Gaza Refugees," is the relevant section.

CASUALTIES AMONG REFUGEES

20. In addition to the disruptions referred to . . . , the occupation of the Gaza Strip by the Israel army resulted in a number of civilian casualties in both the refugee and local populations, and caused anxiety and fear among the refugees, particularly during the first weeks.

21. In other circumstances, it would have been a logical course for the United Nations Truce Supervision Organization to investigate and report upon casualties resulting from an armed attack across the demarcation line. In the present emergency, that organization was unable to do so, as the movements of its officers in the Gaza Strip had been restricted by the Israel authorities. The [United Nations Relief and Works] Agency has, therefore, made every effort to ascertain the facts concerning the various incidents affecting the refugees and it has sought to prevent any repetition of violence against the refugee population. The Agency has been compelled to rely upon its own sources of information. These were necessarily limited, but they included eye-witness accounts by UNRWA employees, both refugees and others.

22. The Director [of UNRWA, Henry Labouisse, an American] sets forth below a summary of the information he has obtained concerning refugee casualties, which he believes to be as accurate a reflection of the facts as prevailing circumstances permitted.

23. **Khan Yunis.** The town of Khan Yunis and the Agency's camp adjacent thereto were occupied by Israel troops on the morning of 3 November. A large number of civilians were killed at that time, but there is some conflict in the accounts given as to the causes of the casualties. The Israel authorities state that there was resistance to their occupation and that the Palestinian refugees formed part of the resistance. On the other hand, the refugees state that all resistance had ceased at the time of the incident and

that many unarmed civilians were killed as the Israel troops went through the town and camp, seeking men in possession of arms. The exact number of dead and wounded is not known, but the Director has received from sources he considers trustworthy lists of names of persons allegedly killed on 3 November, numbering 275 individuals, of whom 140 were refugees and 135 local residents of Khan Yunis.

24. **Rafah.** On 12 November, a serious incident occurred in the Agency's camp at Rafah. Both the Israel authorities and UNRWA's other sources of information agree that a number of refugees were killed and wounded at that time by the occupying forces.

25. A difference of opinion exists as to how the incident happened and as to the numbers of killed and wounded. It is agreed, however, that the incident occurred during a screening operation conducted by the Israel forces. These screening operations have been carried out in each UNRWA camp, as well as among the non-camp population. The stated purpose of the Israel authorities was to find persons who were members of the so-called "Palestine Brigade" or who participated in *fedayeen* operations. The procedure was to institute a twenty-four-hour curfew in the area being screened and to call all men between certain specified ages to gather at designated places; meanwhile, soldiers went through the houses and huts looking for suspects who might have remained at home.

26. The Israel authorities in Gaza state that the attitude of the refugees in Rafah camp was hostile and that there was some resistance to the screening operations, during which the casualties occurred. The refugees deny any such resistance. The facts appear to be as follows: Rafah is a very large camp (more than 32,000 refugees) and the loudspeaker vans which called upon the men to gather at designated screening points were not heard by some of the refugee population. Realizing this, an UNRWA official went personally to one section of the camp to inform the inhabitants of the Israel announcement. Moreover, sufficient time was not allowed for all men to walk to the screening points and get there before the designated hour. In the confusion, a large number of refugees ran toward the screening points for fear of being late, and some Israel soldiers apparently panicked and opened fire on this running crowd.

27. The Director has received from sources which he considers trustworthy lists of names of persons allegedly killed at Rafah on 12 November, numbering 111, of whom 103 were refugees, seven local residents, and one an Egyptian.

PROTEST BY THE AGENCY

28. Upon learning of the Rafah incident, the Agency protested to the Israel Government stating that, unless immediate measures were taken to put an end to such happenings, it would be impossible for UNRWA to continue its work among and on behalf of the refugees in the Gaza Strip. The Agency was assured by the Israel Foreign Office that the Government was taking urgent steps to establish the facts and was doing its best to ensure that there would be no repetition of such incidents.

29. To the best of the Agency's information, the two incidents mentioned above

are the only major ones of their kind which have taken place. There have been, however, a number of refugees killed or wounded in smaller incidents—some during the fighting, some in connexion with breaches of curfew restrictions, and some accidentally. The exact number is not known, but the Director has received a list, from sources which he considers trustworthy, numbering sixty-six individuals, of whom forty-eight were refugees, killed in the period 1 to 21 November (exclusive of those mentioned above).

30. It has not been possible to verify individually each listed death, nor has it been possible to complete a list of all refugees who may have been killed or who are missing. Further information may be obtained in the weeks to come, but it is most unlikely that lists of casualties can ever be made complete. One of the reasons for this is that, particularly in the early phase, many burials were made without identification.

Note here the references to eyewitness accounts, lists of casualties, and claims by Israeli authorities in Gaza. Presumably this material was written down. Perhaps these documents still exist and will be found by an intrepid researcher in the UNRWA archives—located mostly in Amman, Jordan—some day.

I asked Mordechai Bar-On, chef de bureau to Moshe Dayan in 1956, who was extensively interviewed for this book, specifically about the killings at Khan Younis and Rafah. Here is the relevant part of the transcript of the interview, which was conducted in English.

Q: *Let's move forward a bit to the actual conquest of Gaza and to what happened in Khan Younis and Rafah.*
Bar-On: What do you refer here to, Khan Younis, Rafah? I know of one case which I heard of and I didn't pursue it in great detail, of some, I think it was in Rafah, not in Khan Younis as far as I know, but it was in one place in which the commander, who happened to be in later years a great peacenik in Israel, Matti Peled. . . . But at that time he was the commander of a brigade, and he was commander of Gaza, so—

Q: *He was the commander of all of Gaza?* [Note: Matti Peled died in 1995.]
Bar-On: Of all Gaza . . . And don't trust this information because it's just what I remember, I never delved into that. . . . But there was some sort of a riot either in a refugee camp or in a prison camp. They tried to sort out the fedayeen or they tried to find those who were culprits of violent activities. And there was a kind of disorder in the place, and then there was [missing word] shooting on the part of the Israelis into the multitude. And as far as I remember something like 100 were killed, which is a great number. . . . I know of one such place. I don't know what you referred [to], Khan Younis. . . . To me, to my mind, [the incident I'm aware of regarding Khan Younis] is the raid at the end of August of 1955. But maybe I'm wrong.

Q: *So reports, when you were with Dayan, reports weren't really coming in about what was going on?*
Bar-On: Reports from?

Q: *Reports on what was going on in Gaza. . . . Because you don't seem to be familiar with what happened in Khan Younis. I'm just wondering, at the time were reports coming in about what was going on in Gaza? Or is it something that . . . you learned later after the war?*

Bar-On: No no no. At the time, of course. But you have to try to imagine how it works.

Q: *Okay.*

Bar-On: If a thing like this happens, first of all you report by telephone. Not by any writing. So it's word of mouth. I mean, they report it to the area command, and the area command reports to the G3, to the operation room . . . if it's important. In this case I guess it was important enough to let Dayan know right away, even by telephone. [The report] will not be of great detail. You do not ask him, how did it happen? . . . Somebody will tell there was a riot in the camp, and we had to open fire, and many were killed, but it's now quiet. Because the whole thing took perhaps a few minutes. The whole event—or maybe half an hour, and then the whole thing was over. So it's over now. . . . Then you've got investigations. Sometimes legal investigations, but very often the upper echelon demands a written report on what happened. So the report will then go by echelon and will reach—in most cases Dayan would not read that report. [It will arrive] two or three days later, and sometimes a week later. There were so many other things to busy himself with. . . . Actually, he knew the facts, he knew the facts exactly the way, what happened. Unless he thought it was something that had to be investigated by a lawyer, by a military lawyer, which he did not, I think, at that time. Then I would remember it much more. I don't remember it much more because for me it was a fleeting event. Somebody told me, I told Dayan, and that's it, finished, the story is over.

Q: *I mean, it is a long time ago. Do you remember how you heard about it?*
Bar-On: No . . .

Q: *But you would have been the one to have told Dayan then?*
Bar-On: I'm not sure. Maybe someone called him directly. And he told me . . .

Q: *And you don't know if a report was written about it or not?*
Bar-On: I'm pretty sure that there was a written report. . . .

Q: *And as far as you know, what happened in Khan Younis, you just don't even remember any—*
Bar-On: It's either there or there. You know, some reports . . . do not register with us, because what registered with me is a case in which 100 Palestinians are being killed, women and children, within an hour, that [registered with] me. The fact that there was some shooting in some place and two Palestinians were killed, would not record in my memory—sadly about my memory. But for them it's another case. And of course, the Palestinians, and I don't blame [them] for that, but the Palestinians have a tendency to inflate those stories because it serves them so they want to inflate them. Now sometimes they don't have to inflate because a hundred killed is a hundred killed.

Q: *I'll tell you, it wasn't women and children. There might have been some women and children killed, but it was [almost all] men. Just so you know.*

Bar-On: Anyway, they make the best out of these stories, especially over the years the story goes and becomes bigger and bigger. The memory becomes bigger and bigger. We have this experience, and it's only natural. So what you hear from people on the locale, you have to . . . take with a grain of salt, because they might report a truthful story, but [exaggerate] the way they tell [it] and the details. In my mind, I know only one mishap or one act of cruelty, if you might call it, or misdeed, and I know of one such case [where] Matti Peled was involved. There were many more—Palestinians were killed here and there over that period. I don't know if it was—I think it was Khan Younis, not in Rafah. So I do not know what do they refer to when they say another event in Rafah.

There is one intriguing reference to the killings in Khan Younis by Israeli professor of philosophy Avishai Margalit in his review of Noam Chomsky's *The Fateful Triangle* (*New York Review of Books*, June 28, 1984). In it, he states:

> Take the case of the massacre at Khan Younis in the Gaza Strip during the war of 1956, one of many unpublicized cases of Israeli brutality that Chomsky mentions. Israel was involved, according to the UN chief inspector, General E.L.M. Burns, in the massacre of at least 275 people. This number is cited by Chomsky although knowledgeable Israeli sources I have talked to believe it is too high. What is missing from this account, however, is the fact that each of the persons who were shot was identified as a *fedayeen* (or terrorist, in Israel's current jargon) according to lists compiled by Israeli intelligence before the killings. Execution without trial is evil, as is the mindless slaughter of innocents by Israelis at Deir-Yassin or by Phalangists at Sabra and Shatila.

In a response in the letters page of the *New York Review of Books* (August 16, 1984), Chomsky stated his sources for the casualty figure at Khan Younis (citing the director of UNRWA, Henry Labouisse) and added that "the official Israeli account" and other reports "denied" that those shot had been identified as fedayeen. "In fact," wrote Chomsky, "it seems that the army simply went on a rampage after the conquest." Margalit replied:

> In my view bureaucratic murder according to pre-prepared lists and without trial is as evil as murder committed by rampageous soldiers hitting innocent civilians. It is no less evil: it is a different evil.

ADDITIONAL NOTES ON SOURCES

p. 36: The Israel Foreign Ministry report cited is from its Middle East department. I found it in Tom Segev's book *1949: The First Israelis*.

pp. 77–78: Dayan's eulogy for Ro'i Rothberg is quoted from Benny Morris's book *Israel's Border Wars, 1949–1956*.

pp. 118–119: Mark Gefen's account of the Khan Younis killings was published in *Al Hamishmar*, April 27, 1982. Riva Hocherman translated the article from the Hebrew.

APPENDIX 2

THE DEMOLITION OF HOMES IN RAFAH: THE ISRAELI VIEW

In May 2003 I interviewed Israel Defense Forces spokespersons and commanders for their comments on the home demolitions in Rafah. What follow are the relevant portions of the transcripts.

Major Sharon Feingold and Captain Jacob Dallal, IDF spokespersons:

Feingold: What concerns us most is the tunnels—this is the biggest problem for us along that border. You have to understand that when we talk about these tunnels, this is a conglomerate, this is an operation, this is a business. . . . For the last two and a half years these tunnels have been used to smuggle both wanted terrorists and weapons and munitions. And . . . we're talking about dozens of tunnels. . . . The average is about 15 meters deep and 300 and 400 meters long. . . . Now they can't dig them out in the open, of course. They would be spotted in seconds. So what they do is they dig them . . . from houses which are closest to the border, which means the tunnels are shorter in length. Most of these structures along the border . . . are used as piers for tunnels. What we [do] is expose the tunnels. After we expose the tunnels we blow them up. So [the Palestinians] move further and further into Rafah itself to dig the tunnels. . . .

Q: *What sort of coordination do you have with the Egyptians on this?*
Feingold: I can't go into that, that's very sensitive, but I can tell you that the Egyptians are doing everything they can to fight this phenomenon from their side. . . . [M]ore than 100 tunnels [have been] exposed. We blow them up, they dig another tunnel. It's a game of, if you want, cat and mouse going after these people. And because they dig the tunnels from people's houses, it's very hard for us to detect these tunnels. Look at this. [She shows a photo on a computer.] This is a tunnel which was dug under the baby's cot, inside a house. This is a normal house in Rafah. You can see it's quite a wealthy house. And this is the pier for the tunnel, under the baby's bed. . . . [It] is not something out of the ordinary. This is what we're facing every single day in Rafah. . . . [T]hese tunnels are the arteries of terror. These tunnels are the ones supplying bullets, the AK-47s, the anti-tank rockets—the RPGs—and people, wanted terrorists.

Q: *I'd like to get a sense of . . . the threat that, from your perspective, the tunnels pose.*
Feingold: Oh, a very big one. [Shows a map of Rafah's border area.] They use these structures. Some of them are abandoned, some of them are not. Some of them have roofs. Some of them do not. Some of them are used as places where they keep their farm animals, you know, the chickens and the goats and

whatever. And in some of them the people are still living, [on the] first floor or the second floor. . . .

Q: *You mentioned a number of things that have been smuggled through. Go over that again. What is generally smuggled through as far as arms or ammunition?*

Feingold: Anything that you can get into the tunnel. It's very easy. When we destroy more tunnels we see that the price for an AK-47 automatic rifle rises from $1,000 to $2,000. You see by the market in Rafah, you see how good we are. Which is quite funny, but it's not funny to us. Basically, these tunnels are not very big. You have to be very small to crawl inside. But there are tunnels which we have discovered which are big, where they had lights in there, where they had a telephone system in there. People could actually walk. . . . We also don't know how many tunnels there are. . . . We do know that they use children to dig the tunnels . . . and pay them very low salaries. . . .

Dallal: In general, the whole question of children, also to lay explosive devices on the border, on the Philadelphi Road itself.

Feingold: They send them because they're small, because children are not something that should raise any suspicion. . . . They run there all the time.

Q: *And the evidence you have of that is what?*

Feingold: We have intelligence that shows that. . . . We know for a fact that they're using children all the time. . . . They send them to try to infiltrate the [Jewish] settlements inside the Gaza Strip. They're not that successful, but some of them have been. We caught a child that's eight years old and 14, if I'm not mistaken. . . .

Q: *Eight and 14?*

Dallal: Those are the youngest.

Feingold: The youngest that we caught, which managed to go, to infiltrate one of our settlements. They were caught.

Q: *And you say the children are also used to plant explosive devices?*

Dallal: [They] actually go up to the border road and leave things. I remember I was there, this was a while back when this happened, but they would see a child put a bag there, a brown bag, and walk away, along the road. And that was a sort of a small explosive device, and [the IDF] would deactivate it . . . later. And what can you do, also, when you see the children do things that are suspicious, we can't shoot, we don't shoot at them. There's nothing we can do. . . . They see it from the outpost, they know children [are] coming forward doing things that look suspicious, digging, leaving things, and also . . .

Feingold: Yep. It's a big problem. And interestingly enough . . . the residents of Rafah organized themselves and they [put] ads in newspapers there [saying], "Stop using our houses, stop using our children. . . ."

Q: *I've seen a number of times homeowners yelling at people with guns, "Get away from my home." Obviously, as you must know, there are a lot of people who don't have tunnels, and who don't want their homes destroyed.*

Feingold: That's something that has to be very clear. Our war is not against the Palestinian people. . . .

Q: *But what would you tell someone, a homeowner who's losing his home, whose home is getting bulldozed, who doesn't have a tunnel. . . .*

Feingold: We don't bulldoze someone's house if we don't have good reason to do that. We only bulldoze a house when that house is used either for intelligence gathering, or shooting [at] our forces, or as a cover for people who are planting explosive devices, or used by the tunnel smugglers. . . . In this asymmetric battle . . . it's not like the old conventional wars where you fight a soldier or you use a tank attack. Here we're fighting a battle of silhouettes and shadows. These people are not wearing uniforms. They're wearing civilian clothes. They assimilate themselves inside a civilian population. They use the civilian population. When you dig a tunnel under a baby's cot, you know fully well that when Israeli [soldiers] will find that tunnel, they will destroy the house. They're actually holding the people of this house hostage. These people are afraid of them. . . .

Q: *So you think some of these homes are used against the homeowner's [wishes]?*

Feingold: I'm sure that they are, I'm sure that they are. And this is tragic. These people are paying a price. . . . They have nothing to do with terror. They wish to live peacefully. . . . But we can't allow this. . . . And people publish ads in the newspaper saying don't use us as hostages, or go away from our neighborhood, it means that they got the message, our message. . . .

Q: *Now you mentioned a number of things that a house could be destroyed for, but according to the Governorate of Rafah, more than seven hundred dwellings or homes have been destroyed along the border.*

Feingold: No . . . I think that's a big exaggeration. I'm not sure that we can share with you all the statistics that we have. I have to ask you, what is a house?

Dallal: Yeah, exactly.

Feingold: What is a house? Is it four walls . . . ?

Dallal: A shed?

Feingold: Where you keep your chickens and your goats? These are not houses in the Western norm . . . with a family. . . .

Dallal: Are they inhabited? That's the other question. If the gunmen have been using them for six months and no one lives there, is that inhabited? Is the house built? Is that a house? And the other thing, all these [things] that [Major Feingold] was explaining to you for the reason why—When a house is used to conduct terror [it can be destroyed]. . . .

Feingold: Under the Geneva Conventions. . . .

Dallal: [As far as any house listed by the Rafah governorate] it could be a shed, it could be a half-built structure, it could be an uninhabited structure. . . .

Feingold: A few tens, a few dozens . . .

Q: *So a few dozen [houses destroyed] from your standpoint?*

Feingold: I would say not even close to [the hundreds mentioned]. And again, these structures we do go after, we do that for a reason. We don't just go there, you know, because we have nothing better to do. It's because we located a house that's been used by the gunmen for the last two months or for the last two weeks. And it could have been used by the gunmen. . . .

Dallal: [Motions to a map and shows houses that are marked as being used by gunmen.] These are standing structures, and these are places in this particular area, the red is: grenades come from those houses, and pink: fire has been shot from those places—regularly. And these are the things that are standard.

Q: *You mentioned uninhabited homes. I'll just tell you from the . . . Palestinian perspective. They say they're fired at by the IDF—their home—just randomly. In other words, bullets just come in every now and then into their home. And after a while it just becomes too dangerous for them. They move out of the home, and they try to visit it during the day. And at this point it becomes abandoned or semi-abandoned. And then they feel they've sort of lost it. And I've even seen Palestinians who've boarded up their homes so that no one can use it to shoot from even though they're not actually living in it. Because they don't want their homes to be demolished.*

Feingold: Obviously not. The accusation that we shoot randomly is absolute nonsense. We understand that the battle that's being conducted against terror—inside these houses there are children and women . . . but when these houses are used to shoot anti-tank rockets at our soldiers—this is a war zone. . . . I don't know any soldier anywhere around the world who's been shot at and will not fire at the source of fire. . . . And as [Captain Dallal] said, once the house is used for combat activity it ceases to become a house. Under the Geneva Convention, it can be targeted. . . . We are only firing at people who are firing at us. . . . It's very sad that these people have to leave their houses. It's very sad. But why are they having to leave their houses? . . . [T]hese people who are in charge of the tunnels are very unhappy when we explode their tunnels. . . . It's an economic operation. Once we cut into their profits they become very agitated, very angry. They are determined to keep this area a combat zone. . . . As in every war, innocent people, bystanders, who have absolutely nothing to do with terror, are paying the price. . . .

Later, Captain Dallal told me that about 45 inhabited homes had been demolished by the IDF to date (May 2003) in Rafah.

Colonel "Pinky" (nickname given) commander of the IDF Southern Brigade of the Gaza Strip Division:

Q: *Let me ask you, do you have a figure of how many homes have been demolished? If you have a permit or permission to destroy every house, you must have a figure for it. Is that available? An IDF figure?*

Pinky: Approximately, I believe that we have destroyed between 300 to 400 houses, and if you check it you'll have the right number. . . . One of the most important things in guerrilla warfare is to learn and to prepare yourself for the next battle, and the next battle could be on the same day. But right now, you know, so many events. So you lose the time, you lose the day, you lose the events. If you ask me how many terrorists my brigade killed in the last year, I don't have the number anymore. In the beginning you count them, but if you go to the books, there is the number of the terrorists that we killed, we got the number of structures we've demolished, we've got everything.

Q: *Let me ask you, from the Palestinian point of view, you've got people who say their homes are hit randomly by gunfire. What's your comment on something like that?*
Pinky: . . . It's a fighting zone.

Q: *They say there's no gunfire from their areas sometimes yet their houses are hit.*
Pinky: It's very easy to say something like this because you can never have the evidence to show that no one shoots from there. Because I can give you examples where they claim that we kill people and we hit people and when you are checking in the hospital, there is no one that arrived to the hospital. I can give you events that they claim that we killed someone and we don't have the name, we don't have nothing, even the place. It's not the place where my soldier was shooting. And I told you sometimes we make mistakes and shoot, but if I investigate every event—I don't want to say all the events—but most of the events when we hit places that we're not supposed to hit, it was by mistake. You don't see that soldiers have an aim to hit innocent citizens. You don't have something like this that you can show me and claim that there are people here who are bad people, bad soldiers. And I admit that sometimes when you are shooting here, there are stray bullets that hit in the wrong targets.

Q: *Now as far as the house demolitions are concerned, I've talked to people whose houses have been demolished who will say there's definitely no tunnel, that they argue with gunmen, they want gunmen to leave their area because they don't want their homes to be demolished, and their homes are demolished anyway.*
Pinky: I hear about this claim, and I know that sometimes maybe we demolished the wrong house. But in most of the cases, I told you, I cannot demolish a house without having a permit to do it. And what's happened, you know, it's like a process. . . . [Some Palestinians] are not going to admit and say that sometimes the gunmen get inside the house and shoot from the houses in the times they were there. And sometimes when people try to resist these kind of people, they shoot [at] them, in the leg. . . . And you know, you're American. Go and see what's happening in the world. I think that, if you check us, and look at our behavior, when people shoot anti-tank missiles at my soldiers, and you have here all the snipers, and you have here all the booby traps, and you will see how much damage we did, you will see that we are very very gentle, if you can say gently about something like this. But when there is [a chance] that my soldier is going [to be] hit by the terrorist, there is only one solution for me: it's to hit the targets and to destroy whatever is creating the situation to be bad [for] my soldier. You can come with me to visit the Cohen family now. I'm going to let them know how their son was killed. And one of the things that they ask—and we are talking about Khan Younis—why did you let the houses that our son was killed from . . . to be established—you didn't destroy it before our son was killed—from this house. So what are you going to say to this mother?

Q: *What do you say?*
Pinky: I say that I'm a soldier, a professional soldier, and I obey the rules. And

there are international rules, and it means if I want to destroy something or demolish something, it means I need to have a permit. And as long as we obey the rules, we are not going to destroy and kill people and demolish structures that do not have [a] connection with the terror operation. And unfortunately the house that [Cohen] was killed from—the sniper shot from this house—was demolished only after it happened. Because before [that], we did not have any evidence that [gave] us the option to demolish this house. . . . We brought the family to the post where he was killed . . . and they were very angry [that] we didn't destroy . . . the neighborhood.

Q: *You're talking about the Toufieh area? . . .*
Pinky: You understand where the post [is]?

Q: *Yes, I know exactly, I know Toufieh quite well.*
Pinky: You see I don't demolish houses there without reason. But if you take what's happened there in Toufieh, I'm sure other armies would destroy all the neighborhood through [to] the hospital.

Q: *All the way up to the hospital?*
Pinky: For sure. Go to Chechnya.

Q: *Oh yeah, well, the Russians.*
Pinky: So you see we are really gentle when we are picking the targets, and we try not to . . . hit the innocent people. I really feel bad about this. But when you take the families, the soldiers, that I [have] responsibility for, there is no option for me as a commander to let them be killed by this opportunity that I give to the other side. And the other side knows it. They know my rules of engagement, and they use it, and they use it in a cynical way, in the fact that they use the families, the innocent people as human shields, and it makes me sorry. . . .

Q: *Let me ask you one more question, and again about house demolitions along the border. It seems like this is gradually going north. Is there a point where this is going to stop or is it just going to keep creeping north, the demolitions, until you feel you're under no threat at all? When does that stop? Is there a limit on this?*
Pinky: When they will stop to shoot on my troops. This is the answer. If I will feel, and I will see, that there is no resistance, and there is no shooting, and there is no risk to my troops. . . . [T]he moment that I understand that they use [a house] to hit my soldiers, I'm there, I'm there. So the only thing that leads me is the confidence and the safety of my soldiers. We don't have [a plan] to destroy Rafah. It's not our aim. We want the smuggling from the tunnels [to] be stopped, we want the conducting of terror operations in this area [to] be stopped. . . .

Lieutenant Colonel "Avi" [full name not given], commander of the IDF Desert Patrol Battalion; Lieutenant "Erez" also present:

Q: *So are you responsible for the border area and Rafah?*
Avi: Yes . . .

Q: *So how would you characterize the responsibilities of your battalion?*

Avi: To guard the international border. . . . Nowadays this means that you have Egypt on one side, Palestinians on the other side, and in between them a corridor which is Israeli. And I'm responsible for this corridor. . . . Until the intifada began, our major activities were just kind of random patrols and random searches. It wasn't nearly as intense. We would find illegal cigars, once in a while drugs, but it was pretty light operations in terms of our patrolling this border, until the intifada began. . . . When the war began and they began to focus their activities, the Palestinians realized that their major source of contraband was being cut off, and they built hundreds of more tunnels, and the tunnels became designated—these are the tunnels for Hamas, these are the tunnels for Fatah, these are the tunnels for Islamic Jihad. . . . This is a war front. It's a central war zone. It has been and still is the front that has the most number of incidents of any place in Israel. . . .

Q: *I realize you can't tell me in specific terms how you know [where] there is a tunnel, but can you give me a general idea?*

Avi: I get intelligence information that there is a tunnel. I don't know exactly where. I begin to dig, not in a built-up area, like where there's homes, rather in the corridor, the Israeli corridor. I put dynamite inside the ground. This is the initial explosion. If I [hit near] a tunnel, the tunnel sucks all the [earth above] inside. And it . . . automatically [traces] a line, shows you on the surface of the earth the line that the tunnel is following.

Q: *Oh, I see, it just sort of collapses.*

Avi: It points to where they are going. It follows the line all the way to the house. . . .

Q: [Referring to a map of Rafah on the wall.] *Can I ask you, the Xs indicate what and the dots indicate what, the red dots?*

Avi: Red is [for] homes that people live in, and black [is for] empty homes. The numbers are mosques. . . . [We document with] recorded footage, every tunnel. Because they constantly claim that we're destroying homes, and we're killing people, innocent civilians, we put a photographer with us at all times. . . . We don't just randomly destroy homes. Every home that on the other side that they say we destroyed, every single home has a history. Either they fired on our troops from there—RPGs, anti-tank fire—or there was a tunnel.

Q: *So you have a record here of every home and its history, then?*

Avi: On the intelligence level of the division for pretty much every house we have the information.

Q: *The colonel described to me the permission process for destroying a home. Can you go over that with me, too?*

Avi: I get information saying that such-and-such tunnel was dug from such-and-such location. That's the first process. . . . Once I find a tunnel, I know what direction it's coming from, I then gather intelligence and information [on] the home, the home that built the tunnel, do people live in [it] or is it vacant? . . . There is a project plan, the project plan goes to [Colonel "Pinky," who] sends the project plan above him to the commander of the area, and the commander of the area sends it all the way up to the legal advisor for the entire army. They either approve it or they don't approve it. There are times they turn me down because the exit of the tunnel is in an area where to destroy it we'd have to destroy many homes, it's in a very crowded area so they say instead of destroying the home, destroy the tunnel itself, the complete tunnel. . . . The best way to do it in the end is to go to the entrance, or the exit, however you want to look at it, the entrance, we'll say, from the Palestinian side, and destroy the entrance. It's not my decision in the end. I have to go through this whole process.

Q: *How often is it turned down?*
Avi: Very very frequently. . . . The problem is that they know we're going after the first row of homes so they simply keep moving the entrance of the tunnels deeper and deeper into the camps. Which means if we want to go to the opening, we have to [go] further and further . . . into the camps. And we will go everywhere. Everywhere we have to go, we will go.

Q: *In the final analysis, do you feel your efforts have been very effective with the tunnels, or do you feel like you keep finding more, which indicates that the Palestinians keep pushing it?*
Avi: We're very very successful. I go in with my Hummer and speak to the Palestinian population. . . . When I go in, I make an announcement on the loudspeakers telling everyone to get out of the area. After we deal with the problem, we distribute flyers . . . saying, "People, if there are no tunnels, we're not coming in here. If you build tunnels, we are coming in here. So don't build tunnels. Protect your homes." I speak to many people over there. . . . I know them, I speak to them.

Q: *When you say you speak to them, do you actually get out of your vehicle . . . ?*
Avi: I move in my Hummer. . . . I'm protected by the Hummer. I see people, I call them over to me, and I speak to them.

Q: *And basically you tell them no tunnels, no problem?*
Avi: I speak to them about the situation, about everything. I explain to them why this is happening. Their greatest concern is to explain to me that they're not the ones involved. They're like apologetic almost. They just can't control it, they say. . . . We're in a defensive situation, not an offensive situation. They who bring us inside, cause us to fight, are the terrorist units. That's why we enter. All the times that we go in are because of the terrorist units or because of the tunnels. . . .

Q: *Why do you think . . . homes [are] abandoned then? Because they were once inhabited.*
Avi: I showed you the map. You asked me about the Xs, the black and red. I work here every day, 24 hours a day. . . . I know where they live and where they don't live, who lives there. I know the father of the home, his children.

Q: *Just with your intelligence?*
Avi: From my eyes, because I'm here constantly. They built their homes before the war. People were living in them. When the war started, people fled their

homes. Not because we came into the homes, but because the other side started using their homes for military operations. They didn't want to get killed. So that's why they left their homes.

Q: *I have to put this to you. I've spoken to Palestinians. They say they leave their homes because bullets come into their homes from the Israeli side. They say that after a while it's just too dangerous.*
Avi: I understand everything you're saying, and I agree that bullets come in. But bullets come in because they're firing at us from those homes. Either from the homes or from the area of the homes. When we know it's a populated house, we do our utmost to not fire into a populated house. And in the end of the day, the owner of the house weighs up his options. If he's in an area where there's fighting around, whether it's from the Israeli side or the Palestinian side, if it's too dangerous . . . there, he leaves.

Q: *When you say "area of the house," what do you mean?*
Erez: [Showing a photo of homes.] An area of a home, we mean by that, if we're talking about 575, for example [the home is numbered], the area is from this wall or from this bush or from the windows.

Q: *In other words the* immediate *area of the home, that's what I want to get at, the yard of the home, from behind the home.*
Erez: Yeah, of course . . .

Q: *You know, those are pretty much my questions, unless you think there's something you should tell me.*
Avi: I'll tell you just one thing. I'm a father of two girls, I have a family, and I have a home. And I know what it is to have a home. Every place I go into I think ten times, one hundred times, should I go inside. But in every place, if there is danger to my soldiers, or if there's a dangerous situation, whether they're bringing in arms and weapons, I'll go in and take care of the situation. It's too bad that the other side, I'm talking about the population of the other side, it's too bad they don't understand after I've been here for two years, I don't understand after two years being here how the other side has not succeeded to kick out the minority that exists there that causes all the suffering.

APPENDIX 3

THE DEMOLITION OF ASHRAF'S HOME

Ashraf's house was finally and completely demolished by the Israeli army on May 17, 2003, after I had finished researching this book.

As it happened, I was back in Rafah at the time on assignment for the *New York Times Magazine*, writing about the smuggling tunnels connecting Palestinian to Egyptian Rafah. Abed and I were sitting with a representative of the governorate of Rafah going over the subject of home demolitions when Ashraf called, telling us to get down to the Block J area because the Israelis were again demolishing homes.

On our way there we ran into Ashraf's brother, who told us, "They demolished the whole house." Here is my truncated journal entry about the incident:

> He's all smiles, all but giggly. You want to see? We turn down the sandy path, we can see the Zorob [tower], we've been hearing gunshots, we peer around a building; again, it's hard to get your bearings when you're looking at a landscape absent of something, and in this case what is absent is Ashraf's house. All I can see is dirt piled up. The brother explains that the bulldozers pushed sand and debris up on the house from two sides and that collapsed the structure. . . . I ask Ashraf's brother how he feels about what's happened. He doesn't seem particularly upset. "Now we are sure," he says. "Before it was in-between..."
>
> We got to Ashraf's home. His father is vaguely smiling. And then Ashraf steps out. . . . Ashraf has draped his arm over Abed. . . . "Life is fucking us," says Ashraf. "It's like shit."

Ashraf's dad, Talil, told me, "Yes, now it's finished. Now I should think about starting something new." Surveying the landscape, reduced to debris and sand, he said, "It was the nicest area in Rafah. Couples that were engaged used to come here to walk. Between day and night it became a ruin. . . . This is a disaster. This is a new migration."

A few days later, I spoke to the battalion commander, Lieutenant Colonel "Avi" (quoted at length in Appendix 2), who was responsible for the operation that destroyed Ashraf's house. My IDF minder, Captain Doron, was also present.

Q: *Three days ago I was in Rafah, and I saw . . . homes demolished. . . . It was west of Block J.*

[We refer to the maps to determine the area in concern. Avi shows images of a bulldozer with damage to its bullet-proof glass.]

. . .

Avi: If you look from those homes to the Egyptian side you'll see a cement wall of the Israelis blocking your view. There's an opening there. There's an opening between that cement, which is the area [from which] we enter [to conduct operations in Rafah]. This is a bullet-proof tractor. He entered into that area to close that opening. Two days before this, there were people who exited through that area, terrorists, who were going to leave the Gazan side, go into Egypt, go all the way down south and [from there back into Israel]. Because of that I wanted to close the opening. . . . The bulldozer entered, and look at the results: There are a huge number of direct bullet hits on the vehicle.

Q: *Was this at night?*
Avi: In the day. At night we had the people going into Egypt from the Gazan side, and the next day we went to close the [opening]. . . .

Q: *I just want to be sure we're talking about the same thing. This happened, I think it was Saturday, when the homes were demolished.*
Avi: Yes. These were not homes that people lived in. These were deserted homes that people were firing on our troops from. And from these homes they constantly fired at us. So from three different directions they hit the vehicle, from every side window and from the front.

Q: *So gunmen were confirmed firing from those homes?*
Doron: Yeah, that's it.
Avi: We are positive those homes were deserted.

[Later, the subject of the bulldozing of Ashraf's and other homes came up again.]

Avi: On Shabbat, the incident you spoke about that Saturday, there were terrorists involved in this action. They were firing from the homes. You call this a home, we call this a military position. It's an empty home, a vacant home that no family is living in. There's nothing inside the house that would make it a home. It's not connected to water or electricity. . . . It's a military position [that] fires at us.

APPENDIX 4

PALESTINIAN FIGURES FOR HOMES DEMOLISHED

The day after Ashraf's home was destroyed, I accompanied the Palestinian officials sent to assess and document the extent of the damage wrought by the Israeli bulldozers. Besides Ashraf's, three other houses were confirmed demolished and two were reportedly demolished and needed to be checked on.

While we were doing our inspection, a man stepped up to tell the officials that his home had been destroyed, too. "There were four rooms," he insisted. "You don't believe me?" "It's not a matter of believing you or not," one of the local government's officials, an engineer, replied. "Come to the governorate. Bring the documents about your house, the plans."

The assessments of the engineer and representatives of Rafah's Distribution Center and the Ministry of Housing were important in determining who would get compensated for what. The governorate was responsible for compensating non-refugee households; UNRWA was responsible for compensating refugees. There was coordination between the two organizations, but their figures for homes demolished were slightly different due to different counting methods.

UNRWA counted each building as one house, no matter how many housing units it contained. The governorate counted all housing units as individual houses. For example, a demolished multi-story building that contained three separate apartments would be counted by UNRWA as one house but by the governorate as three.

UNRWA (with the lower figures) counted 459 refugee and 94 non-refugee homes completely demolished in Rafah from September 2000, the start of the Second Intifada, until May 2003, when I last visited. A further 72 houses were considered partially destroyed and unsafe. The total of homes that had been damaged but could be repaired was 883.

In the same period, UNRWA had built 97 replacement homes.

According to UNRWA, in Rafah, up to April 2003, 4,781 people from 874 families had their homes completely demolished.

When I mentioned to Isa Qarra, public information officer for the Gaza Field Office of UNRWA, who gave me the above figures, that an IDF spokesman claimed that only about 45 inhabited houses in Rafah had been destroyed, he said, "I have no comment. These are the numbers we have."

BIBLIOGRAPHY

For the big-picture sweep of events—political, diplomatic, and military—leading up to and beyond the 1956 Suez Canal Crisis I relied on two books, Kennett Love's *Suez: The Twice-Fought War* (McGraw-Hill Book Company, 1969) and Donald Neff's *Warriors at Suez* (The Linden Press/Simon & Schuster, 1981). By placing the Gaza raid of February 28, 1955, in their respective first chapters, both authors helped me understand its centrality in the context of what happened in Khan Younis and Rafah in November 1956.

For the Israeli point of view, I turned to Tom Segev's *1949: The First Israelis* (Owl Books/Henry Holt and Company, 1998) and Benny Morris's *Israel's Border Wars: 1949–1956* (Oxford University Press, 1993). Despite his right-wing politics and slant, Morris is considered an objective historian and a careful examiner of archival records. I relied on his book in particular for insight into Israeli responses to border incidents and the fedayeen campaigns. I quote from his figures for Israeli and "infiltrator" casualties. Morris was gracious enough to meet me in Jerusalem when I needed tips on approaching the Israeli historical record.

My other two important Israeli sources were Mordechai Bar-On's *The Gates of Gaza* (St. Martin's Press, 1994) and Moshe Dayan's *Diary of the Sinai Campaign* (Schocken Books, 1967). Mordechai Bar-On was personally very helpful to me, and my interview with him figures prominently in this book.

For the U.N. perspective on the events of the time, I relied on Lieutenant General E. L. M. Burns's *Between Arab and Israeli* (George G. Harrap & Co, 1962). Burns was the chief of staff of the United Nations Truce Supervision Organization (UNTSO) and later the commander of the United Nations Emergency Force (UNEF).

ARCHIVES AND PEOPLE CONSULTED

U.N. Archives, New York
UNRWA Photo Archive, Gaza City
Israel Defense Forces Archives, Ramat Gan IDF Base
Israel State Archives (Ginzach Hamedina), Jerusalem
Knesset Archives, Jerusalem
The Press Archive, Municipal Library, Tel Aviv
Kol Ha'am Archive, Tel Aviv

A number of Israelis—former military men, families of deceased military men, and historians—were contacted to see if more light could be shed on the events in Khan Younis and Rafah in 1956. Both Meron Rapoport, my researcher, and I spoke to Mordechai Bar-On and to Lieutenant Colonel Meir Pa'il, former commander of the 51st Battalion of the Golani Brigade, which was active in the Rafah area. In addition,

Meron spoke to Zvi Al-Peleg, a former governor of the northern Gaza Strip; the family of the late Matti Peled, military commander of the Gaza Strip; and the family of Lieutenant Colonel Haim Gaon. I consulted historians Benny Morris, Ilan Pappe, and Uri Milstein, among others. Meron talked to Uri Avnery, ex–chief editor of the weekly *Ha'olam Hazeh*, former Knesset member, writer, and historian, and Professor Avishai Margalit, whose comments on Noam Chomsky's *The Fateful Triangle* are noted in Appendix 1.

A NOTE ON NAMES, PORTRAITS, AND INTERVIEWS

Most of the people I interviewed for this book agreed to give their full names. Some wished to remain anonymous. Others gave partial names, and in those cases I have stuck to whatever portion they preferred to use.

For the portraits, I worked from photographs for most of the interviewees. In the cases of people who did not wish to be identified, I generally drew quick sketches to approximate the look of the individual without rendering him or her identifiable. Where a name is indicated but there is no portrait at all, the likely explanation is that my camera malfunctioned.

Regarding language, I have tried to be faithful to the words people used when they were interviewed, even though it meant reproducing choppy word choices. Where a reader might have been left confused, I have smoothed the language somewhat, though as little as necessary.

ACKNOWLEDGMENTS

Chris Hedges has been a close friend since we first met in Bosnia. Our trip to Gaza together in 2001 was my first step on the road that led to this book. His moral conviction has always been an inspiration to me. I would also like to thank Azmi, our fixer on that occasion.

Mark Dennis and Christine Hauser very generously offered me places to stay and introduced me to many interesting people when I was transiting through Jerusalem.

This book could not have been written without the help of Toufic Haddad and Abed Elassouli. Toufic paved my way. He accompanied me to Gaza on my exploratory visit for this book and introduced me around. Through Toufic I met Abed, and Abed agreed to become my translator and guide. Abed and I were barely out of each other's sight during my later two-month sojourn in Khan Younis and Rafah. I consider his contributions invaluable. Years after I had visited Gaza he still answered questions and checked spellings for me. Like me, he probably thought the process would never end.

Hani and Khaled, two characters in the book, were also very helpful in introducing me to their communities in Rafah and Khan Younis.

As I cannot speak Hebrew, I had the help of two Israeli researchers, Oshri Netev and especially Meron Rapoport, in digging into Israeli archives. Meron also contacted a number of Israelis who figured significantly in the 1956 story, or, if deceased, their families.

All the good people at the U.N. Archives in New York and at UNRWA headquarters in Gaza City were enormously helpful.

Riva Hocherman, my friend and editor at Metropolitan Books, did double duty, helping me cut down my manuscript to a manageable length and translating numerous Hebrew-language articles and documents. Her attention to detail and enormous efforts have made this book much better.

Nicole Aragi, my friend and agent, kept my spirits up during my mid–comic book crisis and somehow kept my income flowing when I wasn't sure I would reach the finish line without putting my things on eBay.

I am indebted to many other people, too numerous to mention: journalists and U.N. people I met and whose company I enjoyed in Jerusalem; NGO personnel here and there, especially Robyn Long; various Palestinians and Israelis who invited me into their homes; numerous Gazans, among the most hospitable people I have ever met; my patient friends back in the States, where I spent years writing and drawing this book; my wonderful parents, my sister Maryanne, as well as Keith and Collin; and my lovely girlfriend, Amalie, who teaches me every day that there is more to life than bad news and awful history.